THE MOVE TO GLOBAL WAR

COURSE COMPANION

Keely Rogers
Jo Thomas

OXFORD
UNIVERSITY PRESS

OXFORD
UNIVERSITY PRESS

Great Clarendon Street, Oxford, OX2 6DP, United Kingdom

Oxford University Press is a department of the University of Oxford. It furthers the University's objective of excellence in research, scholarship, and education by publishing worldwide. Oxford is a registered trade mark of Oxford University Press in the UK and in certain other countries

British Library Cataloguing in Publication Data

Data available

978-0-19-831018-1

10 9 8 7 6 5 4

Paper used in the production of this book is a natural, recyclable product made from wood grown in sustainable forests.
The manufacturing process conforms to the environmental regulations of the country of origin.

Printed in India.

Acknowledgements

The publishers would like to thank the following for permissions to use their photographs:

p14: Bettmann/Corbis; p16: Bettmann/Corbis; p17: Philadelphia Museum of Art/Corbis; p21: Keystone/Getty Images; p24: Chris Hellier/Corbis; p26: Philadelphia Museum of Art/Corbis; p28: Chris Hellier/Corbis; p29: Keystone/Getty Images; p36: Popperfoto/Getty Images; p37: Hulton Deutsch Collection/Corbis; p43: Roger-Viollet/Rex Features; p44(L): Adoc-photos/Corbis; p44(TB): Richard Jones/Rex Features; p44(TR): Quirky China News/HAP/Rex Features; p45: Associated Newspapers Ltd. / Solo Syndication/British Cartoon Archive; p48: Express Syndication Ltd/British Cartoon Archive; p50: Bettmann/Corbis; p51: Everett Collection/Rex Features; p54: Associated Newspapers Ltd. / Solo Syndication/British Cartoon Archive; p60: Corbis; p61: Bettmann/Corbis; p63: Associated Newspapers Ltd. / Solo Syndication/British Cartoon Archive; p66: Associated Newspapers Ltd. / Solo Syndication/British Cartoon Archive; p69: Carl Mydans/The LIFE Picture Collection/Getty Images; p71: Associated Newspapers Ltd. / Solo Syndication/British Cartoon Archive; p73: Ralph Townsend; p77: Granger, NYC — All rights reserved.; p78: Bettmann/Corbis; p82: FPG/Archive Photos/Getty Images; p88: Topfoto; p94: Bettmann/Corbis; p98: Bettmann/Corbis; p105: Bettmann/Corbis; p101: Associated Newspapers Ltd/Solo Syndication/British Cartoon Archive; p106: Associated Newspapers Ltd/Solo Syndication/British Cartoon Archive; p110: SuperStock; p111: Scherl/SZ Photo/Mary Evans; p121: Austrian Archives/Corbis; p124: Photo12/UIG/Getty Images; p127: Photo12/UIG/Getty Images; p129: Age Fotostock; p139: Andrea Jemolo/Scala Archives; p140: Associated Newspapers Ltd/Solo Syndication/British Cartoon Archive; p144: Associated Newspapers Ltd/Solo Syndication/British Cartoon Archive; p147: Bettmann/Corbis; p151: Fair Use; p153: DeAgostini/Getty Images;

p160: Alfred Eisenstaedt/Pix Inc./The LIFE Picture Collection/Getty Images; p155: Everett Historical/Shutterstock; p161: Nazi Party; p163: Hulton Archive/Getty Images; p168: Punch Limited; p170: STF/AFP/Getty Images; p171: Imagno/Getty Images; p173: ZUMA Press, Inc/Alamy; p175: Sueddeutsche Zeitung Photo/Mary Evans; p177(T): Sueddeutsche Zeitung Photo/Mary Evans; p177(B): Bettmann/Corbis; p178: Corbis; p179: Keystone/Getty Images; p182: Luce/Keystone/Getty Images; p183: The Herb Block Foundation; p184: Hulton Archive/Getty Images; p186: Associated Newspapers Ltd/Solo Syndication/British Cartoon Archive; p190: Associated Newspapers Ltd/Solo Syndication/British Cartoon Archive; p192: Spencer Arnold/Getty Images; p194: Associated Newspapers/Rex Features; p195(TL): Carl Mydans/The LIFE Picture Collection/Getty Images; p195(TR): Corbis; p195(BL): Ray Illingworth/AP Images; p195(BR): Illustrated London News Ltd/Mary Evans; p197: INTERFOTO/Alamy; p199: Corbis; p200: Swarthmore College Peace Collection; p202: Associated Newspapers Ltd/Solo Syndication/British Cartoon Archive; p207: Associated Newspapers Ltd/Solo Syndication/British Cartoon Archive; p210: FPG/Hulton Archive/Getty Images; p215: Associated Newspapers Ltd/Solo Syndication/British Cartoon Archive; p219: Associated Newspapers Ltd/Solo Syndication/British Cartoon Archive; p213: Associated Newspapers Ltd/Solo Syndication/British Cartoon Archive; p225: Associated Newspapers Ltd/Solo Syndication/British Cartoon Archive; p229: Punch Limited.

Cover illustration by Karolis Strautniekas, Folio Illustration Agency.

Artwork by QBS Learning and OUP.

The authors and publisher are grateful for permission to reprint the following copyright material:

Norman H. Baynes: *The Speeches of Adolf Hitler April 1922 – August 1939* (Oxford University Press, 1942), reprinted by permission of Oxford University Press.

Herbert P. Bix: *Hirohito and the Making of Modern Japan*, copyright © 2000 by Herbert P. Bix, reprinted by permission of HarperCollins Publishers.

Jeremy Black and Donald M. MacRaild: *Studying* History (Palgrave Macmillan, 2007), copyright © Jeremy Black and Donald M. MacRaild, reprinted by permission of Palgrave Macmillan.

Martin Blinkhorn: *Mussolini and Fascist Italy* (Routledge), copyright © 1984, 1994, 2006 Martin Blinkhorn, reprinted by permission of Taylor & Francis Books UK.

J. H. Boyle: *Modern Japan: the American Nexus*, (Harcourt Brace, 1993) Javonovich, copyright © Cengage Learning.

G. Bruce Strang: On the Fiery March: Mussolini Prepares for War (2003), reprinted by permission of ABC-CLIO Inc., permission conveyed through Copyright Clearance Center, Inc.

J. Calvitt Clarke and C. Foust: *Russia and Italy against Hitler: the Bolshevik-Fascist Rapprochement of the 1930s* (1991), reprinted by permission of ABC-CLIO Inc., permission conveyed through Copyright Clearance Center, Inc.

Winston Churchill: Quotation copyright © The Beneficiaries of the Estate of Winston S. Churchill, reprinted by permission of Curtis Brown, London on behalf of the Beneficiaries of the Estate of Winston S. Churchill.

Martin Clark: *Modern Italy - 1871-1982*, (Longman, 1985), copyright © 1984 Taylor & Francis, reprinted by permission of Taylor & Francis Books UK

Gordon A. Craig: *Germany 1866–1945*, 1978, copyright © 1978 by Oxford University Press, Inc., reprinted by permission of Oxford University Press.

R. De Felice: *Mussolini il Duce II. Lo Stato Totalitario, 1936-40* (1981), Einaudi, Turin, Italy, © **1981, 1996, 2008 Giulio Einaudi editore s.p.a., Torino,** reprinted by permission.

Continued on back page

Course Companion definition

The IB Diploma Programme Course Companions are resource materials designed to support students throughout their two-year Diploma Programme course of study in a particular subject. They will help students gain an understanding of what is expected from the study of an IB Diploma Programme subject while presenting content in a way that illustrates the purpose and aims of the IB. They reflect the philosophy and approach of the IB and encourage a deep understanding of each subject by making connections to wider issues and providing opportunities for critical thinking.

The books mirror the IB philosophy of viewing the curriculum in terms of a whole-course approach; the use of a wide range of resources, international mindedness, the IB learner profile and the IB Diploma Programme core requirements, theory of knowledge, the extended essay, and creativity, activity, service (CAS).

Each book can be used in conjunction with other materials and indeed, students of the IB are required and encouraged to draw conclusions from a variety of resources. Suggestions for additional and further reading are given in each book and suggestions for how to extend research are provided.

In addition, the Course Companions provide advice and guidance on the specific course assessment requirements and on academic honesty protocol. They are distinctive and authoritative without being prescriptive.

IB mission statement

The International Baccalaureate aims to develop inquiring, knowledgable and caring young people who help to create a better and more peaceful world through intercultural understanding and respect.

To this end the IB works with schools, governments and international organizations to develop challenging programmes of international education and rigorous assessment.

These programmes encourage students across the world to become active, compassionate, and lifelong learners who understand that other people, with their differences, can also be right.

The IB learner Profile

The aim of all IB programmes is to develop internationally minded people who, recognizing their common humanity and shared guardianship of the planet, help to create a better and more peaceful world. IB learners strive to be:

Inquirers They develop their natural curiosity. They acquire the skills necessary to conduct inquiry and research and show independence in learning. They actively enjoy learning and this love of learning will be sustained throughout their lives.

Knowledgable They explore concepts, ideas, and issues that have local and global significance. In so doing, they acquire in-depth knowledge and develop understanding across a broad and balanced range of disciplines.

Thinkers They exercise initiative in applying thinking skills critically and creatively to recognize and approach complex problems, and make reasoned, ethical decisions.

Communicators They understand and express ideas and information confidently and creatively in more than one language and in a variety of modes of communication. They work effectively and willingly in collaboration with others.

Principled They act with integrity and honesty, with a strong sense of fairness, justice, and respect for the dignity of the individual, groups, and communities. They take responsibility for their own actions and the consequences that accompany them.

Open-minded They understand and appreciate their own cultures and personal histories, and are open to the perspectives, values, and traditions of other individuals and communities. They are accustomed to seeking and evaluating a range of points of view, and are willing to grow from the experience.

Caring They show empathy, compassion, and respect towards the needs and feelings of others. They have a personal commitment to service, and act to make a positive difference to the lives of others and to the environment.

Risk-takers They approach unfamiliar situations and uncertainty with courage and forethought, and have the independence of spirit to explore new roles, ideas, and strategies. They are brave and articulate in defending their beliefs.

Balanced They understand the importance of intellectual, physical, and emotional balance to achieve personal well-being for themselves and others.

Reflective They give thoughtful consideration to their own learning and experience. They are able to assess and understand their strengths and limitations in order to support their learning and personal development.

A note on academic honesty

It is of vital importance to acknowledge and appropriately credit the owners of information when that information is used in your work. After all, owners of ideas (intellectual property) have property rights. To have an authentic piece of work, it must be based on your individual and original ideas with the work of others fully acknowledged. Therefore, all assignments, written or oral, completed for assessment must use your own language and expression. Where sources are used or referred to, whether in the form of direct quotation or paraphrase, such sources must be appropriately acknowledged.

How do I acknowledge the work of others?

The way that you acknowledge that you have used the ideas of other people is through the use of footnotes and bibliographies.

Footnotes (placed at the bottom of a page) or endnotes (placed at the end of a document) are to be provided when you quote or paraphrase from another document, or closely summarize the information provided in another document. You do not need to provide a footnote for information that is part of a 'body of knowledge'. That is, definitions do not need to be footnoted as they are part of the assumed knowledge.

Bibliographies should include a formal list of the resources that you used in your work. The listing should include all resources, including books, magazines, newspaper articles, Internet-based resources, CDs and works of art. 'Formal' means that you should use one of the several accepted forms of presentation. You must provide full information as to how a reader or viewer of your work can find the same information. A bibliography is compulsory in the extended essay.

What constitutes misconduct?

Misconduct is behaviour that results in, or may result in, you or any student gaining an unfair advantage in one or more assessment component. Misconduct includes plagiarism and collusion.

Plagiarism is defined as the representation of the ideas or work of another person as your own. The following are some of the ways to avoid plagiarism:

- Words and ideas of another person used to support one's arguments must be acknowledged.

- Passages that are quoted verbatim must be enclosed within quotation marks and acknowledged.

- CD-ROMs, email messages, web sites on the Internet, and any other electronic media must be treated in the same way as books and journals.

- The sources of all photographs, maps, illustrations, computer programs, data, graphs, audio-visual, and similar material must be acknowledged if they are not your own work.

- Works of art, whether music, film, dance, theatre arts, or visual arts, and where the creative use of a part of a work takes place, must be acknowledged.

Collusion is defined as supporting misconduct by another student. This includes:

- allowing your work to be copied or submitted for assessment by another student

- duplicating work for different assessment components and/or diploma requirements.

Other forms of misconduct include any action that gives you an unfair advantage or affects the results of another student. Examples include, taking unauthorized material into an examination room, misconduct during an examination, and falsifying a CAS record.

Contents

YOUR GUIDE FOR PAPER 1

The years 1931 to 1941 saw the development of nationalist and militarist governments in both Europe and Asia. As these regimes began to pursue aggressive foreign policies, the hopes for a peaceful world following the First World War collapsed. Increasingly, the idea of "collective security" proved to be inadequate and by 1941 much of the world was involved in a devastating conflict which would cost the lives of millions.

This book deals first with the growth of Japanese nationalism and militarism, the resulting expansion of Japan into East Asia and the response of the Western democracies to Japan's actions. It examines the events that led to the Japanese attack on Pearl Harbor in 1941; an event that transforms the European conflict into a global war.

The second case study examines Italian Fascism and German Nazism. It looks at how the expansionist aims of these governments led to the break down in collective security among the European powers and the descent into a European war in 1939.

Historical concepts

The content in this unit is linked to the six key IB concepts.

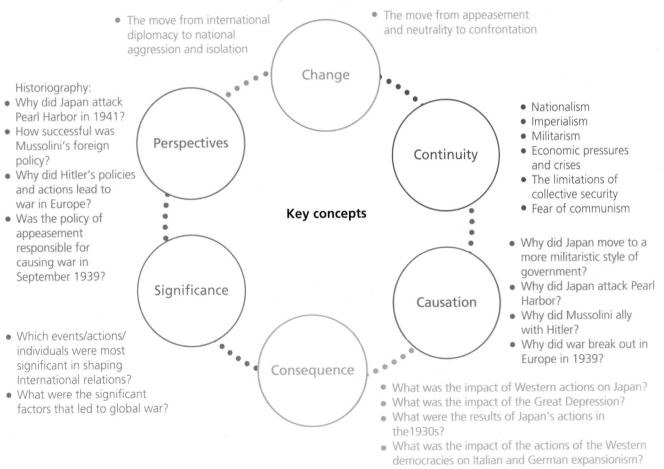

- The move from international diplomacy to national aggression and isolation

- The move from appeasement and neutrality to confrontation

Change

Historiography:
- Why did Japan attack Pearl Harbor in 1941?
- How successful was Mussolini's foreign policy?
- Why did Hitler's policies and actions lead to war in Europe?
- Was the policy of appeasement responsible for causing war in September 1939?

Perspectives

Key concepts

Continuity

- Nationalism
- Imperialism
- Militarism
- Economic pressures and crises
- The limitations of collective security
- Fear of communism

Significance

Causation

- Why did Japan move to a more militaristic style of government?
- Why did Japan attack Pearl Harbor?
- Why did Mussolini ally with Hitler?
- Why did war break out in Europe in 1939?

- Which events/actions/individuals were most significant in shaping International relations?
- What were the significant factors that led to global war?

Consequence

- What was the impact of Western actions on Japan?
- What was the impact of the Great Depression?
- What were the results of Japan's actions in the1930s?
- What was the impact of the actions of the Western democracies on Italian and German expansionism?

"The move to global war" is a prescribed subject for Paper 1 of your IB History examination. This book focuses not only on helping you to cover and understand the content relating to this topic, but will also help you to develop the skills necessary to answer the source questions.

The content of this prescribed subject may also be relevant to the topics that you are studying for Papers 2 and 3.

Each chapter in this book includes:

- analysis of the key events in each case study
- activities to develop your understanding of the content and key issues
- links between the content and historical concepts (see previous page)
- timelines to help develop a chronological understanding of key events
- a summary of relevant historiography
- a range of sources for each topic
- practice source questions along with examiner's hints

How to use this book

This first chapter will explain how to approach each question on the IB Paper 1; there will then be source exercises to try throughout the book which will give you the opportunity to practise your Paper 1 skills.

 Where you see this icon, you will find extra help answering the question, either at the end of the chapter or next to the question itself.

Where you see this icon, go to www.oxfordsecondary.com/ib-history-resources to find extra help answering full document questions.

Preparing for Paper 1: Working with sources

As historians, our training and discipline is based on documentary evidence.

— David Dixon

When you work with sources you are practising a key component of historians' methodology. Paper 1 skills are the skills that historians apply when they research a question and attempt to draw conclusions.

In Paper 1 you will:

- **demonstrate** understanding of historical sources
- **interpret and analyse** information from a variety of sources
- **compare and contrast** information between sources
- **evaluate** sources for their value and limitations
- **synthesize** evidence from the sources with your own detailed knowledge of the topic.

ATL Thinking skills

Read the following comment on sources and then answer the questions that follow.

"The practice of history begins with evidence and with sources. The availability of sources is often the key determinant of what becomes most popular, because some areas, for example nineteenth-century France, benefit from a greater volume of documents than others, such as ancient Germany. Whereas historians of early modern and medieval popular culture face a constant battle to find material ... those concerned with modern political history face a veritable forest of official documents – more than any one person could marshal in a lifetime. It is vital, therefore, that students of history become aware of the scope of historical sources, and the methods which historians use to order them."

Black J and Macraild, D M. 2007. *Palgrave Study Skills – Studying History*. 3rd edn, page 89. Macmillan. Basingstoke, UK

1   According to Black and Macraild, what makes certain historical subjects more popular than others?

2   What problems do contemporary historians face?

Communication skills

Following the catastrophe of the First World War the new Bolshevik government in Russia published all the Tsarist documents relating to the outbreak of the war. This led to other European governments publishing volumes and volumes of documents – in what became known as the "colour books" – but in most cases attempting to demonstrate how their country had **not** been responsible for causing the war. Historians have subsequently had vast quantities of documents to use as more government and military sources were declassified and released. However, as recent historiography has revealed, there is still no consensus among historians as to the key causes of the First World War.

3 In pairs discuss whether each generation of historian can move closer to "historical truth" and can be more objective because they are further away in time from an event and have more sources to work from.

4 Listen to this discussion on the historiography of the causes of the First World War: http://www.bbc.co.uk/programmes/b03srqz9?p_f_added=urn%3Abbc%3Aradio%3Aprogramme%3Ab03srqz9

What different interpretations do historians have on the causes of the First World War? What factors have affected their interpretations?

TOK

Following on from your discussions for question 3 and 4, get into small groups and consider *what is the role of the historian?* To what extent do you agree that the key role of historians is to bring us closer to historical truth? Or do historians, selection of evidence and use of language tell us more about their own eras and societies than those of the past?

What can you expect on Paper 1?

Paper 1 has a key advantage for students as the question format is given in advance; you can predict the nature and style of the four questions on this paper. This means that you can also learn and practise the correct approach for each of these questions and maximize the marks you attain technically. The majority of marks on this paper are awarded for skills.

This book deals with the prescribed topic of global war. As this is an IB prescribed topic you will need to ensure you have learned all of the content in this book which is linked to each sub-topic from the bullet point list set down in the syllabus:

Case studies	Material for detailed study
Case study 1: Japanese expansion in East Asia (1931–41)	Causes of expansion ● The impact of Japanese nationalism and militarism on foreign policy ● Japanese domestic issues: political and economic issues, and their impact on foreign relations ● Political instability in China Events ● Japanese Invasion of Manchuria and Northern China (1931) ● The Sino-Japanese War (1937–41) ● The Three Power/ Tripartite Pact; the outbreak of war; Pearl Harbor (1941) Responses ● The League of Nations and the Lytton Report ● Political developments within China – the Second United Front ● International response, including US initiatives and increasing tensions between the US and Japan

Case study 2:	Causes of expansion
German and Italian expansion (1933–40)	• Impact of fascism and Nazism on the foreign policies of Italy and Germany
	• Impact of domestic economic issues on the foreign policies of Italy and Germany
	• Changing diplomatic alignments in Europe; the end of collective security; appeasement
	Events
	• German challenges to the post-war settlements (1933–1938)
	• Italian expansion: Abyssinia (1935–1936); entry into the Second World War
	• German expansion (1938–1939); Pact of Steel, Nazi–Soviet Pact and the outbreak of war
	Responses
	• International response to German aggression (1933–39)
	• International response to Italian aggression (1935–36)
	• International response to German and Italian aggression (1940)

The four sources on the examination paper will be a selection of both primary and secondary sources. The length of each source may vary – but the total length of the paper should not exceed 750 words in total. One of the four sources will be a "visual" rather than text-based source, for example a photograph, cartoon, table of statistics, graph or map.

This book will thus give you plenty of practice with a wide range of different sources on the topic of global war.

How to approach the source questions on Paper 1

Refer to the guidelines below when attempting the source-based questions in each chapter of the book.

First question

This is in two parts. It is made up of a 3-mark and a 2-mark component – giving you a possible total of 5 marks. It is assessing your *historical comprehension* of the sources. You do not need to give your own detailed knowledge in your response.

This is the only question that asks you to **explain** the content and meaning of the documents

Part a

The 3-mark question asks you to comprehend, extract and possibly infer information. Here are some suggestions for answering this question:

• Write: firstly …, secondly …, thirdly … to ensure that you make at least three separate points.

• Do not repeat the same point you have already made.

• Do not overly rely on quotes – make your point and then briefly quote two or three words of the source in support.

Part b

• You should try to make two clear points for this question.

• For each point, refer specifically to the content of the source to provide evidence for your answer.

For parts a and b you should not need to bring in your own knowledge; however your contextual understanding of the topic and sources should enable you to understand more clearly the content and message of each source.

Second question

As you know, historians need to use and evaluate sources as they research a historical era or event.

For the second question, you need to evaluate one source in terms of its "value" and "limitations" by examining its origin, purpose and content. This question is worth 4 marks.

To find the origin and purpose look carefully at the provenance of the source:

For origin	**Who** wrote it/said it/drew it?
	When did the person write it/say it/draw it?
	Where did the person write it/say it/draw it?
	What is the source – a speech/cartoon/ textbook, etc.?
For purpose	**Why** did the person write it/say it/draw it?
	Who did the person write it/say it/draw it **for**?
For content	Is the language objective or does it sound exaggerated or one-sided?
	What is the tone of the source?
	What information and examples do they select or focus on to support their point?

From the information you have on the origins of the source, and what you can infer about the document's *purpose*, you must then explain the value and limitations the source has for historians researching a particular event or period in history.

The grid on pages 7 and 8 gives you an idea of the kinds of values and limitations connected with different primary sources.

Examiner's hint: *Note that value and limitations given in the grid are general or generic points that could be applied to these sources. However, your contextual knowledge and the specific provenance of any source that you get in the examination will allow you to make much more precise comments on the value and limitations of the source that you evaluate in a document question. Notice also that the value of the source will always depend on what you are using it for.*

What are the values and limitations associated with secondary sources?

The most common secondary source that you will have to deal with is one from a text book or historian. Again the key questions of "What is the origin of the source?" and "What is the source's purpose?" need to be addressed in order to work out the value and limitation of the source in question.

Here are some points you could consider regarding the value and limitations of works by historians and biographers:

Source	Values	Limitations
Historians	• are usually professionals or experts in field • have the benefit of hindsight which is not present in contemporary sources • may offer sources based on a range of documents; the more recent the publication, the more sources will be available	• might have a broad focus to their work or might have a very specific and narrow focus • might be an expert in a different region or era from the one they are writing about • may be influenced by their nationality, experience, politics or context
Biographers	• will have studied the individual in question in much detail • may provide sources that have value due to tone, use of language and expression • sometimes have the benefit of hindsight	• might have become too involved with their subject and have lost objectivity • may focus on the role of the subject of their biography at the expense of other individuals or factors • might not have direct access to the subject and/ or other relevant sources (the place and date will be key here) • may have limitations due to tone, use of language and expression

ATL Thinking skills

Consider the following provenance:

Kenneth Pyle, a professor of History, writing in the academic book, *The Making of Modern Japan* **(1996)**

1 Using the points on the previous page, consider the value and limitations of this source for a student analysing Japanese history in this period. (Remember to research Pyle's credentials as a historian of Japan.)

2 How would a school history textbook differ in value and limitations compared to the work of a historian?

ATL Communication and thinking skills

Task 1

Find a biography of one key figure from the period of history that you are studying. With reference to the questions above, analyse the value and limitations of the source in providing extra insight into the role and impact of this individual.

Task 2

What questions would you ask about an **autobiography** to assess its values and limitations to your research

ATL Thinking skills

Read the following extract:

Part of the problem for historians is defining what a source is. Although primary sources are usually closest, or indeed contemporary, to the period under observation, and secondary sources those works written subsequently, the distinction is actually quite blurred. Once we move away from simple cases [such as politicians' diaries, or cabinet minutes] which are clearly primary, difficulties do arise. Take Benjamin Disraeli's novel of 1845, *Sybil; or the Two Nations*. This is first and foremost a piece of fiction … For historians … however, Sybil is something of a primary source: it typifies the milieu (social setting) of the young Tory Radicals of the day [of whom Disraeli was one] …

Black J and Macraild, D M. 2007. *Palgrave Study Skills – Studying History*. 3rd edition, page 91. Macmillan. Basingstoke, UK.

Note: Disraeli was a 19th-century British Conservative Party leader, and British Prime Minister from 1874–80.

Question

What is the problem with trying to define sources as "primary" or "secondary"?

Examiner's hint: *Note that for the purposes of evaluation, a source has no more or less intrinsic value to historians just because it is primary or secondary.*

Always focus on the specific origins and purpose of a source – not whether it is primary or secondary. You do not need to give this distinction in your answer.

ATL Communication and thinking skills

Read the following statements. Why would these statements be considered invalid by examiners?

- A limitation of this source is that the translation could be inaccurate.

- This source is limited because it doesn't tell us what happened before or after.

- This source is limited because it is biased.

- This textbook was written over 70 years after the event took place so it is unlikely that the author had first-hand experience. This is a limitation.

- A value of this source is that it is an eyewitness account.

- This source is only an extract and we don't know what he said next.

- This is a primary source and this is a value.

- As it is a photograph, it gives a true representation of what actually happened.

Refer back to the Examiner's hint on page 5 regarding this table.

Source	Values These sources:	Limitations These sources:
Private letters (audience – the recipient) Diaries (audience – personal not public at the time of writing)	• can offer insight in to *personal* views or opinions • can indicate the affects of an event or era on an individual • can suggest motives for public actions or opinions • can, through tone, use of language and expression give insight into perspective, opinion or emotions	• only give individual opinion, not a general view or government perspective • may give an opinion that changes due to later events or may give a view not held in public • might have the motive of persuading the audience (in the case of private letters) to act in certain way • may have limitations because of tone, use of language and expression
Memoirs to be published (audience – public)	• can offer insight into *personal* views, suggest motives for public actions and might benefit from hindsight – an evaluation of events after the period • might show how the individual *wants* his or her motive or actions to be viewed by the public	• may revise opinions with the benefit of hindsight, i.e. now the consequences of actions are known • might be written because the author wants to highlight the strengths of his or her actions – to improve the author's public image or legacy • may have limitations because of tone, use of language and expression
Newspapers, television or radio reports Eyewitness accounts	• could reflect publicly held views or popular opinion • might offer an expert view • can give insight into contemporary opinion	• could be politically influenced or censored by specific governments or regimes • may only give "overview" of a situation • might only give a one-sided narrow perspective • could emphasize only a minor part of an issue • may have limitations because of tone, use of language and expression (Note that eyewitnesses are not useful just because they are at an event; each eyewitness will notice different aspects and may miss key points altogether, which could be a limitation)
Novels or poems	• could inform contemporary opinion • might offer insight into emotional responses and motives	• could provide a "dissenting" voice, i.e. not popular opinion • could exaggerate the importance of an event or individual • could have political agenda • may have limitations because of tone, use of language and expression

Statistics	<ul><li>can offer insight into growth and decline</li><li>might suggest correlations between indicators, e.g. unemployment and voting patterns</li><li>might suggest the impact of an event or its results over time</li><li>make comparisons easier</li></ul>	<ul><li>are gathered for different purposes (e.g. political, economic) and could be deliberately distorted</li><li>might relate only to one location or time period</li><li>might suggest incorrect correlations; there could be another causal factor not included in some sets of statistics</li></ul>
Photographs	<ul><li>can give a sense of a specific scene or event</li><li>can offer insight into the immediate impact of an event on a particular place, or people's immediate response</li><li>might offer information on the environment</li></ul>	<ul><li>are limited as we cannot see beyond the "lens"</li><li>might distort the "bigger" picture because of their limited view</li><li>might be staged</li><li>might reflect the purpose of the photographer; what did he or she want to show?</li></ul>
Cartoons or paintings	<ul><li>can inform public opinion as cartoonists often respond to popularly held views</li><li>can portray the government's line when there is censorship</li></ul>	<ul><li>could be censored and not reflect public opinion</li><li>often play on stereotypes (particularly cartoons) and exaggeration</li><li>could be limited to the viewpoint and experience of the cartoonist or artist (or the publication the cartoon or painting appears in)</li><li>may have limitations because of tone, use of language and expression</li></ul>
Government records and documents Speeches Memoranda	<ul><li>might show the government's position on an issue</li><li>can offer insight into the reasons for decisions made</li><li>might reveal the motives for government policies</li><li>can show what the public has been told about an event or issue by the government</li><li>might be a well-informed analysis</li></ul>	<ul><li>often do not offer insight into the results of policies and decisions</li><li>might not reveal dissent or divergent opinion</li><li>might not show public opinion</li><li>can be used to keep sensitive information classified for many years</li><li>may not explain the motives for a decision or political purpose</li><li>may have limitations because of tone, use of language and expression</li></ul>

ATL Research skills

Find primary sources of the types listed in the grid above for the topic that you are currently studying. Using the notes in the grid above, analyse the values and limitations of each of these sources.

For the sources that you have assessed, also look at the content and the language being used. How does the tone, style or content help you to assess the value and limitations of the sources?

Third question

This will ask you to **compare** and **contrast** two sources. Your aim is to identify similar themes and ideas in two sources, and to also identify differences between them. It is marked out of a total of 6 marks.

The key to this question is *linkage*, i.e. you are expected to discuss the sources together throughout your response. The examiner is looking for a *running commentary*. At no time should you talk about one source without relating it to the other. "End-on accounts" – where you write about the content of one source followed by the content of the second source – do not score well.

How do you approach this question?

You must find **both** similarities and differences. This is best presented as two separate paragraphs – one for comparisons and one for contrasts. Here are some tips:

- You could practice using highlighter pens – highlight the similarities in each source in one colour and the differences in another colour.

- You must make sure that you mention **both** sources in every sentence you write. The skill you are demonstrating is linkage.

- Always be clear about which source you are discussing.

- Find both the more "obvious" similarities and differences, and then go on to identify the more specific comparisons and contrasts.

- Deal with similarities in your first paragraph and differences in your second.

- Ensure that each point you make is clearly stated. If you quote from the sources, make this brief – quote only two or three words to support your point.

- Do not introduce your answer or attempt to reach a conclusion. This is not necessary and wastes time.

- Do not waste time explaining what each source says.

- Do not discuss **why** the sources are similar or different.

Examiner's hint: *Note that you must make more than **one** comparison and more than **one** contrast. You should attempt to identify **six** points of linkage as this is a 6-mark question. This might mean there are three points of comparison and three points of difference. However, there might not be balance – there could be two points of comparison and four points of contrast, or four points of comparison and two points of contrast.*

How to draw comparisons/show similarities

Both Source A and Source B …

Source A suggests … ; similarly, Source B suggests …

Source A supports Source B …

Like Source B, Source A says …

In the same way that Source B argues … , Source A points out that …

How to draw contrasts / show differences

Source A suggests … ; however, Source B says …

Source B disagrees with Source A regarding …

Source A claims … as opposed to Source B which asserts …

Source B goes further than Source A in arguing … while A focuses on…

Examiner's hint – what *not* to do: *The focus of this question is **how** the sources are similar or different – it is asking you to look at the content of the source. This question is **not** asking you **why** the sources might be similar or different.*

Do not use grids, charts or bullet points – always write in full paragraphs.

*It is **not** a full valid contrast to identify what is simply mentioned in one source but not the other (i.e. "Source A mentions that … played a role, whereas Source B does not mention this" is not developed linkage).*

Question Three will be assessed using generic markbands, as well as exam specific indicative content. The markbands are:

Marks	Level descriptor
5–6	• There is discussion of both sources. Explicit links are made between the two sources.
	• The response includes clear and valid points of comparison **and** of contrast.
3–4	• There is some discussion of both sources, although the two sources may be discussed separately.
	• The response includes some valid points of comparison **and/or** of contrast, although these points may lack clarity.
1–2	• There is superficial discussion of one or both sources.
	• The response consists of description of the content of the source(s), and/or general comments about the source(s), rather than valid points of comparison or of contrast.
0	• The response does not reach a standard described by the descriptors above.

Examiners will apply the "best fit" to responses and attempt to award credit wherever possible.

Fourth question

This is worth the most marks, 9 of the total of 25. It requires you to write a mini-essay. The key to this question is that an *essay* is required – not a list of material from each source. However, you are required to *synthesize* material from the sources with your own knowledge in your essay.

How do you approach this question?

It is recommended that you plan your answer as you would any essay question. The difference here is that you will use evidence from the sources as well as from your own detailed knowledge to support your arguments.

- First make a brief plan based on the sources and group them into either those which support the point in the essay title and those which suggest an alternative argument, or group them under themes if the question is open, e.g. "Examine the reasons for the changing alliances…". Add the sources to the grid as shown below.

- Then add your own knowledge to the grid. This should be detailed knowledge such as dates, events, statistics and the views of historians.

- When you start writing, you will need to write only a brief sentence of introduction.

- When using the sources, refer to the them directly as Source A, Source E and so on.

- You can quote briefly from the sources throughout the essay but quoting two or three words is sufficient.

- Use *all* the sources.

- Include own detailed knowledge

- Write a brief conclusion which should answer the question and be in line with the evidence you have given.

Sources that suggest X	Sources that suggest other factors
Source A	Source B
Own knowledge: events, dates, details	Own knowledge: events, dates, details
Source D	Source C
Own knowledge: historian	Own knowledge: events, dates, details
Source E	Source A makes more than one point, can be used to support more than one argument or theme
Own knowledge: events, dates, details	

▲ Planning grid for the fourth question – mini-essay

The Fourth question will be assessed using generic markbands, as well as exam specific indicative content. The markbands are:

Marks	Level descriptor
0	• The response does not reach a standard described by the descriptors below.
1–3	• The response lacks focus on the question. • References to the sources are made, but at this level these references are likely to consist of descriptions of the content of the sources rather than the sources being used as evidence to support the analysis. • No own knowledge is demonstrated or, where it is demonstrated, it is inaccurate or irrelevant.
4–6	• The response is generally focused on the question. • References are made to the sources, and these references are used as evidence to support the analysis. • Where own knowledge is demonstrated, this lacks relevance or accuracy. There is little or no attempt to synthesize own knowledge and source material.
7–9	• The response is focused on the question. • Clear references are made to the sources, and these references are used effectively as evidence to support the analysis. • Accurate and relevant own knowledge is demonstrated. There is effective synthesis of own knowledge and source material.

Examiners will apply the "best fit" to responses and attempt to award credit wherever possible.

Here is a summary of the key points for each question with the kind of language that is useful when answering each question.

First question, part a

Remember you have to show your understanding of the source and come up with three points. Here are some useful sentence starters:

> This source says that …
>
> Secondly …
>
> It also suggests that …

First question, part b

Always start with your key point.

> One message of this source is …
>
> This is supported by … *here refer to specific details in the source.*
>
> Another message of the source is …
>
> *You need to make a separate point, not an elaboration of the first point: you need two clear points about the message of the sources.*

Second question

This question is assessing your ability to analyse a source for its value and limitations by looking at its origin and purpose and content.

> Make sure that you use the words "origin", "purpose" or "content" in each of your sentences to ensure that you are focused on what the question needs, e.g.
>
> A value of the source is that its author …
>
> A value of the purpose is that it …
>
> The language of the content of this source indicates that …
>
> The content also seems to focus on, or use, examples which are …
>
> On the other hand, there are also limitations to using this source for finding out about … This is because (*explain here how origin and purpose can cause problems for the historian*) **or**
>
> A limitation of the origin is …
>
> A limitation of the purpose is …
>
> The content of this source makes it less valuable because …

Third question

This is designed to assess your cross-referencing skills.

When comparing two sources you could use the following structures:

> Sources A and B agree that …
>
> Moreover, the two sources are also similar in that … This is supported by … in Source A and … in Source B …

For a contrasting paragraph:

> Source A differs from Source B in that Source A says … while Source B argues that …
>
> Another difference between the two documents is that …
>
> Moreover, Source B goes further than Source A when it suggests/says that …

Fourth question

This is a mini-essay and is assessing your ability to synthesize sources with your own knowledge as well as your ability to give supported arguments or points that address the specific essay question.

Use your essay writing skills and vocabulary for this question.

In addition, as you are using sources as well as your own knowledge, you could use the following to help tie in the sources to your own knowledge:

> As it says in Source C …
>
> This is supported by the information given in Source …
>
> Source A suggests that … and this is supported by the fact that in the Soviet Union at this time …
>
> Historians have argued that … This viewpoint is supported by the information in Source E concerning …

How should I distribute my time in the Paper 1 examination?

A key issue for this paper is managing your time effectively in the examination. If you do not work through the questions efficiently you could run out of time. You must allow enough time to answer the fourth question; after all this is worth the most marks on the paper.

You will have one hour to complete the paper. At the beginning of the examination you have five minutes reading time when you are not allowed to write anything.

We recommend that you use your five minutes reading time to read through the questions first. This will give you an initial understanding of what you are looking for when you read the sources. Read through the questions and then begin to read through the sources.

How much time should I spend on each question?

Some examiners have suggested that the time you spend on each question could be based on the maximum number of marks that the answer could receive. The following is a rough guide:

First question, parts a and b	10 minutes	5 marks
Second question	10 minutes	4 marks
Third question	15 minutes	6 marks
Fourth question	25 minutes	9 marks

1 JAPANESE EXPANSIONISM IN EAST ASIA

1.1 The impact of nationalism and militarism on Japan's foreign policy: the origins, 1853–1930

Conceptual understanding

Key concept

→ Causation

→ Significance

Key questions

→ Assess the origins of Japanese nationalism and militarism.

→ Examine the reasons for Japan following an expansionist foreign policy in the 19th century.

▲ General Tojo bowing to Emperor Hirohito, 1940

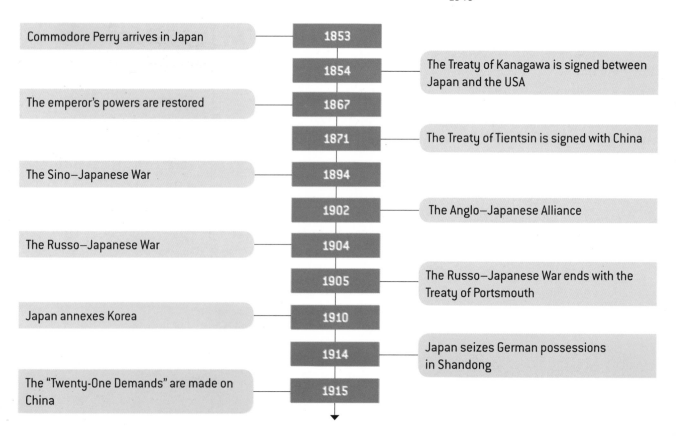

Commodore Perry arrives in Japan	1853	
	1854	The Treaty of Kanagawa is signed between Japan and the USA
The emperor's powers are restored	1867	
	1871	The Treaty of Tientsin is signed with China
The Sino–Japanese War	1894	
	1902	The Anglo–Japanese Alliance
The Russo–Japanese War	1904	
	1905	The Russo–Japanese War ends with the Treaty of Portsmouth
Japan annexes Korea	1910	
	1914	Japan seizes German possessions in Shandong
The "Twenty-One Demands" are made on China	1915	

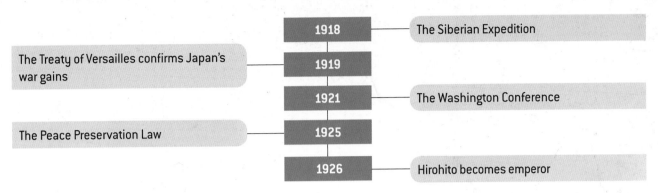

	1918	The Siberian Expedition
The Treaty of Versailles confirms Japan's war gains	1919	
	1921	The Washington Conference
The Peace Preservation Law	1925	
	1926	Hirohito becomes emperor

What were the origins of Japanese nationalism and militarism?

In order to understand the events of the 1930s in Asia, it is important to look at the roots of Japanese **nationalism** and **militarism**, which started in middle of the 19th century.

Several factors contributed to the growth of Japanese nationalism:

- the determination to transform Japan into a Western-style power, which was linked to the desire for equality with Western powers

- Japan's belief in its destiny as the leader of Asia

- the need to obtain raw materials and to secure markets in East Asia, and to stop other countries from doing this

- the need for strategic security

- the actions of the Western powers

- growing popular support for militarism and expansionism within Japan.

The impact of these factors was not only to promote nationalism in Japan but also to link that nationalism with an **imperialist** foreign policy as Japan took over other Asian territories in pursuit of its nationalist goals. Nationalism in Japan also became linked with militarism because Japanese expansion was dependent on the military taking action and making political decisions.

Japanese nationalism began in the second half of the 19th century when Japan had its first contact with the West. Up until this time, it had been isolated from the outside world in an attempt to shield its civilization from the perceived threat posed by Christianity. This had been the policy of Japan's rulers, the **shogun**, who had effectively ruled the country since 1192.

Nationalism
When the people of a country strongly support the interests of their own nation, possibly to the detriment of the interests of other nations.

Militarism
When a government or the people of a country believe that it is necessary to have a strong military in order to both defend and to promote the interests of their country.

The Shogun
Since 1192, Japan had been ruled by a feudal military dictatorship called the bakufu. Although the emperor was still officially the ruler, in practice the power lay in the hands of the Shogun who was a military dictator. Beneath the Shogun were the daimyo or feudal lords, and under the daimyo were the samurai or warriors.

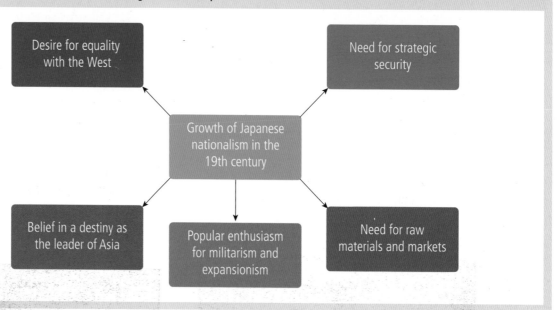

Communication skills

Copy out this mind map. As you read through this chapter, identify motives and events that support each of the five factors given below. Add this evidence to your mind-map.

- Desire for equality with the West
- Need for strategic security
- Growth of Japanese nationalism in the 19th century
- Belief in a destiny as the leader of Asia
- Popular enthusiasm for militarism and expansionism
- Need for raw materials and markets

▲ A representation of a factory in Meiji, Japan

However in 1853, an American naval officer, Commodore Matthew Perry, arrived on the shores of Japan with several US steamships. He was determined to get Japan to open up to US demands for trade. Intimidated by Perry's "Black Ships", and mindful of what had happened to China which had attempted to resist the West and had been forced to sign a series of humiliating treaties, the ruling Shogun, Tokugawa Yoshinobu, signed the Treaty of Kanagawa with the USA in 1854.

The effects of this treaty on Japan were immense. Political power now returned to the emperor, who became known as the Meiji or "enlightened" emperor. His government began modernizing Japan, dismantling the feudal system and establishing a limited form of democracy. Major reforms took place in all areas: industry, education, fashion and, perhaps most significantly, the military. At the same time, the Meiji government promoted national unity and patriotism; the reforms were led with the cry of "rich country, strong military".

Japan's military reforms included modernizing the army and adapting German military tactics. Japan also established a new navy with the help of the British. The results of modernization were significant. In the Sino–Japanese War of 1894–95, Japan defeated China, thus positioning itself as a world power with an empire. The Treaty of Shimonoseki gave the Pescadores Islands, Formosa and Liaodong Peninsula to Japan, recognized Korean independence and obliged China to pay a large indemnity, to open additional ports and to negotiate a commercial treaty.

Source skills

Source A

An extract from a memoir, written in 1931, by Ubukata Toshiro, a journalist-novelist, who was a teenager at the start of the Sino–Japanese War.

... Everybody agreed that it would be very difficult to capture Pyongyang, since the city held huge British cannons. However, in August, the Japanese army overpowered Pyongyang with so little effort that it almost was disappointing – and the Japanese people were enraptured. My home town had no telephone system back then. News of victories came to the police before the newspaper received it, thanks to a telegraph line between the post office and police station. All news was put upon the message board in front of the police station, and we children ran to check it several times a day. The excitement of the Japanese people was beyond imagination. After all, China was thirty times as big as Japan, and its population was over 200 million, compared to our 30 million. It had such a competent leader in Li Hongzhang… and this was our first war with a foreign country, a country supported moreover by the British. Everyone – adults, children, the aged, the women – talked about war and nothing else, day and night … no one ever had been as happy as when we learned of the fall of Pyongyang...

Source B

A Japanese artist depicts Chinese officials surrendering to naval officers in 1895.

First question, part a – 3 marks

According to Source A, why were the Japanese so excited about the victory over China in 1895?

First question, part b – 2 marks

What is the message of Source B?

Second question – 4 marks

With reference to its origin, purpose and content, assess the values and limitations of Source A for historians studying the impact of the Sino–Japanese War of 1895.

The effects of the First Sino–Japanese War on nationalism and militarism

Germany, Russia and France, concerned with Japan's growing power and its impact on Asia as a whole, forced Japan to give up the Liaodong Peninsula in what was known as the Triple Intervention. Much to Japan's fury, Russia then took the Liaodong Peninsula for itself, while Germany secured control over Shandong Province. France and Great Britain took advantage of the weakened China to seize port cities on various pretexts and to expand their spheres of influence. The impact of this can be seen in the sources below.

Source skills

Source C

An extract from Japanese government official Hayashi, written in June 1895 following the Triple Intervention.

We must continue to study and make use of Western methods … If new warships are considered necessary we must, at any cost, build them; if the organisation of our army is inadequate we must start rectifying it from now; if need be, our entire military system must be changed.

At present Japan must keep calm and sit tight, so as to lull suspicions nurtured against her; during this time the foundations of her national power must be consolidated; and we must watch and wait for the opportunity in the Orient that will surely come one day. When this day arrives Japan will decide her own fate; and she will be able not only to put into their place the powers who seek to meddle in her affairs; she will even be able, should this be necessary, to meddle in their affairs.

Source D

John Hunter Boyle. *Modern Japan: The American Nexus* **(1993).**

Speaking for many of his countrymen, journalist Tokutomi wrote that the Triple Intervention was to transform him psychologically and dominate the rest of this life. "Say what you will, it had happened because we weren't strong enough. What it came down to was that sincerity and justice didn't amount to a thing if you weren't strong enough." Japan had learned to emulate the West. It had played by the rules. From the standpoint of the victim, they were not particularly fair rules, but they were the established rules of imperialism. Now, in Japan's moment of victory, it found that it was reviled by yellow-peril sloganeering and denied equal membership in the imperialist club. Japanese, even those who had been most enthusiastic about Western models, became convinced, as Marius Jensen writes, that international law and institutional modernization alone would never bring full respect and equality from the West.

Third question – 6 marks

Compare and contrast the views expressed in Source C and Source D regarding the views of the Japanese towards Western countries.

The military success of the Sino–Japanese War, the gaining of land and also the frustration at having to give up some land to a Western power, encouraged the growth of nationalism and also militarism in Japan. It reinforced the idea that a strong military was necessary for Japan to be successful as a world power and to defend itself against other Western powers and against the Russians. Japanese military expansion increased between 1895 and 1905, and ministerial representatives of the army and navy were now to be drawn only from the upper ranks of the armed forces. This kept a military presence at the heart of the government.

There was a determination to strengthen Japan in all respects. Industrial production soared as Japan sought to become less reliant on imports of iron and steel. The population was told to "endure through hardship" as huge amounts of money were spent on the army and navy. A patriotic society, the Amur River Society, was established to promote the idea of Japanese expansion on the mainland.

Japan after 1900

How did international events contribute to the growth of nationalism and militarism?

Japan's position was further strengthened by the signing of an alliance with Britain, the Anglo–Japanese Alliance, in 1902. This not only ended Japan's diplomatic isolation but was also the first time a military alliance had been signed between a Western and a non-Western nation.

When Japan and Russia clashed over their interests in Korea and Manchuria, Japan went to war, with a surprise attack against the Russians in 1904. It was successful in its land battles, although with great loss of life; however, it was the war at sea that was decisive. The Russian fleet sailed halfway round the world from its base in the Baltic Sea to Vladivostok. When it arrived in the Tsushima Strait, it was destroyed by Admiral Togo and the new Japanese fleet.

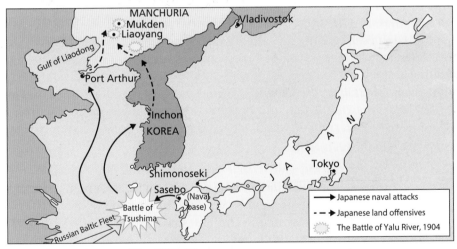

▲ The Russo–Japanese War, 1904–05

Why was Manchuria so important to Japan?

Manchuria was the area of China closest to Japan. Four times larger than the Japanese islands, it was agriculturally rich with mineral resources. This meant it provided important opportunities for the supply of resources to Japan. Manchuria also offered the possibility of providing living space for the rapidly growing Japanese population and, strategically, it could act as a buffer against the threat from Russia.

ATL Thinking skills

The Russo–Japanese War

An extract from Kenneth B. Pyle, 1996. *The Making of Modern Japan*, page 191.

The [Russo–Japanese] war required an unprecedented mobilization of the nation's resources. The government mobilised one-fifth of the male working population for some form of war service and sent 1 million men to the front. Casualties amounted to more than 100,000 and the financial cost was immense. Its cost was ten times that of the Sino-Japanese War and stretched the economy to the limit. To sustain so heroic an effort, the war was justified as a great popular undertaking. Nothing in the nation's history had so heightened political awareness as this war.

Questions

1 According to this source, what effects did the Russo–Japanese War have on Japan?

2 Discuss how Pyle has used language to present his argument.

An extract from Kenneth B. Pyle, 1996. *The Making of Modern Japan*, **page 196.**

Japanese imperialism was driven by continuing preoccupation with strategic advantage and a peculiar combination of nationalist pride and insecurity … This pursuit of empire and status as a great power coloured all other aspects of Japan's national development … If the drive for industry and empire was to be sustained, national loyalties would have to be continuously reinforced and every effort made to overcome the forces of disintegration.

Question

What are the implications of Pyle's assessment of Japan by 1906?

The Russians were forced to accept the Treaty of Portsmouth. Many Japanese were disappointed with the terms of this treaty as they had been led to expect much more. However, Japan gained control of Korea and much of South Manchuria, including Port Arthur. It also gained railway rights in Manchuria along with the southern half of Sakhalin Island.

The war earned Japan not only the respect of the West but also the admiration of other Asian countries, who saw the Japanese as a role model for how they, too, might take on the West and win. It also affirmed Japan's own belief in its destiny as leader of Asia.

Some Japanese were worried about the impact that such imperialism was having on Japanese society. The cost of the wars had an impact on its economy, and the need to defend its new territories brought with it the demand for a stronger army and fleet. However, the voices of those who argued for a less ambitious foreign policy were overwhelmed by those who wanted to improve Japan's position in Asia.

How did Japan benefit from the First World War?

The First World War gave Japan the opportunity to expand its influence in Asia further. Japan demanded German colonial territory in China and when this demand was ignored, Japan declared war on Germany, seizing Germany's military bases on the Shandong Peninsula in the north of China in 1914. Meanwhile, its navy occupied Germany's South Pacific possessions.

With the Allies distracted, Japan then issued China with the "Twenty-One Demands". The most important of these required China to agree to the Japanese remaining in Shandong and to grant Japan extra commercial privileges in Manchuria. China was also not to lease any more coastal territory to other powers, and was to accept political, financial and military advisers sent from Japan. These demands caused a sharp reaction from Britain and the USA, and also angered those within the Japanese government who believed that such actions stood only to damage Japan's reputation. As a result, the demands were modified.

Economically, Japan was able to take advantage of the First World War by supplying goods to the Allies and also by supplying orders to Asian markets that the Allies were unable to fulfil. Thus, exports flourished. Japan also became more self-sufficient as it developed industries to produce goods previously imported.

Another opportunity for Japan to expand came with the Bolshevik Revolution in Russia in 1917. Following the Russian withdrawal from the war, after it had signed the Treaty of Brest–Litovsk with the Germans, the Allies sent an invading force to support the Whites in the Russian Civil War against the Red Army of the Bolsheviks. The Japanese sent 70,000 men to support the Whites, even though they had originally agreed that they would send only 7,500 men. The Japanese also stayed on after the end of the civil war and after the British, US and French forces had left. Ultimately, however, they were defeated by the Bolsheviks and had to withdraw in 1922. The whole venture encouraged mistrust of Japan in the USA and Britain. At home, there were attacks on the government because of the cost of intervention in Russia, the loss of prestige and the failure to control the army, which had largely acted independently of the government during the expedition.

The results of the First World War for Japan

At the Versailles Conference that followed the First World War, Japan secured the former German Pacific islands as a mandate and Germany's former economic privileges on the Shandong Peninsula of China. These gains firmly established Japan as an important economic power on the Asian mainland and as the main naval power in the Western Pacific.

However, Japan was reminded that it was not fully a member of the "Western Club" by its failure to get racial equality clauses included in the Charter of the League of Nations. This was because leaders in Britain and the USA were afraid of the implications this would have for Japanese immigration into their countries (see right for more details).

ATL Social skills

Look back at the six factors, listed on page 15, that contributed to the growth of Japan's nationalism after 1853. In pairs or small groups, copy out the spider diagram and work together to add evidence from pages 15–21 to support these factors.

Japan in the 1920s

How peaceful was Japan in the 1920s?

Influenced by Shidehara Kijuro, who was ambassador to Washington in 1921 and foreign minister in 1924–27 and 1929–31, Japan changed to a foreign policy of internationalism during the 1920s. This aimed to develop Japan's economy via peaceful means: keeping good relations with the USA, a key trading partner, and continuing to seek economic advancement in China, but within the framework of international agreement.

Thus Japan was a signatory to several international agreements. At the Washington Conference of 1921, the Americans insisted that the Anglo–Japanese Alliance of 1902 should be replaced by a Four-Power Treaty; in this treaty Britain, Japan, the USA and France agreed to confer should the rights or possessions of any of the four countries be threatened in the Pacific. A Nine-Power Treaty, signed by China, Belgium, Italy, the Netherlands and Portugal as well as the signatories of the Four-Power Treaty, was concluded in February 1922. This undertook to respect Chinese independence and integrity, and to respect the "sovereignty, the independence and the territorial and administrative integrity of China". Japan agreed to return the German concessions in Shandong seized during the First World War.

Meanwhile, the Five-Power Naval Treaty restricted competition in battleships and aircraft carriers by setting a ratio of 5:5:3 for Britain, the USA and Japan respectively. France and Italy would each be allowed a 1.75 ratio. This treaty required Japan's Imperial Navy to abandon its plans for a massive expansion and was deeply opposed by the Navy General Staff.

These treaties together formed the Washington Treaty System and indicated that Japan was committed to international cooperation in the 1920s.

Japanese immigration to the USA

The flow of Japanese immigrants to the USA increased substantially after 1900. They worked mainly in unskilled jobs and faced discrimination in all areas. A growing fear of "the yellow peril", perpetuated by the US press, drove various anti-Japanese laws; the Japanese were not allowed to become US citizens and in states such as California were prevented from owning land. The 1924 Immigration Act discriminated against Japan by making it the only country not to be allowed **any** quota of immigrants into the USA.

▲ Shidehara Kijuro

The Washington Treaty System

Four-Power Treaty:	Five-Power Naval Treaty:	Nine-Power Treaty:
This ended the Anglo–Japanese Alliance. The USA, Britain, France and Japan were to confer if there was a crisis in the Pacific.	This limited the tonnage of the US, British, Japanese, French and Italian navies.	Japan, the USA, Britain, France, Italy, China, Portugal, Belgium and the Netherlands were to respect China's integrity and independence and abide by "open door" principles.

This change to a more international approach in foreign affairs was supported by internal developments that seemed to point to a more liberal and more democratic Japan. The term "Taisho democracy" referred to a series of reforms instituted during the latter years of Emperor Taisho's reign. As part of Taisho democracy, it became common for the prime minister's position to be given to the leader of one of the two main political parties that controlled the Diet in the 1920s. This was significant because it meant that those now gaining political power were doing so because of their experience rather than because they were members of the elite. Meanwhile, the electorate was extended until, in 1925, all adult males were given the vote. Society became more open and mass media more influential.

Prime Minister Hara's government lasted from 1918 to 1921 and introduced social and economic reforms. The military was contained and Hara's government led Japan into the League of Nations, where its membership of the Council showed that it was accepted as one of the world's leading powers.

What problems did Japan face in the 1920s?

Despite the moves towards democracy and internationalism in the 1920s, there were underlying problems in Japanese government and society, which came together in the 1930s to lead Japan towards a military dictatorship.

1. A fragile democracy

Japan's democratic reforms remained fragile. Financial scandals and election law violations eroded public support for the political parties. The links of each party with either the country's big business in the cities or landlords in the countryside also deepened the public's suspicions. The system no longer inspired respect.

In addition, there was a fear of left-wing radicalism. The year that saw the extension of the franchise also saw the government, via the Peace Preservation Law, clamping down on anyone who opposed Japan's political structure. This was aimed particularly at the Communist Party, which had been established in 1920. The passing of these two laws, one extending the franchise and the other limiting the public's right to engage in open discussion, indicated a dilemma in the Meiji government's ruling circles as to how much political freedom to allow.

2. Opposition to Shidehara's internationalism and the growing influence of the military on foreign policy

Many Conservative groups in the government, along with the army, questioned Shidehara's approach to international relations, seeing it as a betrayal of Japan's interests. The Washington Treaty System, for example, was seen as *"an Anglo-Saxon 'iron-ring' preventing Japan from expanding abroad"* (Bix, 2001: 226). They continued to advocate an aggressive policy in China and to see Japan's destiny as being the leadership of Asia.

The conservatives' dislike of Shidehara's policies was confirmed when the USA passed a bill limiting immigration from all countries to 150,000 a year, and specifically excluding "Asiatics" from the quota (see information box on page 21). This was very offensive to the Japanese and provoked strong protest from the Japanese press who called it a "grave insult" and "deliberate slap in the face". It played into the hands of the military and other opponents of Shidehara's policies, who saw the immigration bill as provocation by the West.

When Emperor Taisho died, the coming of new Emperor Hirohito was celebrated with a revival of the idea of the emperor as a living god, along with the revival of nationalism and the idea of Japan's special destiny in the world.

3. A growing economic crisis

The economic boom of the war years lasted only until the middle of 1921, when Europe began to revive and take back lost markets. Unemployment and industrial unrest developed and, in 1921, a bitter strike paralysed Japan's docks. There was a large divide between the cities and rural areas, and farmers suffered from the falling price of rice caused by good harvests and cheap imported rice. When farmers and workers tried to organize themselves politically, they were suppressed by the police. This again increased dissatisfaction with a political system that crushed the left and that seemed to be intimately associated with the *zaibatsu* (big business companies) and the landlords. The real economic crisis, however, came with the outbreak of the global depression following the Wall Street Crash in the USA in 1929.

Indeed, by the end of the 1920s, following a series of domestic and foreign crises, the Japanese government would come down on the side of repression rather than democracy.

What was the role of political instability in China in encouraging Japanese nationalism before the 1930s?

China's political instability was key in encouraging imperial competition on its mainland and preventing Japanese expansion into Korea and Manchuria.

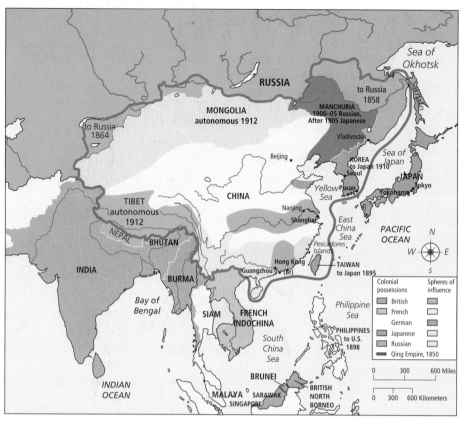

▲ A map depicting how colonial powers carved up China, 1850–1910

During the course of the 19th century, as European powers competed to gain colonies, China had been forcibly opened up for trade by the West. Although this had also been the case for Japan, following Perry's arrival, it had managed to turn this situation to its advantage, borrowing Western ideas to become a strong country after 1868.

However, China went on to become a semi-colonial country. Following China's defeat by the British in the Opium Wars (1839–42 and 1856–60), European powers gained extraordinary economic, military and legal privileges on Chinese soil, especially along the coast in the treaty ports. Officially, the Chinese Empire was still an independent power, but in reality it was at the mercy of other powers and their treaties, which were backed up by "gunboat diplomacy" or armed power. In addition, Christian missionaries flooded into the country

As we have seen, Japan wished to achieve equality with the West which, of course, also meant acquiring colonies. The Meiji ambition to be a "first-class country" helped to encourage the drive for expansion on the mainland. Naturally, this would also help provide economic benefits: the raw materials and the markets of East Asia. Japan could see the European powers sharing out the spoils of China and they were concerned that they would lose out if they did not also stake claims on the mainland. Strategically, Japan was also alarmed at the possibility of other powers having political control in Korea (seen as "a dagger thrust at the heart" of Japan) and China; it believed that Japan's security depended on it having a dominant influence in such areas. The Sino–Japanese War (see page 18) was fought over influence in Korea, and China's weakness compared to the newly modernized Japan was evident in its quick defeat. A revolution in China in 1911 toppled the Manchu dynasty. However, the country remained weak and divided. It was dominated by warlords who had fought among themselves and prevented any kind of national unity.

By the 1920s, the main political force in China was the Guomindang Nationalist Party (GMD) which, after 1925, was led by General Jiang Jieshi. However, the Communist Party of China (CCP) had been set up in 1921. The rivalry between these two political groups was to cause further instability in China in the late 1920s and 1930s, as you will read in the next chapter.

Source skills

A French political cartoon from 1898.

First question, part b – 2 marks

What is the message of this cartoon with regard to China in the 19th century?

Research and thinking skills

1 Add more evidence to your spider diagram (see page 16) on factors that had contributed to the growth of Japanese nationalism by the end of the 1920s.

   Which of these factors do you consider to be the most important?

2 Identify the factors that encouraged the influence of the military to grow in Japan during this period.

3 In pairs, discuss the role of China in encouraging Japanese expansionism in this period. Be ready to feed back your discussion to the class.

TOK

After you have discussed the review questions consider the following:

Did your class agree on which events were most significant? How might your choice of events impact the conclusions you draw about historical events?

Now discuss more generally who decides which events are historically significant and how this impacts our understanding of the past.

Source help and hints

You need to find three clear points to answer part a of Question 1 on the document paper. When reading through the source it is a good idea to first underline or highlight these points before writing them out.

First question, part a – 3 marks

(See page 17.)

According to Source A, why were the Japanese so excited about the victory over China in 1895?

Source A

An extract from a memoir, written in 1931, by Ubukata Toshiro, a journalist-novelist, who was a teenager at the start of the Sino–Japanese War.

Everybody agreed that it would be very difficult to capture Pyongyang, since the city held huge British cannons. However, in August, the Japanese army overpowered Pyongyang with so little effort that it almost was disappointing – and the Japanese people were enraptured. My home town had no telephone system back then. News of victories came to the police before the newspaper received it, thanks to a telegraph line between the post office and police station. All news was put upon the message board in front of the police station, and we children ran to check it several times a day. The excitement of the Japanese people was beyond imagination. After all, China was thirty times as big as Japan, and its population was over 200 million, compared to our 30 million. It had such a competent leader in Li Hongzhang… and this was our first war with a foreign country, a country supported moreover by the British. Everyone – adults, children, the aged, the women – talked about war and nothing else, day and night … no one ever had been as happy, as when we learned of the fall of Pyongyang.

> Cited in *Modern Japan, A History of Documents.* J.L. Huffman, OUP, 2004

Once you have found three clear points, it is an easy process to write your answer:

Example answer

Firstly, according to Source A, the Japanese were excited about the victory over China because the capture of Pyongyang was achieved very easily, "with so little effort", despite the fact that they had thought it would be "very difficult". Secondly, the Japanese were excited because China was so much bigger than Japan and had a good leader; this made the victory seem even more remarkable. Finally, they were excited because they had been successful in their first war with a foreign country.

Examiner's comment: *This answer would be likely to achieve three marks because there are three clear points. Note the brief quotes to support points, though you do not need to quote the sources directly. Make sure that you do not repeat the same point.*

First question, part b – 2 marks

(See page 17.)

Standing upright, taller than Chinese

Bowing

Western-style uniform

Fists clenched

Traditional dress

What is the message of Source B?

When you have a visual source, annotate the source to help you pick out the key points.

Your annotations should help you work out the overall message of the source and can be used as evidence to support your points.

Note that the phrases or words that are in bold in the example answer are key to making your answer clear to the examiner.

Example answer

The first message of this painting is that the Japanese are superior to the Chinese. **This is shown by** the Japanese standing tall and upright, in a commanding position with feet apart and fists clenched. **Conversely,** the Chinese are shown as being subservient by the fact that they are bowing. **Second,** the artist is also **giving the message** that the Japanese have successfully Westernized and thus modernized. **This is shown by** the fact that the Japanese are wearing Western uniforms, whereas the Chinese are in traditional dress.

Examiner's comment: *The message of the source is clearly stated and supported with details from the painting and so this answer would be expected to gain full marks. Two clear points are made.*

Second question – 4 marks

(See page 17.)

With reference to its origin, purpose and content assess the values and limitations of Source A for historians studying the impact of the Sino–Japanese War of 1895.

The key to this question is to look at the introduction to the source. This will give you the origin of the source and thus clues as to its purpose. The important point to pick up here is that this is a memoir written some years after the First Sino–Japanese War. Also note that it was written by a Japanese journalist who is recalling an event of his childhood.

Example answer

This source was written by a Japanese journalist who is recalling a key event of his childhood: the victory of the Japanese over the Chinese in 1895. A value of this origin is that the author experienced the event at first hand and so he can give us an eye-witness account of the impact it had on a small town. The purpose has value in that it is a memoir and it gives an insight into

how this event was remembered by some in Japan. It also has value as an example of what was being published about such events in the 1930s.

However, the source has some limitations relating to its origin and purpose. As it is a memoir, written some 35 years after the event, it is possible that Ubukata has forgotten some aspects, or that some events have taken on greater importance, especially as he is writing in 1931 when Japan is a great power. Memoirs are written with the purpose of being published and so it is possible that he is exaggerating some aspects to make his memoir more interesting. This limitation can be seen in the language, "no one had ever been so happy".

Examiner's comment: *This answer deals with both values and limitations, and refers to the origin, the purpose and the content.*

Note that expressions such as "it is possible that" are useful, as you may not know for sure.

Third question – 6 marks

(See page 18.)

Compare and contrast the views expressed in Source C and Source D regarding the views of the Japanese towards Western countries.

Again, for compare and contrast questions, annotate the sources when you read them to help you pick out the comparisons and contrasts. You can do this in different colours. This will make it easier to write your answer.

Below, as an example, two of the comparisons are picked out in blue and green; one contrast is shown in purple.

Source C

An extract from Japanese government official Hayashi, written in June 1895 following the Triple Intervention.

We must continue to study and make use of Western methods … If new warships are considered necessary we must, at any cost, build them; if the organisation of our army is inadequate we must start rectifying it from now; if need be, our entire military system must be changed.

At present Japan must keep calm and sit tight, so as to lull suspicions nurtured against her; during this time the foundations of her national power must be consolidated; and we must watch and wait for the opportunity in the Orient that will surely come one day. When this day arrives Japan will decide her own fate; and she will be able not only to put into their place the powers who seek to meddle in her affairs; she will even be able, should this be necessary, to meddle in their affairs.

Source D

John Hunter Boyle. *Modern Japan: The American Nexus*. (1993).

Speaking for many of his countrymen, journalist Tokutomi wrote that the Triple Intervention was to transform him psychologically and dominate the rest of this life. "Say what you will, it had happened because we weren't strong enough. What it came down to was that sincerity and justice didn't amount to a thing if you weren't strong enough." Japan had learned to emulate the West. It had played by the rules. From the standpoint of the victim, they were not particularly fair rules, but they were the established rules of imperialism. Now, in Japan's moment of victory, it found that it was reviled by yellow-peril sloganeering and denied equal membership in the imperialist club. Japanese, even those who had been most enthusiastic about Western models, became convinced, as Marius Jensen writes, that international law and institutional modernization alone would never bring full respect and equality from the West.

Example answer

Comparisons

- One similarity is that both sources refer to the Japanese use of Western methods. Source C talks of using Western methods and Source D says that "Japan had learned to emulate the West".
- Both sources are also, however, critical of the West's intervention. Source C accuses the West of interfering in Japanese affairs, while Source D says that Japan had found itself "reviled" by the West or "the imperialist club". Both sources focus on the humiliation faced by the Japanese following the Triple Intervention in the war and emphasize the bitterness felt by this.
- The tone of the sources is similar. Source C uses such language as "meddle" with regard to the West, while Source B quotes the journalist who accuses the West of not playing by the rules.

Contrasts

- The difference in the sources is that Source A focuses on a plan to remedy the situation, which involves continuing to copy the West, "we must continue to study and make use of Western methods … keep calm and sit tight …". Conversely, Source B focuses on the fact that Western methods haven't worked and the belief among the Japanese that, however much they copied the West, they would never get "full respect and equality".
- Connected to this is the sense that Source C is very positive about the future and believes that an "opportunity" for Japan to "decide her own fate" will definitely come, whereas Source D is much more negative about the future, implying that it will be very difficult to ever achieve equality.

Examiner's comment: *You should attempt to find six points of similarity and difference (indicated here for you in the answer). This could be three contrasts and three similarities. However, there is not always a balance between similarities and differences; there could be only two comparisons and four contrasts, or vice versa. The student has good "linkage" here, which means that the student has compared the sources throughout the question. This is key: do not talk about each source separately and then do the comparison at the end. Each and every point should refer to both sources. It should be a clear running commentary on both.*

The student also has some good, short quotes to support the points made. Review the markbands for the Third Question. Does this answer best fit the top boundary marks?

First question, part b – 2 marks

(See page 24.)

What is the message of this cartoon with regard to China in the 19th century?

It is important that you get used to interpreting cartoons. Cartoonists often use well-known caricatures or symbols to represent countries, so you should know what these are. For example, in this cartoon, France is shown as a woman with the revolutionary rosette on her hat; this is very common in cartoons. Britain here is shown as Queen Victoria, but is sometimes shown as the caricature of John Bull.

The cartoon has been annotated here for you. Use the annotations to help you write an answer to the question.

Western countries competing to get the largest slice of China

China unable to stop the Western powers; racist portrayal of China, indicating weakness

China shown as a pie being cut up into slices

Japan on sidelines watching with interest

References

Boyle, JH. 1993. *Modern Japan: The American Nexus*. Harcourt Brace Jovanovich. New York, USA

Pyle, K. 1996. *The Making of Modern Japan*. DC Heath and Company. Lexington, USA

Toshiro, U. 1931. "Promulgation of the constitution and the Sino–Japanese War". *Modern Japan, A History of Documents*, J.L. Huffman, 2004. OUP

1.2 Japanese expansion in South-east Asia, 1931–1941

Conceptual understanding

Key concepts

→ Causation

→ Change

→ Perspective

Key questions

→ Assess the impact of nationalism and militarism on Japan's foreign policy in the 1930s.

→ Examine the impact of economic factors on Japan's foreign policy.

→ Discuss the impact of the political instability within China on Japan's actions in Manchuria and mainland China.

▲ Japanese forces in Manchuria, 1931

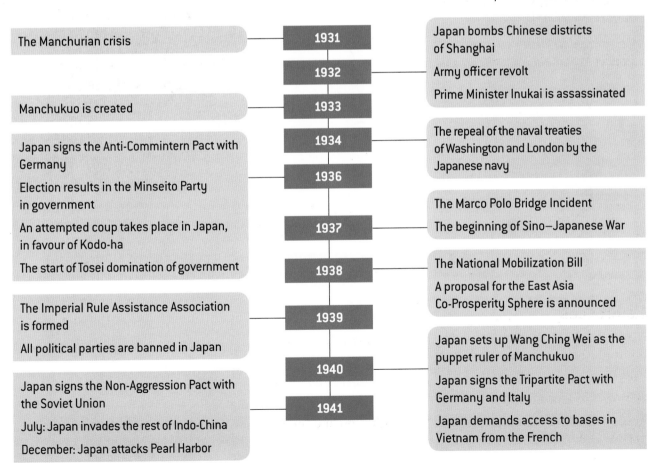

The Manchurian crisis	**1931**	Japan bombs Chinese districts of Shanghai
	1932	Army officer revolt
		Prime Minister Inukai is assassinated
Manchukuo is created	**1933**	
Japan signs the Anti-Commintern Pact with Germany	**1934**	The repeal of the naval treaties of Washington and London by the Japanese navy
Election results in the Minseito Party in government	**1936**	
An attempted coup takes place in Japan, in favour of Kodo-ha	**1937**	The Marco Polo Bridge Incident
		The beginning of Sino–Japanese War
The start of Tosei domination of government	**1938**	The National Mobilization Bill
		A proposal for the East Asia Co-Prosperity Sphere is announced
The Imperial Rule Assistance Association is formed	**1939**	
All political parties are banned in Japan		Japan sets up Wang Ching Wei as the puppet ruler of Manchukuo
	1940	Japan signs the Tripartite Pact with Germany and Italy
Japan signs the Non-Aggression Pact with the Soviet Union		
July: Japan invades the rest of Indo-China	**1941**	Japan demands access to bases in Vietnam from the French
December: Japan attacks Pearl Harbor		

Between 1931 and 1941, Japan's foreign policy continued to be defined by the growth of nationalism and the growing power of the military that you read about in Chapter 1.1. This led to intervention in China, a deteriorating relationship with the West and, ultimately, to the Japanese attack on Pearl Harbor in 1941 and the development of global war.

There are different perspectives regarding what led to the war between the USA and Japan in the Pacific:

- It could be argued that from the early 1930s, Japan had planned a war with the aim of dominating Asia. Japan's aims in the region could only be achieved through war; therefore, war in the region was inevitable. Japan used negotiations to delay an international response to their expansion for as long as possible.

- However, it could also be argued that although Japan did plan to expand its empire in Asia, war was not inevitable. This was because Japan was willing to achieve its objectives through negotiation. If possible, war with the major powers was to be avoided. However, if negotiation failed, Japan needed to be prepared for war.

- In addition, it could be argued that Japan was forced into war by the actions of the USA. Japan had legitimate aims for the region. The USA and Britain were determined to contain Japan.

▲ Growth of Japan's Empire

Causes of expansion

By the 1930s, Japan had fully modernized and gone a long way towards achieving equality with the West. The forces of nationalism and militarism had taken hold and were popular with the Japanese people; these forces had been given a boost by successes in wars against China and Russia, which had established Japan's position in mainland China. Most Japanese, by the 1930s, saw Japan's position in Asia as essential, not only for economic and strategic reasons, but because they believed it was Japan's destiny to be the leader of the region.

Throughout the 1930s, the impact of militarist and nationalist thinking in Japan continued to be important in encouraging an expansionist foreign policy. Furthermore, crises at home in the government and in the economy allowed these forces to have the upper hand. Another key factor that encouraged an expansionist foreign policy was the continuing political instability that existed in China.

Political instability in China

By the late 1920s, a new situation had emerged in China. It was this situation, combined with the growing strength of the military and the economic crisis in Japan, that precipitated the Manchurian crisis of 1931.

Encouraged by public outrage concerning the behaviour of foreigners in China, Chinese nationalism had grown. The Nationalist Party in China, the Guomindang (GMD), led by Jiang Jieshi, began a campaign of national unification. This included anti-foreigner rhetoric and demands to end the unequal treaties that the great powers, including Japan, had forced China to sign.

By 1921, a new political party, the Communist Party, had been set up in China. Initially, the Communists, led by Mao Zedong, joined with Jiang Jieshi to form the United Front. The United Front launched a "Northern Expedition" to consolidate central government control and wrest power from the **warlords**. However, ultimately, the Nationalists and the Communists were to clash in an all-out civil war which, from 1927, directed the energies and focus of Jiang towards defeating the Communists rather than the Japanese.

This changing situation in China was to have an impact on the actions of the Japanese government and military.

> **The warlords**
>
> The warlords were local or regional military leaders that had their own armies. They would rule areas of China as their own territories. Rivalries and competition between warlords meant that at times they were at war with each other.

Japanese domestic issues before 1932: Political crises and the growing influence of the military

The Northern Expedition, which had been launched by Jiang Jieshi with the Communists, was regarded with some degree of concern by the Japanese government. The Japanese had backed the warlord in Manchuria, Zhang Zuolin. However, Zhang had become very powerful and attempted to expand into Northern China, which made him a target for Jiang. If Jiang defeated Zhang, this could impede Japan's special interests in Manchuria.

The Japanese government planned to use its army in Manchuria, the Kwantung Army, to disarm Zhang and to force him to retreat back to Manchuria before he was defeated by Jiang. The policy was to let Jiang's GMD have China while Japan focused on its interests in Manchuria. However, some Kwantung leaders thought that Zhang should not be treated so leniently and decided to take action themselves. First, they forced Jiang's Northern Expedition to halt at Jinan. They then assassinated Zhang on 4 June 1928. Some of the Kwantung assassins believed that the fallout from this act would provide the excuse they wanted to conquer Manchuria.

Japan's Prime Minister Tanaka was instructed by the emperor to enforce discipline in the army. However, despite Tanaka's anger at this interference by the Kwantung Army in government policy, the General Staff were unwilling to punish the perpetrators as they claimed it would weaken the prestige of the army. In July 1929, Tanaka was forced to resign as he was unable to implement the emperor's wishes. Therefore, as early as the summer of 1929, it was clear that the army could ignore

> **The Kwantung Army**
>
> Since 1906, the southern Manchurian railway had been guarded by the Kwantung garrison, which in 1919 developed into the Kwantung Army. The Kwantung Army became a stronghold of the radical Kodo-ha or "Imperial Way" faction, with many of its leaders advocating the violent overthrow of the civilian government to bring about a military dictatorship (see page 39). They also advocated a more aggressive and expansionist foreign policy.

the government with impunity. This fundamentally undermined liberal democracy in Japan.

The leader of the Minseito Party, Hamaguchi Yuko, became prime minister but had to call an election in 1930 as he did not have a majority in parliament. He won a sound majority from the public on his manifesto of good relations with China, disarmament and an end to corruption. However, his government soon faltered as the impact of the Great Depression started to affect the economy (see below). Hamaguchi did not have the funds to help industry and so he cut government salaries for both the civil and military sectors. The military were unhappy with this move, but were then outraged when Hamaguchi agreed to the decisions made at the London Naval Disarmament Conference to limit Japan's naval growth. Criticism of the government, particularly in military circles, grew. In November 1930, things came to a head when Hamaguchi was shot by a right-wing radical. His injuries forced him to resign in April 1931 and he died in August.

Japanese domestic issues: Economic crisis

The global economic crisis which started in 1929 following the Wall Street Crash in the USA called into question the whole international economic order. This, in turn, cast doubts on the trustworthiness of the USA and other democratic nations, and on Japan's own parliamentary government.

Japan was dependent on world trade and its exports fell drastically as countries put up tariffs to protect their own industries. The Smoot–Hawley Tariff Act, signed into law by President Herbert Hoover in 1930, brought in the highest protective tariffs in US peacetime industry. Duties on Japanese goods rose by as much as 200%.

The worst hit industry was the silk industry. By 1932, the price of silk had fallen to less than one-fifth of what it had been in 1923. Farmers were hit particularly badly since over half of them relied on silk production. The result was desperate poverty as unemployment rose to 3 million.

The responsibility for Japan's plight was placed squarely on the shoulders of the liberal reforms of the 1920s. Taisho democracy and Taisho internationalism, never very robust and possibly doomed anyway, were about to become two more victims of the world depression. — Boyle, 1993

In this dire economic situation, Manchuria became even more important to Japan's interests. As you have read in Chapter 1.1, Japan had gained control of Port Arthur, as well as control of railway and mineral rights, when it defeated Russia in the Russo–Japanese War in 1904–05. Manchuria's wealth of resources (coal, iron and timber) were increasingly enticing to a Japan suffering the deprivations of the depression. If Japan took over Manchuria it would control these resources and also gain a market for its manufactured goods.

Manchuria could also provide living space for an over-populated Japan. In fact, Manchuria was depicted by the diplomat Yosuke Matsuoka (who became Foreign Minister in 1940) as a "lifeline" and "our only means of survival".

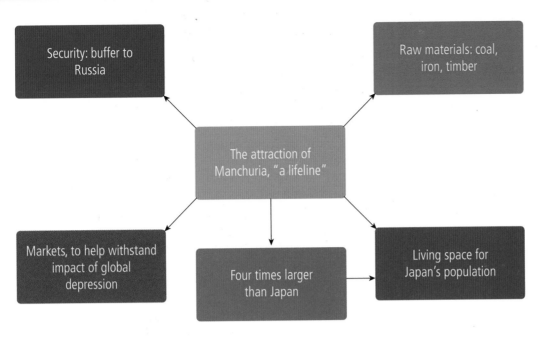

- Security: buffer to Russia
- Raw materials: coal, iron, timber
- The attraction of Manchuria, "a lifeline"
- Markets, to help withstand impact of global depression
- Four times larger than Japan
- Living space for Japan's population

Source skills

Source A

A graph showing Japanese exports 1926–38.

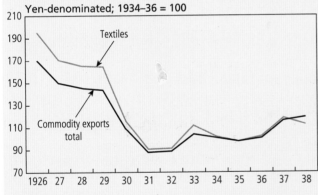

Yen-denominated; 1934–36 = 100

Textiles

Commodity exports total

I. Yamazawa and Y. Yamamoto. 1978. *Estimates of Long-term Economic Statistics of Japan since 1868. 14: Foreign Trade and Balance of Payments.*

Source B

Contemporary observation, 1929.

In this climate of economic despair and political decline, the military emerged as a seemingly shining and pure example of the true spirit of the nation. Aided in part by decades of indoctrination, the military found its most fervent support in the down-trodden rural areas. For many rural youths, military service was their escape from poverty and degradation. Military leaders and organizations such as the Imperial Reservists' Association promoted the idea that the "soldiers were the arms and legs of the empire …" and better than civilians. It stated that young peasant men struggling to survive "consider it to be the greatest honour attainable, once they enter the army to become a private superior class."

Source C

Herbert Bix, an American historian who specialises in Japanese history, in an academic book *Hirohito and the Making of Modern Japan* (2000).

Thus ideas advanced by Japan's leaders to justify their actions in Manchuria gained reinforcement from the breakdown of global capitalism, emergent monetary and trade blocs, and contending domestic systems of politics and ideology. In a lecture delivered at court before Hirohito and his entourage on 28 January, 1932, former army minister General Minami emphasized national security, raw materials, and the need for territory to explain the army's creation of an independent

Manchurian state. "Japan-Manchuria joint management", he told the emperor, would enable Japan to "withstand an economic blockade from abroad" and continue "indefinitely as a great power". The acquisition of Manchuria in its entirety would also solve the Japanese "population problem" by providing space for Japan's rapidly increasing people, whose numbers by the end of the decade were expected to reach 70 million.

First question, part a – 3 marks

According to Source B, why did the military have a particular appeal for the Japanese peasants?

First question, part a – 3 marks

According to Source C, why was Manchuria important for Japan?

First question, part b – 2 marks

What is the message of Source A?

Second question – 4 marks

With reference to its origin, purpose and content, assess the values and limitations of Source C for historians studying the Manchurian crisis.

Despite Japan's plans for Manchuria, it became clear that, given the aims of the Northern Expedition, China would fight for Manchuria. The Kwantung Army's hope that the assassination of Zhang would destabilize the situation and allow for Japan to seize control was not fulfilled, as the warlord was succeeded by his son, Zhang Xueliang, who allied himself with Jiang. Indeed, the Chinese Nationalists rallied behind anti-Japanese propaganda. While the Japanese government still aimed to follow peaceful principles to maintain Japan's position in the North-East of China, militants in the Kwantung Army were concerned that their objective of taking over Manchuria would become more difficult to achieve.

Thus, a group of Kwantung Army officers hatched a plot to seize Manchuria once and for all, against the policies of their own government. Prime Minister Wakatsuki was warned of the plan by Japanese consul officials in Manchuria. He informed the emperor, who ordered the minister of war, General Minami, to restrain the Kwantung Army.

Minami responded by writing an urgent letter to the commander of the Kwantung Army, but this letter was intentionally held back by the general tasked with delivering it. The plotters therefore executed their plan before receiving the emperor's command to cancel any action against the Chinese. As the historian Herbert P. Bix writes: "*[Emperor] Hirohito and his top palace advisers … never imagined that the Kwantung army would seize the initiative, completely overturn the Minseito cabinet's policies, and undermine the emperor's authority*" (Bix, 2000).

ATL Social skills

In pairs or groups, use the sources and the information in this section to assess the impact of the economic crisis on

- the political situation in Japan
- the position of the military
- the overall foreign policy of Japan.

Events in Manchuria, 1931

The impact of nationalism and militarism on Japan's foreign policy

On the evening of 18 September 1931, near Mukden, there was an explosion on a section of the Japanese-owned South Manchurian Railway. Immediately afterwards, officers of the Kwantung Army claimed that the railway had been blown up by the Chinese. However, there is evidence that the perpetrators were members of the Kwantung Army.

The Kwantung Army had its "excuse". Within hours, the Japanese had forced the Chinese to retreat from Mukden. The following day, the Kwantung Army entered Changchun to the north.

Wakatsuki's government attempted to regain control and declared a policy of "non-expansion of hostilities", but the Kwantung Army was relishing its victories and did not heed the orders coming from Tokyo. It began to seize more territory. On 24 September, the government declared that the army would fall back to the railway zone, but again the Kwantung Army ignored the government and pushed further into the Manchurian countryside.

Source skills

Source A

An extract from Kenneth B. Pyle,
The Making of Modern Japan, **page 189 (1996).**

The weakness of the government, the diffuseness of decision-making power, the general confusion and uncertainty attending both the domestic and foreign turmoil – all created an opportunity for resolute action by the Kwantung Army. It pushed ahead to conquer all of Manchuria and establish a Japanese puppet state, Manchukuo. Wakatsuki resigned and was replaced by a Seiyukai cabinet headed by Inukai Tsuyoshi. It was the last party government in pre-war Japan.

Source B

Prime Minister Wakatsuki's appeal to the secretary of the respected Prince Saionji Kinmochi in 1931.

I am not being kept informed by either the Foreign Ministry or the Army Ministry … I have just warned them through Chief of Cabinet Secretary Kawasaki … The Chinese forces in Manchuria and Mongolia number more than two hundred thousand [sic] while we have only some ten thousand. I asked the army minister, "What are you going to do if, by chance, your challenge causes something you haven't anticipated – something that given you are so outnumbered you can't stop?"

The army minister told me, "We'll send in troops from Korea … indeed, they may have already gone in." I rebuked him: "How can you allow dispatch of soldiers from Korea without government authorization?" He said, "Well, the fact is that during the Tanaka cabinet [1927–29] troops were dispatched without imperial sanction." I gathered he had not foreseen any problem at all … under these circumstances I am quite powerless to restrain the military. How can his majesty's military act without his sanction? What can I do? Maybe I should not be talking to you like this, but can you do anything? … I am in serious trouble.

Cited in *Hirohito and the Making of Modern Japan,* page 236, by Herbert P. Bix

First question, part a – 3 marks

According to Source A, why was the Kwantung Army able to seize control of Manchuria?

First question, part a – 3 marks

According to Source B, what problems did Wakatsuki face in responding to events in Manchuria?

Third question – 6 marks

Compare and contrast the views in Source A and Source B regarding the weakness of the Japanese government during the Manchurian Crisis.

ATL Thinking skills

In pairs, identify the factors in Japan and China, which led to the Mukden Incident in Manchuria.

What were the results of the Manchurian crisis?

The results for Japan's international relations

To the outside world, Japan's proclamations of peaceful intent seemed deceitful, as its army continued to expand in Manchuria. The breakdown of control over the Kwantung Army had not been fully appreciated.

Thus there followed, in the 1930s, a marked deterioration in relations between Japan on the one hand and the USA and Britain on the other. Although, as you will read in the next chapter, the West's response to the Manchurian crisis in 1931 was rather cautious, nevertheless, its condemnation of Japan for using force caused Japan to leave the League of Nations.

The historian Kenneth Pyle sees the Manchurian crisis as a "turning point" for Japan. Indeed, it led to Japan's isolation as it now seemed to have abandoned international cooperation and the Washington Treaty System. Within Japan, the League of Nations, international law and the West were attacked not only by the military but also by politicians. The League's resolutions on the Manchurian crisis were compared to the Triple Intervention of 1895 (see page 18) and Foreign Minister Uchida claimed that "*Recognition of the new state* [of Manchukuo] *in no way conflicts with the Nine-Power Treaty*". As in 1895, the West was seen as holding back the legitimate needs of Japan for racist reasons, as upholding international law only when it suited themselves and allowing their own imperialist actions to go unchallenged.

Following on from this, and as the military gained more power in the 1930s, there was a degree of admiration within Japan for Nazi Germany which had also walked out of the League of Nations. In contrast, the new Soviet communist regime was both an ideological and a territorial threat to Japan, with its interests in Manchuria. By the 1930s, the Japanese viewed the Soviets as their key potential opponent in the region. Increasingly concerned by the relationship between

Source skills

Japanese troops marching into a Chinese town, Manchuria, circa September–October 1931.

First question, part b – 2 marks

What is the message of this photograph?

China and the Soviet Union, Japan signed the Anti-Comintern Pact with Nazi Germany in November 1936. However, it is important to note that unlike Italy and Germany, Japan never had a Fascist Party leading the government nor did it abandon elections or cabinet governments, even during the Second World War.

The results for Manchuria and China

By the beginning of 1932 Manchuria was wholly under the control of Japanese forces. The Japanese in Manchuria set up an independent government under the puppet rule of Pu Yi (the last emperor of China) and called the new state "Manchukuo".

In January 1932, fighting had also broken out between Japanese and Chinese forces in Shanghai. The city was bombed by the Japanese with widespread devastation of the Chinese districts. The intense bombing over the densely populated residential area of Chapei, with the thousands of casualties and refugees that were created as a result, intensified Chinese outrage and helped turn world opinion against Japan. Four divisions of Japanese troops landed to assist the navy stationed in Shanghai. After six weeks, Chinese forces were forced to withdraw.

▲ Smoke rises from buildings in Shanghai's native business district, where Japanese troops launch an attack against defending Chinese, 1932.

ATL Thinking skills

Extract from Herbert P. Bix, *Hirohito and the Making of Modern Japan*, page 251 (2000).

Neither army nor navy drew any conclusions from the heavy losses they incurred in this first large battle with a modern Chinese army. They continued as before – utterly contemptuous of the Chinese military and people, whom they saw as a rabble of ignorant, hungry peasants, lacking racial or national consciousness, that could easily be vanquished by one really hard blow.

Quesion

What point is Bix making regarding the attitude of the Japanese military in China?

The results for the Nationalist Party in China

China's response to the Manchurian crisis was to call on the League of Nations. Jiang Jieshi, the leader of the Nationalist Party, was now focused on defeating the Chinese Communists and did not want to get involved in another conflict. He knew that he was unlikely to receive

ATL Thinking skills

I. Hsü, *The Rise of Modern China*, page 550. Published in 1995 by Oxford University Press, Oxford, UK

In retrospect, one cannot help feeling that such a negative approach could hardly achieve positive results. If the government had authorised the Northeastern army to resist the invader, the glamour of aggression might have been dimmed, thus providing a chance for the more moderate civilian government in Tokyo to have had a greater voice in the China affair. Moreover, if Nanking [Nanjing] had pursued an active policy of negotiations with Tokyo, it might have reaped more positive results. Unfortunately, it followed neither course. Instead it placed its reliance on protests to Tokyo and on appeals to the League of Nations.

According to Hsü, how could events have been different if China had been more active in solving the Manchurian issue itself?

The Monroe Doctrine was a 19th-century US policy, which set out to prevent the European powers expanding their colonial interests in North or South America. Japan's version of the Monroe Doctrine would be a policy limiting European influence in Asia.

the kind of support he needed from the Western powers, but hoped nevertheless that he could gain time to organize his defences. He also did not directly negotiate with the Japanese government. This combination of "non-resistance", no-compromise and non-direct negotiation was unlikely to benefit the Chinese position (see historian Immanuel Hsü's view to the left).

Although Jiang was reluctant to confront Japan directly, the Chinese people responded with fury at Japan's actions. There was a boycott of Japanese products, which had an impact on Japan as it reduced sales of its goods in China by two-thirds. This did little to stop Japan's actions, however, or to change Jiang's priorities in dealing with the Communists first before dealing with the Japanese. Thus, following the bombing of Shanghai and Japan's continued expansion in the north, China continued to cede territory. Japanese control of Manchuria was accepted in May 1933 in the Treaty of Tanggu. Jiang further agreed to the seizure of parts of inner Mongolia and, in June 1935, agreed to remove all troops from Hebei province. Jiang's strategy against Japan derived from his belief that, given the size of China, Japan would exhaust itself in the process of trying to occupy it. He believed that the Japanese "were a disease of the skin while the communists were a disease of the heart"; thus, he considered "selling space to buy time", a viable strategy.

The results for the Japanese government

Japan benefited economically from the occupation of Manchuria. However, the cost of maintaining a sizeable army on the Chinese mainland to some extent negated the benefits and there was an increase in taxation back home in Japan. Indeed, by going it alone internationally and also declaring its responsibility for maintaining peace in Asia through the "Asia Monroe Doctrine", Japan was potentially overstretching itself. It needed to be able to protect itself against the Soviet Army and the US navy, and also to make the Chinese government accept its position in Manchuria and Northern China. This precarious situation was the result of decision-making by the army rather than the government and of the nationalist sentiment that had been growing in Japan.

Following the Manchurian crisis, there was little hope that the government would regain the upper hand. Indeed, the Japanese government's position was further undermined by public support for the Kwantung Army's actions in China. There was a celebration of the "heroes" of Manchuria; the embarrassed Japanese government had to go along with the wave of popular opinion and accept the conquests rather than demonstrate the loss of control it had over the army. Foreign criticism and condemnation also galvanized Japanese nationalist sentiments.

ATL Communication skills

Go to the link www.youtube.com/watch?v=OExOfMNK-R4, or search "Evidence of Japanese accusation at WW2 #1", to watch Japanese Foreign Minister Matsuoka at the League of Nations , February 1933, defending Japan's China Policy

Source skills

Saburo Ienaga, a Japanese historian, in an academic book *The Pacific War (Taiheiyo Senso) 1931–45*, page 129 (1968).

The Imperial Army's march into Manchuria was presented as an act of self-defence to guard "Japan's lifeline", which had been acquired at great cost in blood and treasure in the Sino-Japanese and Russo-Japanese wars. Next, North China and Inner Mongolia had to be controlled to guard Manchuria. Protecting these areas required further advances into the heartland of China. This pattern of ever-expanding military operations confirmed a truism about international conflict: once started, a war escalates uncontrollably in the quest for elusive victory.

How could China be brought to its knees? That was an intractable problem.

First question, part a – 3 marks

What points are made by Ienaga regarding the impact of Japan's takeover of Manchuria?

Second question – 4 marks

With reference to its origin, purpose and content, assess the values and limitations of this source for historians studying the Manchurian crisis.

Years of turmoil: The descent into "the Dark Valley"

After 1932, there was division not only between the military and the politicians but within the military itself. This further destabilized the political situation at the time and would ultimately lead to the establishment of a military government and the descent into what the Japanese call "the Dark Valley".

Japanese domestic issues after 1932

Political crises and the growing influence of the military

Although some generals did not want to replace the government with a military junta, there was growing momentum behind the militarist groups that did. There were two key groups that wanted more influence for the military: the Koda-ha or Imperial Way faction, and the Tosei-ha or Control faction. Both groups were imperialist and wanted Japanese expansion. However, the Koda-ha was generally the more radical of the two. The Koda-ha faction believed in a military dictatorship that would deliver state socialism. Its leading officers viewed the Soviet Union as Japan's main enemy. They saw war with the Soviet Union as inevitable and the conquest of Manchuria as the first step towards this. They emphasized national "spirit" over material force.

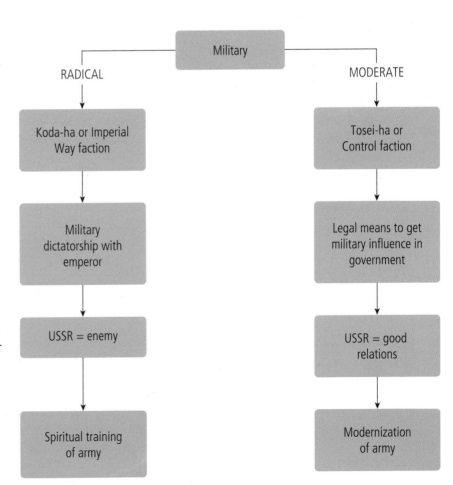

The Tosei-ha were against terrorism and the use of force to remove the government. They wanted to use legal means to foster military power and influence over the government. They did not see war with the Soviet Union as inevitable and wanted to maintain good relations with the Soviets. Their objective was conquest in China, which would require the modernization of the army and industry as well as the mobilization of the whole nation.

As part of this internal contest for power in Japan, three major assassination plots destabilized the government between 1932 and 1936. One of these took place in May 1932, when a number of army and navy officers attacked banks, party officers and the police headquarters in Tokyo. Prime Minister Inukai was shot and killed.

The trial of the conspirators demonstrated widespread support for their actions and a general disillusionment with the ruling political parties. Therefore, the "May 15th Incident", as it became known, enhanced the influence of the army and further undermined the democratic government. The subsequent governments of Admiral Saito and Admiral Okada were interim governments, during which the army played out its power struggle between the Koda-ha and the Tosei-ha factions.

Admiral Saito's government (May 1932–July 1934) seemed to favour the Kodo-ha faction, as it appointed three of its leaders into high positions. However, Saito took a firm stance against the Kodo-ha's radical factions and, after a plot against him was discovered, he promoted a member of the Tosei-ha to minister of war.

Admiral Okada took over in July 1934. During his leadership, the Kodo-ha produced a publication promoting the idea that the army should control the economy. When a Kodo-ha minister was sacked for not keeping control of his young officers, a Kodo-ha officer assassinated the leader of the Tosei-ha, General Nagata.

There was sympathy for the assassin, Aizawa, at his trial but he was found guilty and executed. In response, a group of young Kodo-ha officers attempted a revolt to seize power in February 1936. 1,500 soldiers marched into Tokyo and took over the parliament buildings, the war office, police headquarters and the prime minister's residence. They brutally murdered many officials. News of their attempted and bloody coup went around the world.

Fifteen of the key conspirators were tried in secret and shot. The Kodo-ha faction was discredited. From then on, members of the Tosei-ha faction were most important in developing army planning, and this meant that the army would now take firmer control of the country.

Admiral Okada resigned after the attempted coup and Hirota Koki became prime minister. From the start, he was weak and had to make compromises with the military, including agreeing to pursue a strong foreign policy. In May 1936, he agreed that the ministers for the army and navy had to be serving officers. He later agreed to a seven-point programme from the army, which basically handed control of the government to the military. Hirota agreed to expand arms production and support the army in Manchuria. He also signed the Anti-Comintern Pact with Hitler in November, 1936. When the National Diet declared its alarm

Communication skills

Go to: www.youtube.com/watch?v=yDv8NxGv9Yg, or search for "The Road to War – Japan".

Watch the Pathé News clip, starting 22.30 minutes into the video. Make notes on how the coup was reported.

at the direction the military was taking, the government was brought down.

The government of General Hayashi was in power between February and June 1937. The Diet was the only instrument of power left that attempted to limit the military's power. However, its politicians were divided. In June, Prince Konoye Fumimaro took over as prime minister and it was hoped that, with his long political experience, he could unite the nation politically.

Konoye wanted to restrain the army, but it was soon apparent that he would not be able to; the Tosei-ha faction was dominant in the government and expansion in China was their objective. A leading Tosei-ha general, General Tojo Hideki, became Chief of Staff to the Kwantung Army in July 1937. Within six weeks of Konoe taking power, Japan's army commanders had ordered the invasion of China. Konoe was powerless to halt it.

> **Class discussion**
>
> Discuss possible reasons for Japan's decision to sign the Anti-Comintern Pact with Nazi Germany in November, 1936.

Year	Prime Minister	Features of the period
1931	Wakatsuki	Party Cabinet; undermined by the Kwantung Army taking over Manchuria
1931–32	Inukai	Party Cabinet; assassinated in 1932
1932–34	Admiral Saito	Moderate admirals; power struggle between Tosei-ha and Kodo-ha factions, which resulted in the supremacy of the Tosei-ha and paved the way for more military control over government
1934–36	Admiral Okada	
1936–37	Hirota Koki	Growing militarism; concessions to the army
1937	General Hayashi	
1937–39	Prince Konoe	Unable to control the military; war with China starts
1939	Baron Hiranuma	
1939–40	General Abbe	Japanese expansion in China and South-East Asia
1940	Admiral Yonai	Tripartite Pact
1940–41	Prince Konoe	Diplomatic activity with the USA; fails to control militarists
1941	General Tojo	Attack on Pearl Harbor

▲ Summary of the political changes, 1931–41

Source skills

Source A

Watch a 1936 Japanese anti-American cartoon, *Evil Mickey attacks Japan*:

www.youtube.com/watch?v=icVu-acHlpU.

Source B

Hirota Koki's government adopted the following principles of national policy:

Japan must become the stabilising force in East Asia both in name and in fact so as to contribute to the peace and welfare of mankind and at the same time manifest the ideals of the nation ... The fundamental principles are described below:

1. Japan must strive to eradicate the aggressive policies of the great powers, and share with East Asia the joy which is based on the true principle of co-existence and co-prosperity. This is the spirit of the Imperial Way ...

2. Japan must complete her national defence and armament to protect her national security and development. In this way, the position of the Empire as the stabilizing

force in East Asia can be secured both in name and in fact.

3. The policy toward the continent must be based on the following factors: in order to promote Manchukuo's healthy development and to stabilise Japan-Manchukuo national defense, the threat from the north, the Soviet Union, must be eliminated; in order to promote our economic development, we must prepare against Great Britain and the United States and bring about close collaboration between Japan, Manchukuo, and China. In the execution of this policy, Japan must pay due attention to friendly relations with other powers.

4. Japan plans to promote her racial and economic development in the South Seas, especially in the outerlying South Seas area.

"Fundamental Principles of National Policy", 11 August 1936 in Lu, David J., 1997. Japan: A Documentary History, pages 418–20.

Source C

Richard Storry, a professor of history, in an academic book *Japan and the Decline of the West in Asia 1894–1943*, page 149 (1979).

For rather more than four years, from the spring of 1933 to the summer of 1937, there was peace of a kind between China and Japan. But there was no abatement of Japanese interference, economic and political, in the affairs of Northern China. And at a Tokyo press conference in 1934 a Foreign Ministry spokesman enunciated what appeared to be, despite disclaimers, a Japanese "Monroe Doctrine", warning foreign powers to keep their hands off China.

First question, part a – 3 marks

What are the key points made in Source B regarding Japanese policy in Asia?

First question, part b – 2 marks

What is the overall message of the cartoon in Source A?

Second question – 6 marks

With reference to its origin, purpose and content, assess the values and limitations of Source C for historians studying the Second World War in the Pacific.

Third question – 4 marks

Compare and contrast the views given in Sources B and C regarding Japanese aims and actions during this period.

The Sino–Japanese War of 1937

At the Marco Polo Bridge, near Beijing, fighting broke out between Japanese and Chinese forces on 7 July 1937. In contrast to the Mukden Incident, there is limited evidence that this clash was deliberately set up by Japanese forces, although the army had drawn forces into China from Korea without consulting the government in Tokyo. The minister of war demanded that more forces were deployed from Korea and Manchuria, and although Prince Konoye attempted to contain the army, reinforcements were sent. This led to the full-scale war with China.

By the end of July, Japanese forces had taken Beijing, and the following month there was fighting in Shanghai. Japan was engaged both in the north and in and around Shanghai, and was thus fighting a war on two fronts.

Although the Marco Polo Bridge Incident has often been described as a repetition of that earlier event which led to the Manchurian Incident, reliable postwar studies have concluded that the 1937 incident was not the result of prearranged planning

Class discussion

Why was the Japanese government unable to prevent a full-scale war developing with China in 1937?

by Japanese authorities – either those in Tokyo or those on the scene …
If historians have excused Japan from the charge of premeditating the Marco Polo
Bridge affair, they have not exonerated it from the more serious charge that it
created by its actions a climate of animosity in China in which a trifling incident
could escalate into an eight-year war.

JH. Boyle. 1983. "Sino-Japanese War of 1937–45" in *Kodansha Encyclopaedia of*
Japan, Vol. VII, page 199

The Japanese attack
was brutal, with more
devastating air raids. Their
forces drove inland along
the Yangtze river and
terrorized Chinese refugees
fled to the interior. Some
historians have suggested
that this amounted to the
largest human exodus
in history.

The Rape of Nanjing

The Chinese nationalist
government had moved
its capital to Nanjing, but
abandoned this also as
the Japanese advanced.
Nanjing fell to the
Japanese on 13 December,
and during the days
that followed, Chinese
soldiers and civilians were
subjected to appalling
atrocities. As the historian
Akira Iriye writes, *"The
'rape of Nanking' would
make it all but impossible for
Japan to still be accepted as
a respectable member of the
international community"*
(Iriye, 1987).

▲ Infamous photograph of South Station in Shanghai, China, 28 August 1937

There followed in Nanjing a period of terror and destruction that must rank
among the worst in the history of modern warfare. For almost seven weeks
the Japanese troops, who first entered the city on December 13, unleashed on
the defeated Chinese troops and on the helpless Chinese civilian population
a storm of violence and cruelty that has few parallels. The female rape
victims, many of whom died after repeated assaults, were estimated by foreign
observers at 30,000; the fugitive soldiers killed were estimated at 30,000;
murdered civilians at 12,000. Robbery, wanton destruction and arson left
much of the city in ruins.

Spence, J. 1990. *The Search for Modern China.*

Source skills

Source A

Japanese soldiers purchasing items from Chinese vendors, Nanjing, China.

Source B

Japanese troops rounding up Chinese, Nanjing, China, 16 December 1937.

1   In pairs discuss the message of Source A.
2   What is the message of Source B?

Source C

Corpses on the shore of the Yangtze River, Nanjing, China, December 1937.

ATL Research skills

3   Refer back to the photograph on the previous page showing the baby on the railway tracks in Shanghai. Research the controversy surrounding this photograph.

ATL Thinking skills

4   With reference to Sources A–C, discuss the challenges facing historians using photographs as evidence.

What were the results of the Sino-Japanese War for Japan?

As the historian Pyle has written, a war with China, *"was not a war that the army General Staff wanted"* (Pyle, p. 198). Indeed, up until this time, the Japanese army had been preparing for a major war with the Soviets rather than the Chinese. However, once the Marco Polo incident had escalated, (partly as a result of Jiang Jieshi's new commitment to resist the Japanese, as you will read in the next chapter) Konoe called for an all-out campaign to "annihilate" the nationalist regime.

The hope was that China would quickly capitulate and would accept Japanese leadership in a new Asian order. This view underestimated the extent of Chinese nationalism and the outrage caused by such events as the Rape of Nanjing.

Source skills

A cartoon by David Low "Further and deeper" published in the UK newspaper the *Evening Standard*, 19 January 1938. The cartoon depicts the Japanese military leading two men, labelled "*Jap industry*" and "*Jap politics*", into China.

FURTHER AND DEEPER.

First question, part b – 2 marks

What is Low's message regarding the impact of the invasion of China on Japan in this cartoon?

Thus, despite their defeats, the lack of effective weapons and industrial support, the Chinese refused to agree terms for peace. This meant that Japan had to fight on and push the Chinese further into the interior. This led to supply lines becoming overstretched and the Japanese forces becoming more vulnerable to Chinese guerrilla attacks. Two centres for Chinese resistance developed, one under Jiang Jieshi at Chongqing and another under Mao Zedong in north-west China. Chongqing would become one of the most intensively bombed cities of the Second World War.

In November 1938 the Japanese government declared the creation of a new political, cultural and economic union between Japan, Manchukuo and China – a New Order in East Asia. Prince Konoe had publicly declared Japan's aim of creating this union, which would mean a new level of political, economic and cultural "cooperation" between Japan, China and Manchukuo. Jiang rejected this idea for a new union, and continued the war.

The key problem for Japan over the next few years was how to end the war in its favour. It pursued a number of strategies including compromised peace terms, decisive military victory and the setting up of an alternative Chinese

TOK

In pairs review the sources you have looked at in this chapter thus far. Look at the historians' views and the primary accounts and photographs. When historians work on developing their accounts of historical events how do they select their sources? How do they select what events and actions are significant? Discuss the difference between *selection* and *bias*.

regime that would agree terms with them. None of these methods worked. Bix concludes that war, *"set the stage for the triumph of Communism in China, and [would] end only after having given seed to Japanese involvement in World War II, and Japan's ultimate defeat"* (Bix, 2000).

ATL Thinking skills

An extract from Max Hastings. 2007. *Retribution: The battle for Japan 1944–45*, pages 5–6. Published by Alfred A Knopf. New York, USA

Inaugurating its "Greater East Asia Co-Prosperity Sphere", Japan perceived itself merely as a latecomer to the contest for empire in which other great nations had engaged for centuries. It saw only hypocrisy and racism in the objections of Western imperial powers to its bid to match their own generous interpretations of what constituted legitimate overseas interests. Such a view was not completely baseless. Japan's pre-war economic difficulties and pretensions to a policy of "Asia for Asians" inspired some sympathy among subject peoples of the European empires. This vanished, however, in the face of the occupiers' behaviour in China and elsewhere. Japanese pogroms of Chinese in South East Asia were designed partly to win favour with indigenous peoples, but these in turn soon found themselves suffering appallingly. The new rulers were inhibited from treating their conquests humanely, even had they wished to do so, by the fact that the purpose of seizure was to strip them of food and raw materials for the benefit of Japan's people.

What are the key points made by the historian Hastings regarding Japan's Greater East Asia Co-Prosperity Sphere in this source?

Why did the conflict deepen after 1938?

The militarists take control

Prince Konoye returned as prime minister in July 1940 having resigned in December 1938. He still aimed to limit the power of the military and he created a unity party called the Imperial Rule Assistance Association which was joined by most political parties. However, he again failed to control the militarists.

Indeed, multi-party politics was suspended in 1940 when the Imperial Rule Assistance Association replaced all political parties. The military were in total control when in October, 1941, Prime Minister Prince Konoe resigned and was replaced by General Tojo.

The impact of the war in Europe

With Hitler's swift victories in Europe in the summer of 1940, the military were drawn to new areas of conquest – Europe's colonies. In November 1940, Japan pressured occupied France into permitting Japan's forces to have troops and airfields in Indo-China. This would be the first stage of its conquest of South East Asia. Similar attempts to pressurize the Dutch failed.

Events 1940–41

The Three Power/Tripartite Pact and the Neutrality Pact

In September 1940, the Japanese, under Foreign Minister Matsuoka Yosuke, signed the Tripartite Axis Pact which agreed that Germany and Italy would dominate Europe and leave Japan to dominate East Asia. If the Axis powers could defeat the Western democracies in Europe their colonies in Asia could be easily seized by Japan.

Furthermore, Japan was able to secure its northern border after signing a pact with the Soviet Union. During the war with China, Japan had clashed twice with the Soviet Union over border disputes – first in 1938

and again, for a more protracted period, in the summer of 1939. The Nazi Soviet Pact of 1939 had been a set-back for Japan. However, in April 1941 Matsuoka also entered into a Neutrality Pact with the Soviets. This was mutually beneficial as the Soviet Union could concentrate its forces in Europe and the Japanese could move its forces further south.

Indeed, the victories of the Nazis in Europe created great opportunities for Japan to take over the Asian colonies of Britain, France and the Netherlands and, on 24 July, Japanese forces moved into southern Indo-China. From there they could threaten Siam (Thailand), Malaya and the Dutch East Indies. The USA and Britain, alarmed at this Japanese move, immediately froze all Japanese assets and this brought foreign trade with Japan to a halt. In addition, they strengthened their defences in the region and increased aid to Jiang in China (see Chapter 1.3).

In 1941, in part fostered by Hitler's impressive early victories in Europe, Japan expanded its ambitions for the Greater East Asia Co-Prosperity Sphere; South East Asia was to be included in this.

It has been suggested that Japan entered into the war with China without a clear plan of how to end it. Indeed, Japan was still fully engaged in this war, with no end to the conflict in sight, when it attacked Western colonies in November 1941.

ATL Social skills

The Tripartite Pact

The Government of Japan, Germany and Italy consider it the prerequisite of a lasting peace that every nation in the world shall receive the space to which it is entitled. They have, therefore, decided to stand by and cooperate with one another in their efforts in the regions of Europe and Greater East Asia respectively. In doing this it is their prime purpose to establish and maintain a new order of things, calculated to promote the mutual prosperity and welfare of the peoples concerned.

It is, furthermore, the desire of the three Governments to extend co-operation to nations in other spheres of the world who are inclined to direct their efforts along lines similar to their own for the purpose of realising their ultimate object, world peace.

Accordingly, the Governments of Japan, Germany and Italy have agreed as follows:

ARTICLE 1   Japan recognises and respects the leadership of Germany and Italy in the establishment of a new order in Europe.

ARTICLE 2   Germany and Italy recognise and respect the leadership of Japan in the establishment of a new order in Greater Asia.

ARTICLE 3   Japan, Germany and Italy agree to co-operate in their efforts on aforesaid lines. They further undertake to assist one another with all political, economic, and military means if one of the three Contracting Powers is attacked by a Power at present not involved in the European War or in the Japanese-Chinese conflict.

ARTICLE 4   With the view to implementing the present pact, joint technical commissions, to be appointed by the respective Governments of Japan, Germany and Italy, will meet without delay.

ARTICLE 5   Japan, Germany and Italy affirm that the above agreement affects in no way the political status existing at present between each of the three Contracting Parties and Soviet Russia.

ARTICLE 6   The present pact shall become valid immediately upon signature and shall remain in force ten years from the date on which it becomes effective.

Lu, David J. 1997. *Japan: A Documentary History*, pages 424-25. M.E. Sharpe Armonk, NY, USA

In pairs or small groups discuss and agree a response to the following questions. Present your answers to the class.

1. How might the terms of this treaty facilitate Japanese foreign policy ambitions?

2. How might the Western powers perceive this agreement?

3. How significant is this agreement in demonstrating Japanese intentions in the region?

Source skills

Source A

A cartoon by Sidney "George" Strube published in the Daily Express, 15 July, 1937. London, UK . Mars, "the God of War", has masks labelled, China, Spain and Abyssinia.

A CHANGE OF PROGRAMME

▲ "So is he going back to that old mask - again"

Source B

Kenneth B. Pyle. *The Making of Modern Japan.* 2nd edition, page 198 (1996).

In the summer of 1937 Japan blundered into war with China. It was not a war that the army General Staff wanted. The truth is that even the most able of the total war planners were acutely aware that it would require considerably more time to develop and integrate an effective industrial structure before Japan would be prepared for all-out war. To them it was critical to avoid hostilities and concentrate on a fully coordinated effort to develop Japan's economy … In June 1937 Konoe Fumimaro was chosen by Saionji to become prime minister. Prince Konoe was a widely respected figure from an old noble family, who might, it was thought, succeed in uniting the country and restraining the military. He spoke of achieving "social justice" in domestic affairs, but he proved a weak and ineffectual leader.

Source C

From K.K. Kawakami. *Japan in China: Her Motive and Aims* **(1938).**

No one can doubt that Japan has a grave case against China … During the last ten years the country reverberated with war songs, veritable hymns of hate, exhorting the troops to destroy Japanese interests in China …

Most Chinese cities were no longer safe for Japanese residents. No longer could the Japanese go out of their homes with a sense of security. Chinese merchants would not handle Japanese goods for fear of reprisal on the part of the anti-Japanese organizations. Chinese who were friendly to Japan or who had business or social relations with Japanese were intimidated, blackmailed, assaulted, even murdered. This whole country was aflame with hatred of Japan – not spontaneous combustion, but a conflagration ignited by the Nationalist Government itself.

First question, part a – 3 marks

According to Source C, what was life like for Japanese people in China during the 1930s?

First question, part b – 2 marks

What is the message of the cartoonist in Source A?

Fourth question – 9 marks

Using the sources and your own knowledge, to what extent do you agree with the following statement: "In the summer of 1937 Japan blundered into war with China."

Examiner's hint: *For the fourth question on the paper, you need to plan out your answer before you start writing. Plan it as you would an essay, with clear paragraphs and two sides to the argument if that is what the question requires. Use the evidence in the sources to support your own knowledge. Remember that you will have four sources rather than three to manage in the examination. (See page 79 for a sample plan for a fourth question.)*

Pearl Harbor and the outbreak of war

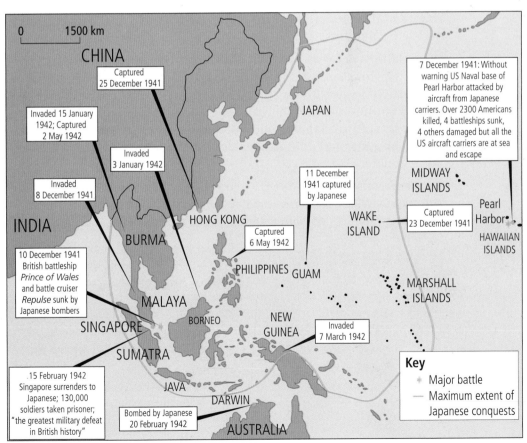

▲ Japanese expansion, December 1941–May 1942

Again, Japan's foreign policy in the crucial year of 1941–42 was determined by domestic issues; in this case the increasing control that the military now had on the government and the economic concerns arising from the US blockade on Japan.

Economic concerns

The economic embargo placed on Japan as a result of its expansion into Indo-China would be fatal in the long term for Japan. The Japanese could not sustain the war in China if their key war supplies were cut off. Therefore, a war of conquest to gain and ensure resources from the European colonies seemed to be the only option. However, opinion in Japan was divided on the question of expanding the war. Some argued that Japan could withdraw its forces from Indo-China and thus get the embargo lifted. Others wanted no retreat and did not view the USA as a real danger to their ambitions.

Negotiations between the USA and Japan continued throughout 1941. Washington wanted Japan to agree to respect the territorial integrity of its neighbours, to pursue its policies by peaceful means and to continue to maintain an "open door" trade policy in the areas under its control. Japan could not agree to these conditions and the deadlock continued into August despite the efforts of Prince Konoe to negotiate.

While negotiations with the USA continued, the military in Japan made alternative plans. The Japanese navy presented its plan for war to the Japanese cabinet – and after some debate, the following was agreed on 4 September, 1941:

> Our Empire will [1] for the purpose of self defence and self-preservation complete preparations for war, [2] concurrently take all possible diplomatic measures vis-a-vis the USA and Great Britain and thereby endeavour to attain our objectives. [3] In the event that there is no prospect of our demands being met by the first ten days of October … we will immediately decide to commence hostilities against the United States, Britain and the Netherlands.

ATL Thinking skills

Saburo Ienaga. 1968. *The Pacific War (Taiheiyo Senso) 1931–45*, page 133. Iwanami Shoten, Japan (translation Random House, New York, USA)

The United States and Japan were inexorably moving toward a bloody collision in the Pacific. Several individuals and groups tried to stop the drift toward war and stimulate productive Japan-US talks. Through the efforts of Bishop James E Walsh, a Catholic Maryknoll priest, and others who had close contacts with Japanese leaders anxious to avert war, negotiations began in Washington between Ambassador Nomura Kichisaburo and Secretary of State Cordell Hull. By this time in 1941, however, Japan had only two grim alternatives: reach a compromise with the US or take the gamble of going to war. The American government was in no mood to compromise and insisted that

Japanese troops be withdrawn from China. Tojo Hideki, army minister in the third Konoe cabinet, spoke for the military: "The army's position is that there can be no compromise on the stationing of troops in China. It affects military morale … Troop withdrawals are the heart of the matter. If we just acquiesce to the American demand, everything we have achieved in China will be lost …". Tojo found these compelling reasons not to budge on China. Premier Konoe, however, "thought it manifestly unwise for Japan to plunge into an unpredictable war at a time when the China incident is still unresolved". He resigned on October 16, 1941.

According to this source, what was the key issue over which the Japanese military were not prepared to compromise?

Even then, the Japanese government continued with negotiations and diplomacy with the USA. A final Japanese mission was sent to Washington to try to agree terms with the Americans. However, at the same time, a huge naval task force prepared secretly to attack the USA should negotiations fail. When negotiations stalled, final preparations were made for an attack on the American naval base in Hawaii.

On 2 November, in a final Imperial Conference, the Privy Council President Hara summed the matter up as follows:

> It is impossible, from the standpoint of our present political situation and of our self-preservation, to accept all the American demands. On the other hand we cannot let the present situation continue. If we miss the present opportunity to go to war, we will have to submit to American dictation. Therefore, I recognize that it is inevitable that we must decide to start a war against the United States.

▲ US Navy file photo showing a small boat rescuing a USS West Virginia crew member from the water after the Japanese bombing of Pearl Harbor, Hawaii, 7 December 1941

> I will put my trust in what I have been told, namely that things will go well in the early part of the war; and that although we will experience increasing difficulties as the war progresses, there is some prospect of success.

President Hara quoted in Jansen, MB. 2002. *The Making of Modern Japan*, page 630.

On 7 December 1941, Japanese bombers attacked US ships and installations at Pearl Harbor in an attempt to destroy the US Pacific fleet. If successful this would have rendered the USA temporarily helpless to resist Japanese expansion. Japan could then conquer and consolidate its control in South East Asia before the USA had time to rebuild its naval capability.

The attack on Pearl Harbor did incur huge losses for the USA, with 90% of the mid-Pacific air and sea power either destroyed or badly damaged. However, the Japanese had not destroyed the US aircraft carrier capability. Indeed, several carriers had been out on manoeuvres and were not hit. This would later prove a fatal mistake for Japan.

The US government was outraged by the attack on Pearl Harbor which was described by President Roosevelt as "dastardly". The duplicitous nature of conducting negotiations in the USA while simultaneously sending an attack fleet across the Pacific was as seen as entirely deceitful and treacherous. The brutal air assault killed 2,403 and injured 1,178 US military personnel and civilians before any declaration of war was made.

However, the Japanese historian Michiko Hasegawa argues that the attack on Pearl Harbor was not in line with Japan's long-term planning and was caused by the oil embargo which forced Japan into war. Revisionist historians go as far as to argue that Roosevelt deliberately provoked Japan into making an attack.

As they attacked Pearl Harbor, Japan simultaneously attacked Hong Kong and Singapore. Japanese forces then went on to attack the Dutch East Indies, the Philippines and Malaya on 8 December. By the end of December, Japan had seized control of Guam, Hong Kong and Wake Island. They also had sunk two important British warships – the *Prince of Wales* and the *Repulse*. Japan had taken Indo-China, Siam, the Dutch East Indies, Malaya, Singapore and the Philippines by mid-1942.

Class discussion

Look back at the newspaper headline on page 50 from the *New York Herald Tribune*. Why might the details in this primary source be inaccurate?

Hull's last Note (see source below)

This was America's final proposal before the attack on Pearl Harbour. It was delivered to the Japanese ambassador by the US Secretary of State, Cordell Hull. One of its conditions demanded the complete withdrawal of all Japanese troops from French Indochina and China.

Source skills

Richard Storry. *Japan and the Decline of the West in Asia 1894–1943* (1979).

When the blow was struck at Pearl Harbour on 7 December the reaction in Japan was compounded of astonishment, relief and joy. For it was the general, if irrational, belief that the Empire was encircled by a ring of grimly hostile powers, that Hull's last Note [see glossary box] had been a further tightening of the noose. The resort to war, then, seemed fully justified as an act of self-defence. Moreover, the tremendous successes of the first few days – the Pearl Harbour strike, the destruction of the Boeings on the Philippine airfields, then landings in Malaya, the sinking of the Repulse and Prince of Wales – appeared to underline the rectitude no less than the inevitability of Japan's plunge into the Second World War. Heaven, so it seemed, was on her side.

First question, part a – 3 marks

According to the source above, what was the reaction of the home-front in Japan to the attack on Pearl Harbor?

Social skills

Write some notes outlining your response to the question on page 52.

Now swap your response with a partner. Mark each other's response out of 3 marks. Give each other feedback.

Perspectives

Historiography

Left-wing Japanese historians date the beginning of the war in the Pacific as 1931 – with the Manchurian Incident. The left in Japan tend to hold the "militarist capitalist clique" responsible for a "15-year war". The Japanese public had been indoctrinated by their pre-war education.

The right-wing historians in Japan identify December 1941 as the starting point for the "Great East Asia War". Many support the idea that was presented in Japanese propaganda at the time, i.e. Japan was freeing Asia from the exploitation of Western colonialism. Furthermore, they argue that without the Japanese invasion of these territories there would have been no successful independence movements in the region in the post-war period. Japan had been forced into a war with the USA by the oil embargo. Historians on the extreme right in Japan, for example Masaaki Tanaka, even argue that the Rape of Nanjing was a fiction. Other historians on the right (Hayashi) have called the war the "Holy War" that was in fact a 100-year struggle with the West following the arrival of the Americans in 1853.

For the orthodox historians in the USA the Pacific War began in 1937 after the Marco Polo Bridge incident. Japan waged a war of aggression and expansion. This perspective on Japan's role in causing the war was the one presented at the Tokyo Crimes Tribunal. Pearl Harbor was key evidence of Japan's aggression and in breach of the Geneva Convention. Japan was wholly responsible for the war in the Pacific. The Japanese historian Saburo Ienaga was also critical of Japan's role in causing the war and argues that Japanese imperialism and militarism were key factors (Ienaga, 1968).

The Japanese historian Michiko Hasegawa asserts that Japan only went to war because of the oil embargo. The starting point for the war was December, 1941. Revisionist US historians, generally writing during the US war in Vietnam, argued that Japan's actions up to 1941 were primarily aimed at purging Asia from Western corruption. Some suggest that as the USA did not act to resist Japan in China in the 1930s, it encouraged Japanese actions. In addition, revisionists such as Boyle identify Roosevelt's role as key in provoking Japan into bombing Pearl Harbor; Roosevelt knew about the Japanese attack as the Americans had broken their codes. The historian Boyle states that: *"[Roosevelt] ignored or even suppressed warnings of military commanders in Hawaii so as to ensure a successful surprise attack on the US fleet"* (Boyle, 1993).

The role of the emperor in Japanese pre-war policies and actions has also been disputed. Traditionalist historians of the emperor's role argue that he had not wanted war but he had had no choice but to submit to the militarists. Revisionists, often writing after Hirohito's death in 1989, suggest that Hirohito was not simply passive but that he was aggressive. The historian Sterling Seagrove, in his book *The Yamamoto Dynasty*, argues that the emperor was a force supporting Japanese expansionism. He could have intervened to stop the expansionists but he did not want to.

Research skills

In pairs research other historians' perspectives on Japan's foreign policy in the 1930s. Try to find historians from different regions and historians writing in languages other than English.

You should spend two hours on this activity. Discuss with your teacher how to reference your sources and provide a brief list of works cited.

TOK

In small groups investigate further into the background and work of the historians named in the perspective box above and those that you find in your research. Discuss how the context within which historians live (time, place and culture) may impact their knowledge, understanding and views of historical events.

Conclusions

The historian Kenneth Pyle sums up the impact of Japan's actions:

Japan paid a terrible price for the bold gamble of its leaders in 1941. Abandoning the cautious realism that had traditionally characterized Japanese diplomacy, the nation entered into a conflict that cost it the lives of nearly 3 million Japanese, its entire overseas empire, and the destruction of one-quarter of its machines, equipment, buildings, and houses. Generations were left physically and psychologically scarred by the trauma.

The outcome was heavy with historic irony. War sentiment in Japan had been impelled by an ultranationalist ideology that sought to preserve the traditional values of the Japanese political order, that vehemently opposed the expansion of Bolshevik influence in Asia, and that wanted to establish the Japanese Empire. Instead, war brought a social-democratic revolution at home, the rise of Communism in China, and – for the first time in Japan's history – occupation by an enemy force.

Pyle, KB. 1996. *The Making of Modern Japan*, page 204

Full document question: The USA's actions with regard to Japan, 1930–41

Source A

A cartoon by David Low. "Dogs of War" published in the *Evening Standard*, London. UK. 31 October 1941

CERTAINLY HON BEASTS, IF STUFFED, APPEAR VERY LIFELIKE . . . .

DOGS OF WAR

Source B

Max Hastings. *Retribution: The Battle for Japan 1944–45* (2007).

A Japanese assault on the Soviet Union in 1941–42, taking the Russians in the rear as they struggled to stem Hitler's invasion, might have yielded important rewards for the Axis. Stalin was terrified of such an eventuality.

The July 1941 oil embargo and asset freeze imposed by the U.S. on Japan – Roosevelt's clumsiest diplomatic action in the months before Pearl Harbor – was partly designed to deter Tokyo from joining Hitler's Operation Barbarossa. Japan's bellicose foreign minister, Yosuke Matsuoka, resigned in the same month because his government rejected his urgings to attack … Japan and Germany were alike fascist states … The common German and Japanese commitment to making war for its own sake provides the best reason for rejecting pleas in mitigation of either nation's conduct. The two Axis partners, however, pursued unrelated ambitions. The only obvious manifestation of shared interest was that Japanese planning was rooted in an assumption of German victory. Like Italy in June 1940, Japan in December 1941 decided that the old colonial powers difficulties in Europe exposed their remoter properties . . . Japan sought to seize access to vital oil and raw materials, together with space for mass migration from the home islands.

Source C

Kenneth B. Pyle. *The Making of Modern Japan.* (1996).

The dilemma that Japanese diplomacy had struggled with ever since the Manchurian Incident now became still more difficult, for as

the China conflict expanded, the nation was the less prepared to deal with the Soviet army on the Manchurian border and the American fleet in the Pacific. A succession of border skirmishes with the Red Army revealed the vulnerability of the Kwantung Army; at the same time the U.S. Navy was now embarked on a resolute program of building additional strength in the Pacific. By the spring of 1940 the Japanese navy General Staff had concluded that America's crash program would result in its gaining naval supremacy in the Pacific by 1942, and that Japan must have access to the oil of the Dutch East Indies in order to cope with American power … In the autumn of 1940 [Matsuoko] signed the Tripartite Pact with Germany and Italy, in which the signatories pledged to aid one another if attacked by a power not currently involved in the European war or in the fighting in China. Matsouka thereby hoped to isolate the United States and dissuade it from conflict with Japan, thus opening the way for Japan to seize the European colonies in Southeast Asia, grasp the resources it needed for self-sufficiency and cut off Chinese supply lines.

Source D

The Japanese Admiral Nagano to the Emperor Hirohito, September 1941

Japan was like a patient suffering from a serious illness … Should he be left alone without an operation, there was a danger of a gradual decline. An operation, while it might be dangerous, would still offer some hope of saving his life … the Army General Staff was in favour of putting hope in diplomatic negotiations to the finish, but … in the case of failure, a decisive operation would have to be performed.

Quoted in Richard Overy. 2009. *The Road to War*, page 342

First question, part a – 3 marks

According to Source D, why did Japan take action at the end of 1941?

First question, part b – 2 marks

What message is conveyed in Source A?

Second question – 4 marks

With reference to its origin, purpose and content, assess the values and limitations of Source D for historians studying the causes of war in the Pacific.

Third question – 6 marks

Compare and contrast the views expressed in Source B and Source C regarding Japanese polices.

Fourth question – 9 marks

Using the sources and your own knowledge analyse the reasons for the Japanese attack on Pearl Harbor in December 1941.

Japanese ~~Overzealo~~
Over zealousness
led to 3 mil + deaths,
scarring of generations,
and reversing of all
national advancements

Review task

Communication and research skills

In small groups use the sources in this chapter, and/or other sources you research online to draft your own version of a Paper 1 examination. You could use the questions in the box here to help you refine the "theme" of your paper.

Remember:

- You will need four sources.
- One source will need to be a non-text source, for example a cartoon, photograph or some statistics.
- You need to ensure that the total word count of your sources does not exceed 750 words.

Here are some ideas for your fourth question.

1 Using the sources and your own knowledge analyse the reasons for the Manchurian crisis in 1931.

2 Using the sources and your own knowledge analyse why the Marco Polo Bridge incident escalated into a full-scale war between Japan and China in 1937.

3 Using the sources and your own knowledge examine the validity of the claim that "in creating the Greater East Asia Co-Prosperity Sphere Japan perceived itself merely as a latecomer to the contest for empire".

4 Using the sources and your own knowledge, to what extent do you agree that Japan's attack on Pearl Harbor was the result of its expansionist foreign policy?

5 Using the sources and your own knowledge examine the role of the failure of Japan's policies in its decision to attack the USA in 1941.

6 "Japan's failure to bring about a victory in the war with China ultimately led to the Second World War in the Pacific." Using the sources and your own knowledge assess to what extent you agree with this statement.

7 Using the sources and your own knowledge assess the extent to which Japan was acting defensively when it attacked Western interests.

Using the information in this chapter, review the impact on Japan's foreign policy of each of the factors on the left-hand side of the following table.

Overall, which factor or factors do you consider to be most important in influencing Japan's foreign policy?

	Causes of the Mukden incident 1928–32	Causes of the Sino-Japanese War 1933–37	Causes of Japan's attack on Pearl Harbor 1938–41
Nationalism			
Militarism			
Political situation in Japan			
Economic situation in Japan			
Situation in China			
Actions of the West (You will need to fill this in after you have read the next chapter.)			
Conclusions			

Source help and hints

First question, part b – 2 marks

(See page 33.)

What is the message of Source A?

To answer this question, you need to work out what you can learn from the graph. Read the details carefully. In this case, you can find out the following.

- The total number of exports fell dramatically after 1929.

- Exports began to rise again from 1932.

- Textiles had been a major part of Japan's exports.

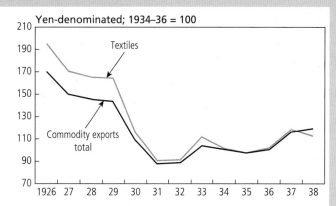

I. Yamazawa and Y. Yamamoto. 1978. *Estimates of Long-term Economic Statistics of Japan since 1868. 14: Foreign trade and balance of payments.*

Second question – 4 marks

(See page 33.)

With reference to origin, purpose and content, assess the value and limitations of Source C for historians studying the Manchurian crisis.

This question is asking you to evaluate the historian's work. It is important that you look carefully at the title of the book, at the date of publication and any information on the historian as these will guide you as to the value of the source for the particular purpose being asked about. Here are some points you could consider.

Values

- The source was written by an academic who is a professional in this field.

- It was written in 2000 which is fairly recent so it may provide good access to recent scholarship.

- It has the benefit of hindsight.

- It is written for the purpose of understanding Hirohito's role in modern Japan and so is likely to have interesting insights on the internal politics of Japan at this time.

- The style of the content suggests an objective approach in use of language and analysis.

Limitations

- The focus of the title and the content is on Hirohito and the political elites, and therefore the book may not fully address non-personal social and economic factors.

First question, part a – 3 marks

(See page 35.)

According to Source A, why were the Kwantung army able to seize control of Manchuria?

You should be able to find the following points:

- The Japanese government was weak.

- There was a lack of clear decision-making power.

- There was a general atmosphere of confusion in Japan.

- There was a sense of domestic and foreign turmoil.

First question, part b – 2 marks

(See page 36.)

What is the message of this photograph?

As with the picture in Chapter 1.1, you need to look carefully at dress, expressions and demeanour of the people in the photograph. From this photograph, you could draw the following conclusions:

- The Japanese are in control.
- The Japanese forces are well ordered.
- There appears to be little support for Japanese forces.
- There seems to be no resistance to Japanese forces.

Second question – 4 marks

(See page 39.)

With reference to the origin, purpose, and content, assess the values and limitations of Source A for a historian studying the impact of the Manchurian crisis.

Notice that many of the points are similar to the answer on page 57 – but the date here is key for allowing you to identify possible limitations.

Values

A value of the source is that it is the work of a Japanese historian, writing in 1968, who has the benefit of hindsight. Also, the purpose is academic and may therefore be objective and well researched. It is also focused on the region and analyses the years 1931–45, which may allow for depth. The content may indicate a Japanese perspective on the conflict that is seen, at least initially, as more defensive in its actions.

Limitations

The date, 1968, is a limitation as more documents may have become available once classified documents from the wartime era were released, which could limit the depth of its interpretation. The focus on the Pacific War may mean the source neglects to include the impact of this event in other regions.

First question, part a – 3 marks

(See page 42.)

What are the key points made in Source B regarding Japanese policy in Asia?

The key points are as follows:

- The Japanese aimed to remove the great powers as an influence in South East Asia and replace them with a "co-prosperity sphere".
- The Japanese government believed that Japan must build up its armaments.
- To protect Manchukuo, the Japanese government wanted to eliminate the threat from the Soviet Union.
- Japan wanted to prepare against Britain and the USA to promote its own economy.
- Japan planned to promote its racial and economic development in South East Asia.

Examiner's hint: *There are several points that you can get from this source – but you only need to explain three to gain 3 marks.*

References

Bix, HP. 2000. *Hirohito and the Making of Modern Japan*. Harper Perennial. New York, USA

Boyle, JH. 1983. "Sino-Japanese War of 1937–45" in Kodansha *Encyclopedia of Japan*, Vol. VII. Kodansha. Tokyo, Japan.

Boyle, JH. 1993. *Modern Japan: The American Nexus*. Harcourt Brace Jovanovich. New York, USA

Hastings, M. 2007. *Retribution: The Battle for Japan 1944–45*. Alfred A Knopf. New York, USA

Hsü, I. 1995. *The Rise of Modern China*, page 550. Oxford University Press, Oxford, UK

Ienaga, S. 1968. *The Pacific War (Taiheiyo Senso) 1931–45*. Iwanami Shoten. Japan (translation Random House. New York, USA)

Iriye, A. 1987. *The Origins of the Second World War in Asia and the Pacific*. Routledge, London, UK

Jansen, MB. 2002. *The Making of Modern Japan*. Harvard University Press, Boston MA, USA

Kawakami, KK. 1938. *Japan in China: Her motives and aims*. John Murray. London, UK

Lu, David J., 1997. *Japan: A Documentary History*, pages 418–20. M.E. Sharpe Armonk, NY, USA

Overy, R. 2009. *The Road to War*. Vintage Books. London, UK

Pyle, K. 1996. *The Making of Modern Japan*. 2nd edn. DC Heath and Company. Lexington, MA, USA

Spence, J. 1990. *The Search for Modern China*. WW Norton and Company. New York, USA

Storry, R. 1979. *Japan and the Decline of the West in Asia, 1894–1943*. Macmillan. London, UK

1.3 The international response to Japanese aggression, 1931–1941

Conceptual understanding

→ Consequence

→ Significance

▲ Franklin D Roosevelt, US president from 1933

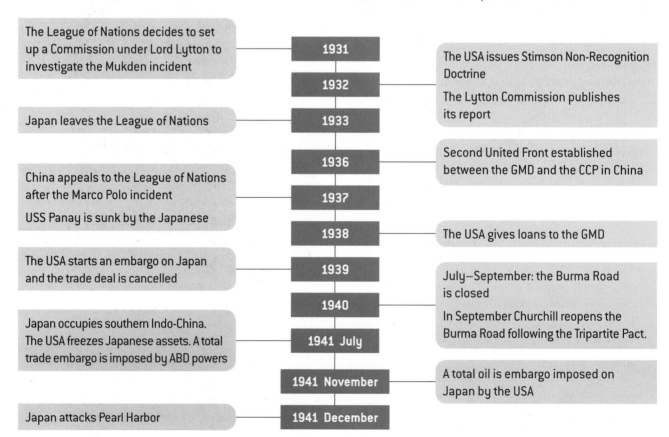

The League of Nations decides to set up a Commission under Lord Lytton to investigate the Mukden incident

1931

The USA issues Stimson Non-Recognition Doctrine

1932

The Lytton Commission publishes its report

Japan leaves the League of Nations

1933

1936

Second United Front established between the GMD and the CCP in China

China appeals to the League of Nations after the Marco Polo incident

USS Panay is sunk by the Japanese

1937

1938

The USA gives loans to the GMD

The USA starts an embargo on Japan and the trade deal is cancelled

1939

1940

July–September: the Burma Road is closed

In September Churchill reopens the Burma Road following the Tripartite Pact.

Japan occupies southern Indo-China. The USA freezes Japanese assets. A total trade embargo is imposed by ABD powers

1941 July

1941 November

A total oil is embargo imposed on Japan by the USA

Japan attacks Pearl Harbor

1941 December

The League of Nations' response to events in Manchuria 1931–36

Japan's action in the Mukden Incident was the first significant challenge by a major power to the new international system that had been set up in Europe after the First World War. This international system centred around the concept of *collective security* – that states would take joint action to deal with aggression. To facilitate such action, the League of Nations, a body where all states could be represented, was established in 1919. In addition, various treaties, such as the Washington Conference System, the Nine-Power Treaty (see page 22) and the Kellogg-Briand Pact reinforced the idea of peaceful international cooperation.

Kellogg-Briand Pact

This pact was signed in 1928 and the signatory states promised not to use *war* to resolve "disputes or conflicts of whatever nature or of whatever origin they may be, which may arise among them". Instead, it called for the peaceful settlement of disputes. Japan signed this pact in 1928 along with 14 other nations. Ultimately, the pact was signed by 62 nations.

Source skills

Source A

Extract from Akira Iriya. *The Origins of the Second World War in Asia and the Pacific* **(1987).**

The term "the Washington Conference system", or "the Washington system" for short, was not in current use in the 1920s, nor was it subsequently recognized as a well-defined legal concept. None the less, immediately after the conference there was much talk of "the spirit of the Washington conference", and a country's behaviour in Asia tended to be judged in terms of whether it furthered or undermined that spirit. … it expressed the powers' willingness to co-operate with one another in maintaining stability in the region and assisting China's gradual transformation as a modern state. It was opposed to a rapid and wholesale transformation of Asian international relations, such as was being advocated by the Communist International and by an increasing number of Chinese nationalists. Rather, the Washington powers would stress an evolutionary process of change so as to ensure peace, order and stability.

Source B

A cartoon published in *Outlook*, a US magazine, in 1931.

First question, part a – 3 marks

What, according to Source A, were the aims of the Washington System?

First question, part b – 2 marks

What is the message of Source B concerning Japan's actions in Manchuria?

The organization and aims of the League of Nations

The League of Nations consisted of the Assembly of the League and the Council of the League. The assembly was made up of the representatives of all member states; it met yearly and each state had one vote. The council consisted of the major powers Britain, France, Italy and Japan plus four other members elected by the assembly. The council made most of the key decisions; in particular it was the body that could take action against a member of the League who resorted to war.

The Covenant of the League of Nations was the document which set out how the League was to achieve its aims of promoting international cooperation and maintaining international peace and security.

ATL Social skills

Read these articles of the Covenant of the League which set out how the League should solve international disputes and so prevent war.

In pairs discuss the following questions. Listen carefully to each other's ideas and agree a joint response.

1 What actions could the League take against aggressor states?

2 Which of these actions do you think would be most effective in solving disputes?

3 Can you identify ways in which these methods might **not** be effective?

Article 10 The Members of the League undertake to respect and preserve as against external aggression the territorial integrity and existing political independence of all Members of the League. In case of any such aggression or in case of any threat or danger of such aggression the Council shall advise upon the means by which this obligation shall be fulfilled.

Article 11 Any war or threat of war, whether immediately affecting any of the Members of the League or not, is hereby declared a matter of concern to the whole League, and the League shall take any action that may be deemed wise and effectual to safeguard the peace of nations …

Article 12 The Members of the League agree that if there should arise between them any dispute likely to lead to a rupture they will submit the matter either to arbitration or judicial settlement or to enquiry by the Council, and they agree in no case to resort to war until three months after the award by the arbitrators or the judicial decision, or the report by the Council. In any case under this Article the award of the arbitrators or the judicial decision shall be made within a reasonable time, and the report of the Council shall be made within six months after the submission of the dispute.

Article 13 The Members of the League agree that whenever any dispute shall arise between them which they recognise to be suitable for submission to arbitration or judicial settlement and which cannot be satisfactorily settled by diplomacy, they will submit the whole subject-matter to arbitration or judicial settlement …

For the consideration of any such dispute, the court to which the case is referred shall be the Permanent Court of International Justice …

The Members of the League agree that they will carry out in full good faith any award or decision that may be rendered, and that they will not resort to war against a Member of the League which complies therewith. In the event of any failure to carry out such an award or decision, the Council shall propose what steps should be taken to give effect thereto.

Article 15 If there should arise between Members of the League any dispute likely to lead to a rupture, which is not submitted to arbitration or judicial settlement in accordance with Article 13, the Members of the League agree that they will submit the matter to the Council. Any party to the dispute may effect such submission by giving notice of the existence of the dispute to the Secretary General, who will make all necessary arrangements for a full investigation and consideration thereof …

Article 16 Should any Member of the League resort to war in disregard of its covenants under Articles 12, 13 or 15, it shall *ipso facto* be deemed to have committed an act of war against all other Members of the League, which hereby undertake immediately to subject it to the severance of all trade or financial relations, the prohibition of all intercourse between their nationals and the nationals of the covenant-breaking State, and the prevention of all financial, commercial or personal intercourse between the nationals of the covenant-breaking State and the nationals of any other State, whether a Member of the League or not.

It shall be the duty of the Council in such case to recommend to the several Governments what effective military, naval or air force the Members of the League shall severally contribute to the armed forces to be used to protect the covenants of the League.

What actions did the League take in response to the Mukden incident?

Following the Mukden incident, China appealed to the League of Nations. This was an example of one member state attacking another; China hoped to invoke the principle of collective security and thus get action taken against Japan as set out in Article 16 of the Covenant.

However, the League acted cautiously. It held several meetings to discuss what action should be taken. These meetings were attended by the Japanese government in China and the USA (who, although not a member of the League, was invited to send representatives to the council). The source on the next page sets out the Japanese government's position on the Manchurian crisis.

While the Japanese government seemed to be cooperating with the League, the army continued to expand its influence over Manchuria in defiance of a request from the League that Japanese troops should withdraw to the railway zone.

The League then decided to send a fact-finding commission led by Lord Lytton to Manchuria. This commission took several months to arrive in Manchuria and then several months to complete its report on the situation. During this time, the Kwantung army was able to continue expanding throughout Manchuria. In March 1932, Manchuria was declared the state of Manchukuo – a puppet state under the control of Japan with China's last emperor, Pu Yi as its ruler. The Japanese claimed that the Manchurians were now free from Chinese domination.

Source skills

A cartoon by David Low published in the UK newspaper the *Daily Mail* on 17 November 1931, "Will the league stand up to Japan?".

WILL THE LEAGUE STAND UP TO JAPAN ?

First question, part b – 2 marks

What is the message of this cartoon concerning the League of Nations' role in the Manchurian crisis?

Source skills

Japanese Government statement, 24 September 1931.

For some years past… unpleasant incidents have taken place in the regions of Manchuria and Mongolia, in which Japan is interested in a special degree… Amidst the atmosphere of anxiety a detachment of Chinese troops destroyed the tracks of the South Manchuria Railway in the vicinity of Mukden, and attacked our railway guards, at midnight on 18 September. A clash between Japanese and Chinese troops then took place… Hundreds and thousands of Japanese residents were placed in jeopardy. In order to forestall an imminent disaster the Japanese army had to act swiftly… The endeavours of the Japanese Government to guard the SMR [South Manchurian Railway] against wanton attacks should be viewed in no other light… It may be superfluous to repeat that the Japanese government harbours no territorial designs on Manchuria.

Second question – 4 marks

With reference to the origin, purpose and content assess the value and limitations of this source for historians studying the Manchurian Incident.

One year after the Mukden incident, the Lytton Commission's Report was published. It stated the following:

- Japan did in fact have special interests in Manchuria but the use of force by the army, and its takeover of the whole of Manchuria, was unacceptable and unjustified.

- Japan should give up the territory and withdraw its forces.

- Manchukuo was not an independent state and could not be recognized as such.

- Manchuria should become independent but under Chinese sovereignty.

The Commission stressed that the problem of Manchuria could only be solved by a general improvement in Sino-Japanese relations. It recommended that, following Japan's withdrawal of troops back to the railway zone, the two countries should negotiate a non-aggression pact and a trade agreement.

Such recommendations ignored the fact that Japan wanted Manchuria and was not prepared to compromise. Japan declared that the League's members were hypocritical in their attitude towards Japanese actions in China; after all, had not the British and French established their enclaves there by force? Japan did not accept the report and withdrew from the League in protest in March 1933. The US Ambassador to Japan, Joseph C Grew, reported that:

The military themselves, and the public through military propaganda are fully prepared to fight rather than surrender to moral or other pressure from the West. The moral obloquy [condemnation] of the rest of the world serves only to strengthen not modify their determination.

Why did the League not take stronger action against Japan?

No further action was taken against Japan. Why? France, as one of the key members of the League, felt that it had no real reason to fall out with Japan. As the colonial power in Indo-China, it also had much to gain from a weakened China.

TOK

Look at the sources on pages 64–66. Make a note of the following:

a the choice of language

b the selection of events and supporting details.

Discuss in small groups in what ways the sources contain *bias*. Do some sources seem to be more objective? Which sources seem the most biased? Feedback to the class. In pairs attempt to write a brief account of the Manchurian Crisis that is without "bias" - attempt to be as objective as possible. Discuss as a class the extent to which it is possible to describe historical events without bias or subjectivity.

Britain was also cautious in its response. Although there were some in the ruling Conservative Party who believed that the principle of collective security should be upheld, it was unwilling to act when its own interests were not at stake. In any case it lacked the military means to resist Japan.

In addition, both countries were suffering from the economic effects of the Great Depression which made them hesitant to spend resources on either economic or military actions. Moreover, the fear of communism in both countries meant that Japan was viewed as an ally in containing communist Russia in the Far East.

Source skills

Source A

Extract from Alan Farmer. *Britain Foreign Affairs, 1919–39* **(1996).**

If action was to be taken, US support was vital, but that support was not forthcoming. Japanese imperialism, although a potential threat to British interests in the Far East, was not an immediate danger. Indeed Japanese expansion in northern China could be seen as reducing the risk of Japanese expansion in other, more sensitive, areas (for example, Southeast Asia).

Economic sanctions were unlikely to achieve much. The Royal Navy was not strong enough to enforce a trade embargo, and the USA, Japan's biggest trading partner, made it clear it would not support any League action. The best policy therefore seemed to be to accept Japan's takeover of Manchuria and to hope that the Japanese threat did not develop.

Source B

Winston Churchill speaking in the House of Commons, 17 February 1933.

Now I must say something to you which is very unfashionable. I am going to say a word of sympathy for Japan, not necessarily for her policy, but for her position and her national difficulties. I do not think the League of Nations would be well-advised to quarrel with Japan. The League has great work to do in Europe … there is no more use affronting Japan than there would be in ordering the Swiss and Czechoslovak navies to the Yellow Sea … I hope we in England shall try to understand a little the position of Japan, an ancient State, with the highest sense of national honour and patriotism, and with a teeming population and a remarkable energy.

On the one side they see the dark menace of Soviet Russia. On the other the chaos of China, four of five provinces of which are now being tortured under Communist rule.

Cited in Ronald Cameron, *Appeasement and the Road to War* (1991)

Source C

Extract from Akira Iriya. *The Origins of the Second World War in Asia and the Pacific* **(1987).**

Unfortunately for China, the international system with which it so strongly identified and to which it turned for help, was itself going through a major crisis of another sort; the beginning of the world depression. Those powers that had constructed and preserved the international system – advanced industrial economics – were in the midst of a severe crisis. Between 1929 and 1931 industrial production, employment, commodity prices, purchasing power – all such indices of economic health, had plummeted, with national incomes cut to nearly one-half in the United States, Germany, and elsewhere. The situation severely affected their economic interactions, and thus the world economy as a whole … international co-operation, in other words, had already begun to break down when the Manchurian Incident broke out.

First question, part a – 3 marks

What, according to Source A, were the reasons why Britain failed to take any further action against Japan?

Fourth question – 9 marks

Using the sources and your own knowledge, examine why the League of Nations did not take stronger action to deal with the Manchurian crisis.

What was the impact of the League's failure to take action over Manchuria?

The failure of the League to respond to the Manchurian incident meant that Japan was able to continue with its expansion; it may also have contributed to Mussolini's decision to invade Abyssinia in 1935.

Source A

Extract from R.J. Overy. *Origins of the Second World War* **(2008).**

In 1933 Japan left the League and effectively removed the Far East from the system of collective security. In 1934, in violation of international agreements to preserve an "open door" policy in China, the Japanese government announced the Amau Doctrine, a warning to other powers to regard China as Japan's sphere of influence and to abandon trade with the Chinese and the provision of technical aid to them. There is no doubt that Japanese leaders, spurred on at home by the military, were encouraged to go further after 1932 than they might otherwise have done because of the weak response from the major powers.

Source B

A cartoon by David Low, "The Doormat", published in the UK newspaper the *Evening Standard*, **19 January 1933.**

THE DOORMAT.

First question, part a – 3 marks

What, according to Source A, was the result of the Manchurian crisis for Japan's future actions in China?

First question, part b – 2 marks

What is the message of Source B?

The response of the League and Europe to events after 1932

China again appealed to the League of Nations after the Marco Polo Bridge incident and the bombing of Shanghai. The League condemned Japan for breaking the Nine-Power Treaty of 1922 but in reality it was now impotent and could take little practical action to help China. In any case, Britain and France were now preoccupied by events in Europe. Britain repeatedly asked the USA for joint diplomatic pressure on Tokyo but to no avail.

In November 1937, the Nine-Power Treaty Conference convened for the last time in Brussels. It condemned the actions of Japan and urged that hostilities be suspended but it produced no measures to stop Japanese aggression.

The response of China to events after 1932

The establishment of the Second United Front

Jiang's insistence on fighting the Communists rather than the Japanese lost him support even from within his own party. In 1933 he had to suppress an uprising among his troops at Fujian who were protesting at his failure to stand up to the Japanese. There were also demonstrations in Beijing over his Japanese policy, the most serious of which was in 1935. Then, in December 1936, while in the middle of a campaign against the Communists, Jiang was kidnapped by troops acting under the orders of General Zhang Xue-liang, the Manchurian warlord and son of Zhang Zuolin. Zhang had been placed in charge of the anti-communist campaign but, like other northern commanders, felt that Jiang should be focusing on the Japanese and not the Communists. The leaders of the CCP became involved in the negotiations over Jiang's release and the prominent communist, Zhou Enlai, flew to Xi'an (Sian) to negotiate a joint alliance against the Japanese. Although Jiang did not sign a formal agreement, he changed his priority of attacking the Communists first before the Japanese. A Second United Front was formed between the Nationalist Party and the Communist Party; the civil war was suspended and instead there was to be a "war of national resistance".

China's actions following the Marco Polo Bridge incident

Following Japan's full-scale invasion of China after the Marco Polo Bridge incident, Jiang announced that "the limits of endurance had been reached" and that "If we allow one inch more of our territory to be lost, we shall be guilty of an unpardonable crime against our race." A national conference was held which included both the Communists and the Nationalists. Mao declared a policy of "total resistance by the whole nation".

Despite Jiang's apparent new approach to the Japanese following the establishment of the Second United Front, the war went badly for the Chinese. By 1938, Beijing, Shanghai, Ghangzhou and Nanjing had all fallen to Japan and the GMD government had to withdraw their capital to Chongqing.

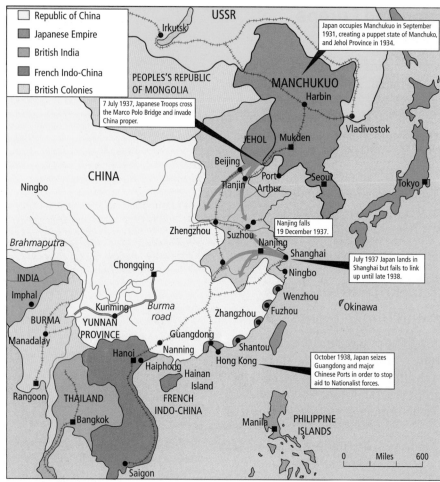

▲ Map showing Japan's advance into China, 1931–1938

Nevertheless, the escalation of the war caused by the Chinese United Front drew the Japanese into a conflict that they did not want and for which they did not have the resources. By 1940, Japan had committed over 750,000 ground troops to the struggle. And despite the lack of any international opposition, the Japanese could not quickly win the war. They were forced to try to consolidate their position by adopting a policy of living off the land with the help of puppet governments. The most important of these was led by Wang Jingwei who was a former GMD colleague, and rival, of Jiang. Believing that China could never win against the Japanese, Wang agreed in 1940 to become the head of "the New Government of China". This regime was recognized by Manchukuo and the three Axis powers but not by any of the Western powers. Thus, by 1938, China was divided into three main areas: Nationalist China based in Chongqing, Communist China based in Shaanxi and Japanese-occupied China in the east and north.

ATL Thinking and social skills

The puppet government of Wang JingWei in central and northern China signed a treaty with Japan on 30 November, 1940

Identify the key terms of this treaty, and highlight which points would be particularly resented by Chinese nationalists. In pairs or small groups compare and contrast your responses. Offer feedback where your partner or a member of your group has missed a point.

Basic Relations Treaty

ARTICLE 2   The Governments of the two countries shall closely co-operate for cultural harmony, creation and development.

ARTICLE 3   The Governments of the two countries agree to engage in joint defence against all destructive operations of communistic

nature that jeopardise the peace and welfare of their countries.

The Governments of the two countries shall, in order to accomplish the purpose mentioned in the preceding paragraph, eliminate communistic elements and organisations in their respective territories, and at the same time co-operate closely concerning information and propaganda with reference to the defence against communistic activities …

ARTICLE 5   The Government of the Republic of China shall recognise that Japan may, in accordance with previous practises or in order to preserve common interests of the two countries, station for a required duration its naval units and vessels in specified areas

within the territory of the Republic of China, in accordance with the terms to be agreed upon separately between the two countries.

ARTICLE 6   The Government of the two countries shall effect close economic co-operation between the two countries in conformance with the spirit of complementing each other and ministering to each other's needs, as well as in accordance with the principles of equality and reciprocity.

With reference to special resources in North China and Mongolian Federation, especially mineral resources required for national defence, the Government of the Republic of China shall undertake that they shall be developed through close co-operation of the two countries. With reference to the development of specific resources in other areas which are required for national defence, the Government of the Republic of China shall afford necessary facilities to Japan and Japanese subjects.

The Government of the two countries shall take all the necessary measures to promote trade in general and to facilitate and rationalise the demand and supply of goods between the two countries. The Governments of the two countries shall extend specially close co-operation with respect to the promotion of trade and commerce in the lower basin of the Yangzi River and the rationalisation of the demand and supply of goods between Japan on the one hand and North China and the Mongolian Federation on the other.

The Government of Japan shall, with respect to the rehabilitation and development of industries, finance, transportation and communication in China, extend necessary assistance and co-operation to China through consultation between the two countries.

ARTICLE 7   … the Government of China shall open its territory for domicile and business of Japanese subjects.

The terms of the Treaty were added to in an Annexed Protocol, 1940.

ARTICLE 3   When general peace is restored between the two countries and the state of war ceases to exist, the Japanese forces shall commence evacuation with the exception of those which are stationed in accordance with the Treaty Concerning Basic Relations between Japan and China signed today and the existing agreements between the two countries and shall complete it within two years with the firm establishment of peace and order.

Treaty concerning basic relations between Japan and China, 1940, in Lu, David J. 1997. *Japan: A Documentary History*, pages 420–22.

Despite the United Front, tensions between the Nationalists and the Communists remained high and there was a deterioration of relations in 1941 when Jiang attacked the Communists. However, with the attack on Pearl Harbour and the declaration of war by the USA against Japan, Jiang realized that Japan would ultimately be defeated. What had been essentially a Sino-Japanese conflict now became part of the Second World War and the global struggle against aggression and totalitarianism.

Source skills

Chinese civilians seeking shelter in a cave during a Japanese bombing near Chongqing, China, circa 1939.

First question, part b – 2 marks

What is the message of this photograph?

The USA's response to Japanese actions 1931–37

The USA's main foreign policy concern in the 1930s was to stay out of international crises and to pursue its own interests; in other words, "isolationism". After the First World War, many in the USA felt that they did not want to get dragged again into disputes which did not directly affect them. The Wall Street Crash of 1929 and the ensuing economic crisis only served to reinforce the United States' concentration on its own issues.

Thus, although the USA was concerned by Japan's actions which were a violation of Chinese territorial integrity and also of the "open door" policy which had been advocated by the US, President Hoover took minimal action. US interests and security were not directly threatened by the Manchurian incident and the focus of the administration was on the economic crisis. In any case, the USA lacked a credible naval force in the Pacific as Congress had refused funds to bring naval strength up to the Washington Treaty and London Treaty limits.

As with Britain, there were other self-interests for the USA to take into account. The USA had trade and investment interests in Japan which it did not want to jeopardize; indeed the USA had far more important trade ties with Japan than with the much larger Chinese Republic. In addition, Ambassador Nelson T Johnson, the US envoy to China, commented that *the development of this area under Japanese enterprise may mean an increased opportunity for American industrial plants to sell the kind of machinery and other manufactured goods that will be needed* (Boyle, 1993: 179). The Chief of the Far Eastern Division of the State Department, Stanley K Hornbeck further commented that *US interests might best be served if the Japanese were kept involved in an indecisive struggle in an area where the United States had no truly vital interests – such as Manchuria* (Boyle, 1993: 179).

The response of the US government was to issue a non-recognition doctrine (also called the Stimson Doctrine after Secretary of State Henry Stimson)

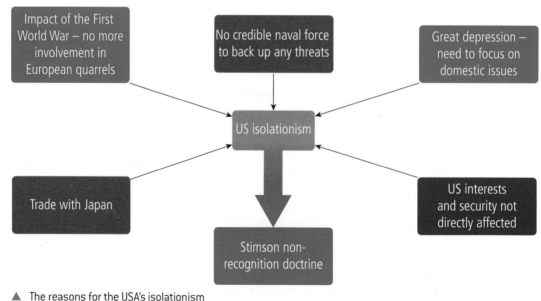

▲ The reasons for the USA's isolationism

on 7 January, 1932 in which the USA declared that it would not recognize any agreement that violated China's territorial or administrative integrity or that went against the open door policy or the Kellogg-Briand Pact. This non-recognition doctrine allowed Hoover to uphold international law but also to avoid committing to economic sanctions.

When Roosevelt was inaugurated as president in March 1933, he continued with the same limited response to Japan. His attention was focused on solving the economic crisis through his "New Deal" policies and, outside of the USA, Hitler's policies took most of the USA's attention. Meanwhile, the USA continued to export strategic materials to Japan throughout the 1930s. The British ambassador in Washington reported:

> [Roosevelt's] view is that there is nothing to be done at present to stop [the] Japanese government and that the question can only be solved by the ultimate inability of Japan to stand the strain any longer. His policy would be to avoid anything that would tend to relieve that strain.

Source skills

A cartoon by David Low, "Silence", published in the UK newspaper the *Evening Standard*, London on 11 November 1938.

▲ The text reads, "League of Nations; Foundation stone of a New Order, laid 1918; *Peace hath her sacrifices*"

First question, part b – 2 marks

What is the message of the cartoonist regarding the Stimson Doctrine?

Source skills

Richard Storry. *Japan and the Decline of the West in Asia 1894–1943* (1979).

> But the Hoover Administration in Washington, so far from contemplating military sanctions of any kind, was not prepared to use America's economic muscle against Japan. Moral force, exemplified by the "non-recognition" policy, was the only weapon; and if one can scarcely, in fairness, blame Stimson for making use of it, especially in the year of presidential elections, the fact remains that it exacerbated nationalist feeling in Japan, was of no practical help to China, and advanced America's own interests in no way at all.

First question, part a – 3 marks

What, according to Storry, was the impact of the USA's "moral force" response to Japanese aggression?

The USA's response to events 1937–38

The hesitant approach of the Americans continued after 1937 despite the fact that Japan's military and economic actions were now becoming a threat to the USA. Japan's ambitious naval building programme, launched in 1936, upset the balance of power in the western Pacific. In addition, the economic penetration into north and central China, following their military invasion threatened US interests in those regions and the whole concept of the "open door" policy.

Class discussion

Review question

Refer back to Source A on page 65. What are the similarities between the motives for the USA's lack of action and the motives for Britain's lack of action over the Manchurian incident?

Neutrality Acts

1935 – If there was a war then the USA would not supply arms to either side.

1936 – No loans could be made to belligerents.

1937 – Warring countries could only purchase arms from the USA if they were paid for and taken away by the purchaser.

Communication skills

Watch the bombing of USS Panay at:

http://www.criticalpast.com/video/65675061828_USS-Panay_Japanese-dive-bombers_manning-machine-guns_motor-sampan, or go to www.criticalpast.com and search "Japanese bombers attack USS Panay".

Roosevelt had some sympathy with China's position, as did the US media. Roosevelt, along with other prominent Americans, gave financial aid. However, none of this translated into political intervention. Indeed, between July and November 1937, the USA rejected ten British appeals for participation in a joint offer of mediation in the Sino-Japanese conflict and to make a show of naval strength. Roosevelt's actions were in any case limited by several laws called Neutrality Acts which enforced the USA's isolationist stance by preventing US involvement in conflicts that did not specifically involve the USA.

A potential crisis which did actually involve US interests and so could have led to more direct US intervention developed when a US gunboat, the Panay, which was escorting three small oil tankers on the Yangtze river, was bombed and sunk by a Japanese aircraft on 12 December 1937. However, when the Japanese quickly apologized and offered compensation, many Americans were relieved that a conflict had been avoided.

Public opinion in 1937 was overwhelmingly in favour of isolation with 7 out of 10 Americans in favour of a withdrawal of US citizens from China in order to avoid the possibility of a confrontation with Japan. The USA sent representatives to the Brussels conference in 1937 (see page 67) but showed itself unwilling to go beyond verbal condemnation against Japan. In one speech in 1937, Roosevelt seemed to promise more than this when he called for a "quarantine" on aggressors to put a stop to the "world of disorder". This "quarantine speech", seemed to indicate a willingness to impose sanctions against Japan. However, if this was his intention, Roosevelt had to quickly back down in the face of public outcry from isolationists.

In fact, not only did the USA *not* impose economic sanctions, its trade with Japan until 1939 played a key role in supporting Japan's war effort against China. The USA bought large quantities of Japanese silk and was a major supplier of oil, scrap iron and automobile parts. It also met nearly 40% of Japan's total needs for metals, cotton and wood pulp.

Why did the USA change its policy towards Japan after 1938?

During 1938, the USA began to carry out a more aggressive policy towards Japan. Roosevelt did not share the sentiments of the isolationists regarding the Neutrality Acts which treated aggressor and victim alike. Thus in 1938, using presidential powers, Roosevelt chose not to apply the Neutrality Acts to China and to give more active support to the nationalists, starting with an oil loan of $25 million. China's Finance Minister HH Kung correctly saw this as a change of policy:

> *The $25 million was only the beginning, further large sums can be expected … this is a political loan … America has definitely thrown in her lot and cannot withdraw.*

Why did America now start to resist Japanese expansion? The announcement by Japan that it wished to create "a new order in East Asia" was the turning point (see page 45). In addition, there was growing concern in the US that Jiang might respond to overtures from Japan to join with them in this "new order". This would put Japan in an invincible position.

Another factor was the possibility that if the USA did not give enough aid to Jiang, the Soviets might increase their support for the Nationalists, thus further increasing their influence in China. US public opinion also began to swing in favour of Roosevelt's campaign to end the neutrality laws.

The international context was key for changing US attitudes. The German victories in the spring and summer of 1940 had encouraged the Japanese in their expansionist policies for fear of "missing the bus" (Hayashi, 1959). In September 1940, Japan entered into a the Tripartite Pact with the European fascist powers Germany and Italy. This stated that if Japan, Germany or Italy was attacked by any third power not then engaged in the European War or the China War, the other two Axis powers would aid the victim of the attack. This convinced many Americans that the war in Europe and the war in Asia were the same war.

Source skills

An American poster supporting a no-sanctions policy against Japan.

FOR AMERICAN LABOR

FOR JAPANESE LABOR

EVERY DOLLAR SPENT HERE FOR SILK GOODS

84c

16c

If this American woman refused to buy silk as usual she would hurt U. S. workers six times as much as she'd hurt Japan.

First question, part b – 2 marks

What is the message of this source concerning any attempt to impose sanctions on Japan?

Communication and thinking skills

"Fireside chat"; a radio broadcast to the people of the USA by Franklin D Roosevelt on 29 December 1940

… Never before since Jamestown and Plymouth Rock has our American civilisation been in such danger as now.

For, on September 27, 1940, by an agreement signed in Berlin, three powerful nations, two in Europe and one in Asia, joined themselves together in the threat that if the United States of America interfered with or blocked the expansion program of these three nations – a program aimed at world control – they would unite in ultimate actions against the United States.

… Does anyone seriously believe that we need to fear attack anywhere in the Americas while a free Britain remains our most powerful naval neighbour in the Atlantic? Does anyone seriously believe, on the other hand, that we could rest easy if the Axis powers were our neighbours there?

If Great Britain goes down, the Axis powers will control the continents of Europe, Asia, Africa, Australia and the high seas – and they will be in a position to bring enormous military and naval resources against this hemisphere. It is no exaggeration to say that all of us, in all the Americas, would be living at the point of a gun – a gun loaded with explosive bullets, economic as well as military.

… We must be the great arsenal of democracy. For this is an emergency as serious as war itself. We must apply ourselves to our task with the same resolution, the same urgency, the same spirit of patriotism and sacrifice as we would show were we at war …

1   What message is Roosevelt attempting to convey to the American people in this radio broadcast?

2   With reference to the origin, purpose and content of Roosevelt's "fireside chat", assess the values and limitations of this source for examining American attitudes towards the international situation.

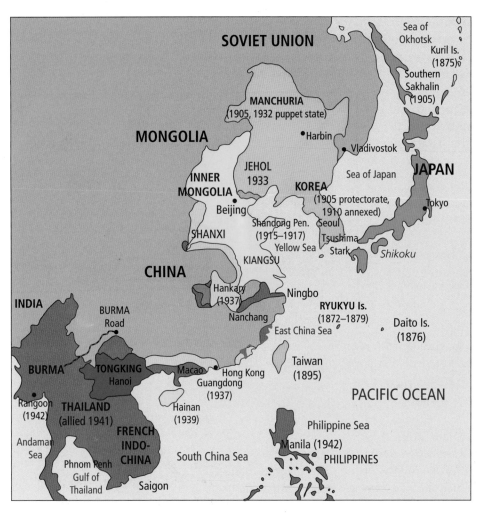

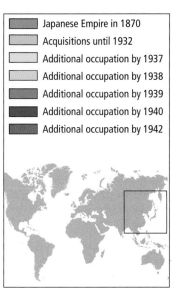

	Japanese Empire in 1870
	Acquisitions until 1932
	Additional occupation by 1937
	Additional occupation by 1938
	Additional occupation by 1939
	Additional occupation by 1940
	Additional occupation by 1942

The advance to war: US pressure on Japan

American reaction to the Tripartite Pact was … unexpectedly strong
– Pyle, 1996: 201

In January 1939 "a moral embargo" was placed on planes and aviation parts sales, and in February 1939 credit to Japan was stopped. In July of the same year a long-standing trade agreement with Japan was suspended. A year later a partial trade embargo on aviation and motor fuel and high-grade melting scrap was put in place.

Throughout 1940 and 1941, as Japan advanced, the USA gave millions of dollars of aid to China. Following the temporary closure of the Burma Road supply route to China in October 1941, the USA agreed more loans to China and, by the summer of 1941, a hundred P-40 US fighter planes were sent to replenish the depleted Chinese air force. Simultaneously, the USA also put economic pressure on Japan.

In July 1941, when Japan moved south rather than moving north to attack the Soviets, the USA responded by freezing all Japanese assets. It then imposed a trade embargo in November which included oil. Britain and the Netherlands also imposed a total trade embargo. As Japan was totally dependent on imported oil from the USA, this created a crisis for the Japanese government who now believed that the Western powers were attempting to encircle Japan and destroy its "rightful place" in the world.

The Burma Road

The **Burma Road** is a road linking Burma with the southwest of China. The road is 717 miles (1,154 kilometres) long and runs through mountainous country. Parts of it were built by approximately 200,000 Burmese and Chinese labourers between 1937 and 1938. The British used the Burma Road to transport materials to China before 1941.

If its oil reserves ran out, Japan would be unable to continue the war in China. Japan could not risk this happening. There followed negotiations and a diplomatic mission to the USA. However, agreement stalled over the fact that the USA insisted that Japan withdraw from China. Japan may have agreed to a withdrawal from southern Indo-China, but could not agree to removing its forces from China as this would be unacceptable to the military and the Japanese people. In order to get the resources they needed the Japanese decided that a war of conquest was necessary (see page 49).

(see page 49)

TOK

In small groups investigate current inter-state tensions. How has the global community responded? Which nation seems to be the aggressor? Explore if the UN has responded, has there been a crisis or issue referred to at the Security Council and was there a UN resolution? Feedback your findings to the class. Consider the international response to Japan's action up to 1941. As a class, debate the extent to which we learn from history.

Source skills

Source A

The US Ambassador to Japan, Joseph Grew, in 1939, offering his assessment of Japan's reaction to sanctions.

A treatyless situation plus an embargo would exasperate the Japanese to a point where anything could happen, even serious incidents which could inflame the American people beyond endurance and which might call for war. The Japanese are so constituted and are now in such a mood and temper that sanctions, far from intimidating, would almost certainly bring retaliation, which in turn would lead to counter-retaliation. Japan would not stop to weigh ultimate consequences … I think that our dignity and our power in themselves counsel moderation, forbearance and the use of every reasonable means of conciliation without the sacrifice of principle … In our own interests, particularly our commercial and cultural interests, we should approach this problem from a realistic and constructive standpoint.

First question, part a – 3 marks

What, according to Source A, were the reasons why sanctions against Japan were a bad idea?

Source B

Max Hastings. *Retribution: The battle for Japan 1944–45* (2007).

It is a fascinating speculation, how events might have evolved if the U.S. and its Philippines dependency had been excluded from Japanese war plans in December 1941; had Tokyo confined itself to occupying British Malaya and Burma, along with the Dutch East Indies. Roosevelt would certainly have wished to confront Japanese aggression and enter the war – the oil embargo imposed by the U.S. following Japan's advance into Indochina was the tipping factor in deciding Tokyo to fight the western powers. It remains a moot point, however, whether Congress and public sentiment would have allowed the president to declare war in the absence of a direct assault on American national interests or the subsequent German declaration of war on the United States.

First question, part a – 3 marks

What key points are made in Source B regarding US policy towards Japan up to December 1941?

What was the reaction of the USA to the attack on Pearl Harbor?

The attack on Pearl Harbor united the American people for a war against Japan. Congress agreed to Roosevelt's request for a Declaration of War on 8 December with only one dissenting vote. This was wonderful news for Churchill who confidently remarked:

Hitler's fate was sealed. Mussolini's fate was sealed. As for the Japanese, they would be ground to powder. All the rest was merely the application of overwhelming force.

Class discussion

Some historians have suggested that Churchill and Jiang had both gambled on the USA entering the war in Europe and the Pacific. Both leaders aimed to hold out until US military and economic force would win the global war. From the evidence in this Chapter, how far do you agree that this was Jiang's position?

President Roosevelt's speech to the United States Congress on 8 December, 1941

Yesterday, December 7, 1941 – a date which will live in infamy – the United States of America was suddenly and deliberately attacked by naval and air forces of the Empire of Japan.

The United States was at peace with that nation and, at the solicitation of Japan, was still in conversation with the government and its emperor looking toward the maintenance of peace in the Pacific.

Indeed, one hour after Japanese air squadrons had commenced bombing in Oahu, the Japanese ambassador to the United States and his colleagues delivered to the Secretary of State a formal reply to a recent American message. While this reply stated that it seemed useless to continue the existing diplomatic negotiations, it contained no threat or hint of war or armed attack.

It will be recorded that the distance of Hawaii from Japan makes it obvious that the attack was deliberately planned many days or even weeks ago. During the intervening time, the Japanese government has deliberately sought to deceive the United States by false statements and expressions of hope for continued peace.

The attack yesterday on the Hawaiian islands has caused severe damage to American naval and military forces. Very many American lives have been lost. In addition, American ships have been reported torpedoed on the high seas between San Francisco and Honolulu.

Yesterday, the Japanese government also launched an attack against Malaya.

Last night, Japanese forces attacked Hong Kong.

Last night, Japanese forces attacked Guam.

Last night, Japanese forces attacked the Philippine Islands.

Last night, the Japanese attacked Wake Island.

This morning, the Japanese attacked Midway Island.

Japan has, therefore, undertaken a surprise offensive extending throughout the Pacific area. The facts of yesterday speak for themselves. The people of the United States have already formed their opinions and well understand the implications to the very life and safety of our nation.

As commander in chief of the Army and Navy, I have directed that all measures be taken for our defense.

Always will we remember the character of the onslaught against us.

No matter how long it may take us to overcome this premeditated invasion, the American people in their righteous might will win through to absolute victory.

I believe I interpret the will of the Congress and of the people when I assert that we will not only defend ourselves to the uttermost, but will make very certain that this form of treachery shall never endanger us again.

Hostilities exist. There is no blinking at the fact that our people, our territory and our interests are in grave danger.

With confidence in our armed forces – with the unbounding determination of our people – we will gain the inevitable triumph – so help us God.

I ask that the Congress declare that since the unprovoked and dastardly attack by Japan on Sunday, December 7, a state of war has existed between the United States and the Japanese Empire.

http://www.let.rug.nl/usa/presidents/franklin-delano-roosevelt/pearl-harbor-speech-december-8-1941.php

Question

In pairs examine the key points made by President Roosevelt in his response to the bombing of Pearl Harbor.

You can also watch Roosevelt's speech here: http://www.youtube.com/watch?v=IK8gYGgOdkE

See an annotated draft of part of the speech at http://www.archives.gov/education/lessons/day-of-infamy/images/infamy-address-1.gif

Listen to the radio address here: http://www.archives.gov/education/lessons/day-of-infamy/images/infamy-radio-address.wav

Full document question: USA's actions with regard to Japan, 1930–41

Source A

Memorandum handed by Secretary of State Henry Stimson to the Japanese ambassador in Washington on 22 September 1931:

This situation [in Manchuria] is of concern, morally, legally and politically to a considerable number of nations. It is not exclusively a matter of concern to Japan and China. It brings into question at once the meaning of certain provisions of agreements, such as the Nine-Power Treaty of February 6, 1922, and the Kellogg-Briand Pact.

The American Government is confident that it has not been the intention of the Japanese Government to create or to be a party to the creation of a situation which brings the applicability of treaty provisions into consideration. The American Government does not wish to be hasty in formulating its conclusions or in taking a position. However, the American Government feels that a very unfortunate situation exists, which no doubt is embarrassing to the Japanese Government. It would seem that the responsibility for determining the course of events with regard to the ending of this situation rests largely upon Japan …

Source B

A US cartoon from 1938 by Clifford Kennedy Berryman (Laocoon refers to a classical Roman statue on which this is based).

Source C

Stimson speaking in 1947 about America's response to Japan's action in Manchuria.

What happened after World War One was that we lacked the courage to enforce the authoritative decision of the international world. We agreed with the Kellogg-Briand pact that aggressive war must end. We renounced it and we condemned those who might use it. But it was a moral condemnation only. We thus did not reach the second half of the question – what will you do with an aggressor when you catch him? If we had reached it, we should easily have found the right answer, but that answer escaped us for it implied a duty to catch the criminal and such a choice meant war. Our offence was thus that of the man who passed by on the other side.

Source D

Herbert P. Bix, an American historian writing in an academic book *Hirohito and the Making of Modern Japan* (2000).

The massacres [of Nanjing] and the sinking of the USS Panay were neither quickly forgotten, nor forgiven – either in China or in the United States … In the depression-racked United States, press reports of the massacres and the sinking of the Panay received rare front-page attention. The Asian news momentarily raised international tensions, stimulating a wave of anti-Japanese, pro-Chinese sentiment that never entirely abated. Since the late nineteenth century, Americans had tended to view China not only as a market to be exploited but also as a proper field for the projection of their idealism and essential goodness in foreign relations. President Roosevelt's refusal to impose sanctions against the vulnerable Japanese economy came under criticism from a new movement to boycott the sale of imported Japanese goods.

First question, part a – 3 marks

According to Stimson in Source A, why should the USA not directly intervene in the Manchurian crisis?

First question, part b – 2 marks

What is the message of Source B with regard to the USA's isolationist position?

Second question – 4 marks

With reference to origin, purpose and content assess the values and limitations of Source C for historians studying the reasons for the USA's isolationist position in the 1930s.

Third question – 6 marks

Compare and contrast the view expressed in Source A and Source C regarding the USA's response to the Manchurian crisis?

Fourth question – 9 marks

Using the sources and your own knowledge examine the reasons for the USA's change of attitude towards Japan between 1931 and 1941.

ATL Thinking skills

Here are wider questions that you could get for a fourth question in the source paper. Using the information and sources in this chapter, discuss each question with a partner, setting out your arguments for and against. What sources in this chapter could you use to help you answer each question?

1 "The League of Nation's failure to take stronger action over the Manchurian crisis encouraged the Japanese to go further in its expansionist policy." To what extent do you agree with this statement?

2 Examine the importance of the actions of the West in determining Japan's actions between 1931 and 1941.

3 To what extent did events in China contribute to Japan's expansionist policy between 1931 and 1941?

4 Discuss the reasons for the changes in US policy towards Japan between 1931 and 1941.

Source help and hints

A cartoon published in Outlook, a US Magazine, in 1931.

First question, part b – 2 marks

(See page 61.)

What is the message of Source B concerning Japan's actions in Manchuria?

> **Examiner's hint:** *Note the symbolism being used in the cartoon – always use your contextual knowledge to help you interpret a source. Here the gateway to Manchuria is not only showing Japan going into China, it also suggests that Japan is violating the "open door" principle as well as the Kellogg-Briand pact.*

Second question – 4 marks

(See page 64.)

With reference to origin, purpose and content, assess the value and limitations of this source for historians studying the Manchurian incident.

Points to consider include the following.

Values

- It is an official government statement, so it has value for showing the Japanese government's position at the time of the incident (1931).

- It was presented at the League of Nations, an international forum, so this shows what the Japanese government wanted the world to think was happening.

Limitations

- This is only the point of view from the government and not the military, so it is only one perspective of what was going on at the time.

- The date of 1931 is before a thorough investigation could have been carried out.

- As this is a speech given to the League of Nations, its purpose is to convince the world of the innocence of Japan, so it may not refer to evidence of Japanese aggression.

- Linked to the above point, the language is quite damning of China and clearly intends to make the Japanese actions seem unavoidable, for example "unpleasant incidents", "atmosphere of anxiety" and "a detachment of Chinese troops destroyed the tracks". Therefore the content is not objective.

Fourth question – 9 marks

(See page 65.)

Using the sources and your own knowledge, assess why the League of Nations did not take stronger action to deal with the Manchurian crisis.

> **Examiner's hint:** *Structure your answer as you would for a standard essay. This means writing a brief introduction and clear paragraphs linked to the question. Your opening sentences should link to the question and make it clear the purpose of the paragraph. Integrate the sources so that they provide extra evidence for the points that you are making.*

The kind of essay structure that you could use to answer this question is shown below.

Introduction

In 1932, the Lytton Commission reported back to the League of Nations on its findings regarding the Mukden incident. As a result of the Commission's findings, the League demanded that Japan should give up the territory that it had taken in Manchuria and withdraw its forces. However, it did not try to force Japan to do this and there are several reasons why it did not take stronger action.

Paragraph 1

Firstly, Europe did not have the means to force Japan into withdrawing. As Source A points out … (include a relevant quote from Source A and then develop it with your own knowledge regarding lack of military strength).

In addition, both Source A and Source B highlight the issue of US isolationism … (explain the relevance of Source B and quote the relevant parts of Source A …)

Paragraph 2

Secondly, there were more self-interested reasons for Britain and France, as two of the most important members of the League, not to put too much pressure on Japan. France, as the colonial power in Vietnam, had much to gain from a weakened China. As Source C highlights, there were also growing concerns about the Soviets and the spread of communism which was seen to be of a greater threat … (here you could quote the relevant part of Source C).

Paragraph 3

Finally, the economic crisis facing Europe following the Wall Street Crash meant that the European powers were more focused on their own internal concerns, rather than dealing with international problems. (Develop with your own knowledge and Source D.)

Conclusion

In conclusion … (make sure you answer the question clearly).

First question, part a – 3 marks

(See page 71.)

What, according to Storry, was the impact of the USA's "moral force" response to Japanese aggression?

The USA's "moral force" response:

- demonstrated to the Japanese that the USA would not use economic sanctions to resist their actions

- increased nationalist feeling in Japan

- did not help China

- failed to support US interests in the region.

Second question – 4 marks

(See page 73.)

With reference to the origin, purpose and content of Roosevelt's "fireside chat", assess the values and limitations of this source in indicating the US government's attitude towards events in Europe in 1940.

Values

- These remarks come directly from the President and therefore the origin has value as the comments are from the Chief Executive of American policy at the time.

- It was broadcast in December 1940 when most of Europe had been taken over by the Axis powers and therefore gives insight into the US position at the time.

- Roosevelt is talking to the American people with the purpose of getting the public to understand the impact of events in Europe on the USA; he needs the support of the public and therefore the source shows how the President attempts to shape public opinion.

- The examples used in the speech focus on and emphasize the aggression of the Axis powers

Limitations

- The president's comments may not reflect the opinion of everyone in the government.

- The date of the origin means that it lacks hindsight.

- The purpose of the "chat" is to get Americans to shift their neutral position and to see that the actions of the Axis powers will affect the USA. Therefore Roosevelt is trying to lead US opinion and so could be making the situation seem worse than he thinks it actually is – he is trying to "shock" the American people.

- This last point is backed up by the style of the "chat"; Roosevelt is trying to make clear the dangers that the world faces, using rhetorical questions, setting out what could happen if there is no intervention and using metaphors that he thinks the US public will understand, for example "all of us in the Americas would be living at a point of a gun …". He is also appealing to Americans' "spirit of patriotism and sacrifice".

References

Boyle, JH. 1993. *Modern Japan: The American Nexus*. Harcourt Brace Jovanovich. New York, USA

Cameron, R. 1991. *Appeasement and the Road to War*. Pulse Publications. Kilmarnock, UK

Farmer, A. 2006. *Britain Foreign Affairs*. Hodder. London, UK

Hastings, M. 2007. *Retribution: The Battle for Japan 1944–45*. Alfred A Knopf. New York, USA

Iriye, A. 1987. *The Origins of the Second World War in Asia*. Longman. London, UK

Lu, David J. 1997. *Japan: A Documentary History*, pages 424–25. M.E. Sharpe Armonk, NY, USA

Overy, R. 2008. *Origins of the Second World War*. 2nd edn. Pearson Education. Harlow, UK

Storry, R. 1979. *Japan and the Decline of the West in Asia, 1894–1943*. Macmillan. London, UK

2 GERMAN AND ITALIAN EXPANSION

2.1 The impact of fascism on Italian foreign policy: the origins, 1870–1933

▲ Benito Mussolini

Mussolini once said of Fascism:
"*action and mood, not doctrine*".

Conceptual understanding

Key concepts

→ Causation

→ Significance

Key questions

→ Examine the reasons for the growth of support for Fascism and Mussolini in Italy after the First World War

→ To what extent did Fascism influence Italian foreign policy in the 1920s?

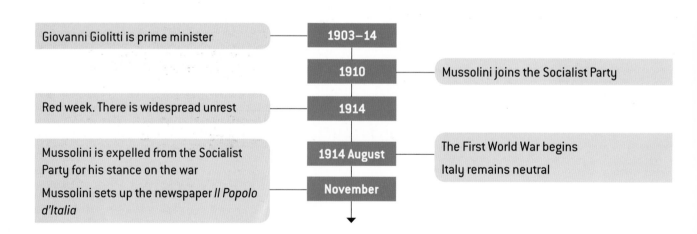

Giovanni Giolitti is prime minister	**1903–14**	
	1910	Mussolini joins the Socialist Party
Red week. There is widespread unrest	**1914**	
Mussolini is expelled from the Socialist Party for his stance on the war	**1914 August**	The First World War begins / Italy remains neutral
Mussolini sets up the newspaper *Il Popolo d'Italia*	**November**	

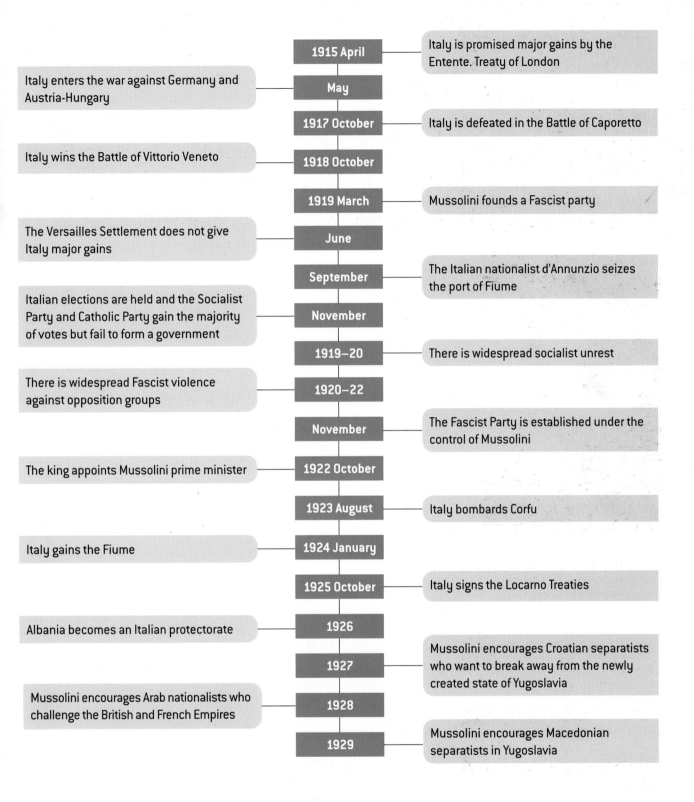

	1915 April	Italy is promised major gains by the Entente. Treaty of London
Italy enters the war against Germany and Austria-Hungary	**May**	
	1917 October	Italy is defeated in the Battle of Caporetto
Italy wins the Battle of Vittorio Veneto	**1918 October**	
	1919 March	Mussolini founds a Fascist party
The Versailles Settlement does not give Italy major gains	**June**	
	September	The Italian nationalist d'Annunzio seizes the port of Fiume
Italian elections are held and the Socialist Party and Catholic Party gain the majority of votes but fail to form a government	**November**	
	1919–20	There is widespread socialist unrest
There is widespread Fascist violence against opposition groups	**1920–22**	
	November	The Fascist Party is established under the control of Mussolini
The king appoints Mussolini prime minister	**1922 October**	
	1923 August	Italy bombards Corfu
Italy gains the Fiume	**1924 January**	
	1925 October	Italy signs the Locarno Treaties
Albania becomes an Italian protectorate	**1926**	
	1927	Mussolini encourages Croatian separatists who want to break away from the newly created state of Yugoslavia
Mussolini encourages Arab nationalists who challenge the British and French Empires	**1928**	
	1929	Mussolini encourages Macedonian separatists in Yugoslavia

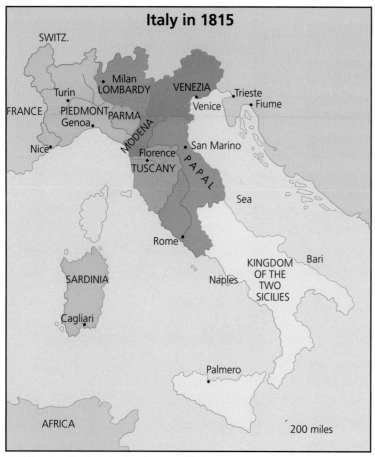

Italy in 1815

SWITZ.

Turin
Milan
LOMBARDY
VENEZIA
• Trieste
• Fiume
Venice

FRANCE
PIEDMONT
PARMA
Genoa•

MODENA

Nice•

Florence•
• San Marino
TUSCANY
PAPAL

Sea

Rome•

SARDINIA

Bari

Naples
KINGDOM
OF THE
TWO
SICILIES

Cagliari•

Palmero•

AFRICA
200 miles

▲ Map showing Italy before it was unified

Italy had only become a unified state in 1861. Before this it had consisted of a number of independent states. It was through the combined diplomatic and military actions of the prime minister of Piedmont Sardinia, Cavour, and Italian patriot Giuseppe Garibaldi, that Italy could be unified in 1861, with Rome and the Papal States finally joining the new Italian Kingdom in 1870.

Despite unification, Italian society after 1870 remained divided across geographical, religious and social lines. These divisions weakened Italian governments and, along with the discontent and unrest caused by Italy's involvement in the First World War, helped facilitate the rise to power of Mussolini and his Fascist Party in 1922.

Once in power, Mussolini pursued an Italian foreign policy that was influenced by a number of factors. These included:

- Italy's geographical position and its limited economic resources
- the Versailles Settlement
- nationalist views on the destiny of Italy to become a great power and to have an empire
- earlier foreign policy humiliations
- the changing international context
- Fascist ideology.

(Fascist ideology will be explored in detail later – see page 89.)

ATL Thinking skills

As you read through the next section consider how each of the factors identified here played a role in helping to formulate Mussolini's foreign policy. Add evidence to a copy of the spider diagram below.

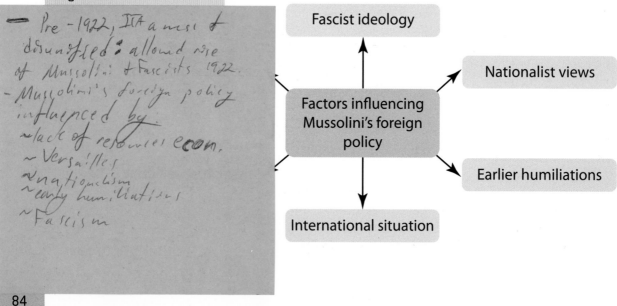

Mussolini's rise to power

What were the long-term weaknesses of Liberal Italy?

The period between 1870 and 1923 is an era known as Liberal Italy and
the inherent weaknesses that undermined Italy during this period would
ultimately facilitate the development of a Fascist dictatorship. Nevertheless, it
was not inevitable that the style of government to replace liberal democracy
would be Fascist rather than socialist or an authoritarian monarchy.

Lack of national identity

Despite the recent unification of the Italian state, Italy lacked a coherent
sense of an Italian identity. Piedmont had been the dominant state, and its
laws and political systems were imposed on the other states. Regionalism
remained a strong force, with many Italians feeling loyalty to their home
towns and cities, particularly in the south. The new capital in Rome had
limited support in this area. There were economic as well as political
divisions between the north and the south, with the majority of peasants in
the south living in abject poverty whilst the industrialized north prospered.

The Catholic Church

The breakdown in relations between Church and State which had
begun during unification also continued to divide Italy. This division
was exacerbated by the anti-clerical policies of the liberal governments.
Indeed, up until 1914, the Vatican had urged Catholics not to vote.

Working-class protest

The middle and upper classes dominated the political system, as the
franchise (the vote) was limited to the wealthy elites until 1930, when
all men over 30 were given the vote. The many liberal governments that
existed before the First World War had a reputation for corruption and
representing the needs of the middle and upper classes only. This led to
growing peasant and working-class unrest, which fermented into a general
strike in 1914. Working-class movements had grown in Italy from the late
19th century, and, in 1892, the Italian Socialist Party (PSI) was founded.

Most politicians at the time wanted to respond to the growing unrest with
force, and by closing down trade unions and banning parties such as the
PSI. One man who dominated Italian politics in the pre-war period, as
prime minister in 1903–05, in 1906–09 and in 1911–14, was Giovanni
Giolitti. Giolitti wanted to win the support of the masses and was willing
to work with the moderate socialists to offer electoral and welfare reform.
He also attempted to gain a rapprochement with the Church by allowing
religious education in schools.

Although Giolitti's policies were initially successful, a serious recession
undermined them and economic issues were compounded by the Italian–
Turkish war of 1911–12. Giolitti pursued this war under pressure from
Italian nationalists and was able to seize Libya from Turkey. However, the
PSI was appalled at such an imperialist war and many on the left rejected
the idea of working with the liberal parliamentary parties. The move away
from the liberals continued after the First World War, when the two
largest parties were the PSI and the Catholic Party (*Partito Popolare
Italiano* or *PPI*).

> **Liberal democracy**
>
> This describes a government
> which is based on both the ideas
> of democracy and of liberalism.
> Thus, people of the country
> can choose the government in
> open and free elections, and the
> individual rights of the people
> are protected by law.

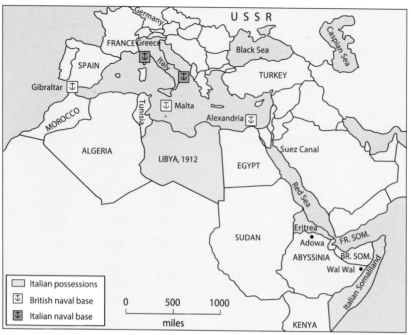

▲ Italy's empire in 1914

Nationalist opposition

The Italian Nationalist Association had been founded in 1910. A poet, Filippo Marinetti, also established the Futurist Movement. This movement glorified war and criticized the weakness of liberal governments for failing to become a "Great Power", which Marinetti believed should have been Italy's destiny after unification. The nationalists also believed that unification was unfinished because the regions of Trentino and Trieste remained under Austrian rule despite containing large numbers of Italian speakers. These were known as the *terre irredente* or "unredeemed lands".

In addition, nationalists also wanted an empire to compete with Britain, France and the new Germany. However, Libya apart, the Italians had made only minor gains in Africa, with Eritea (in 1885) and part of Somaliland (in 1889). They also failed in their attempt to conquer Abyssinia in 1896; indeed, the Italians were humiliatingly defeated by the Abyssinians at the infamous Battle of Adowa.

What was the impact of the First World War on Italy, 1915–18?

Italy's reasons for joining the Entente Alliance

In 1914, Europe was divided into two alliances, the Triple Entente and the Triple Alliance. Italy had been a member of the Triple Alliance with Germany and Austria–Hungary since 1882; however, Italy's politicians were deeply divided during the intervention crisis that developed after the First World War broke out, and at first Italy remained neutral. However, right-wing liberals hoped that, if Italy joined the Entente (the alliance block of Britain, France and Russia established in 1907), they would gain the Italian-speaking territories of the Austro–Hungarian Empire. The prime minister, Antonio Salandra, favoured this action and signed the Treaty of London with Britain, France and Russia in April 1915.

The Italian king, Victor Emmanuel III, was persuaded to back the Treaty of London, and intervention was supported by both Nationalists and Futurists. Intervention caused division on the left; the PSI was against intervention, viewing the conflict as an "imperialist's war", but others on the left supported intervention because they believed that it would destroy Liberal Italy and could foster revolution. The *fasci di azione rivoluzionaria* or "revolutionary action groups" were set up by left-wing interventionists to support the war. Benito Mussolini was a leading member of the PSI who changed his opinion during the intervention crisis, initially opposing the war, but by October arguing in favour

of intervention. Mussolini was expelled from the PSI, and from his editorship of its newspaper, *Avanti!*

Giolitti and many liberals, including most of the Chamber, opposed the war, as did the Catholic Church. The liberals saw that Italy had little to gain from entering the war, while the Church did not relish a war against a fellow Catholic state, Austria.

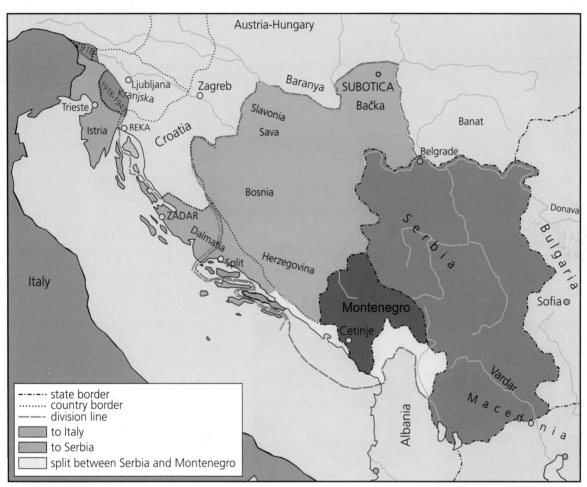

▲ Land offered to Italy, Serbia and Montenegro in London, 1915

Source skills

The Treaty of London, signed by Britain, France, Italy and Russia on 26 April 1915

ARTICLE 4

By the future treaty of peace, Italy is to receive the district of Trentino; the entire Southern Tyrol up to its natural geographical frontier, which is the Bremner Pass; the city and district of Trieste; the Country of Gorizia and Gradisca; the entire Istria.

ARTICLE 9

France, Great Britain and Russia admit in principle that fact of Italy's interest in the maintenance of the political balance of power in the Mediterranean, and her rights, in case of a partition of Turkey, to a share, equal to theirs, in the basin of the Mediterranean.

ARTICLE 11

Italy is to get a share in the war indemnity corresponding to the magnitude of her sacrifices and efforts.

First question, part a – 3 marks

What, according to the Treaty of London, did Italy expect to gain by entering the First World War?

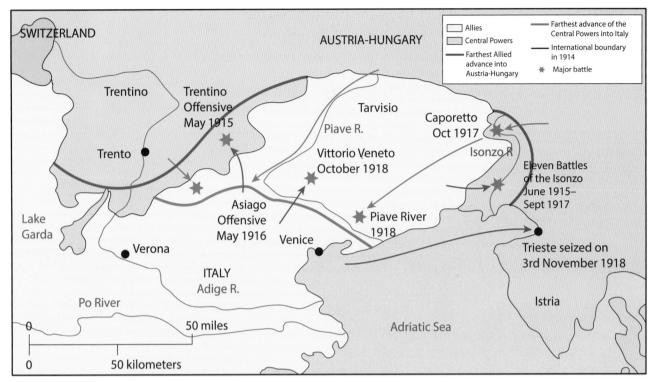

▲ Map of the Italian front during the First World War

▲ Italian troops killed in an Austrian chlorine gas attack

The impact of war

The Italians fought the Austrians and the Germans across a front in Northern Italy. As was the case on the Western Front in France and Belgium, trenches developed and for most of the three years of engagement the war was static. However, at the Battle of Caporetto in October 1917, the Italians suffered huge losses when they were pushed back by the Austrians and Germans, who advanced more than 100 kilometres.

At the end of the war, in October 1918, Italy finally achieved a victory at the Battle of Vittorio Veneto against the Austrians. However, the human cost of the war had been horrendous: more than 600,000 men were dead and hundreds of thousands wounded.

The war made Italy more politically divided. Many of the 5 million men that served in its army were politicized, resenting the liberal government for their mismanagement of the war. Many also resented the PSI's anti-war stance. The workforce was mobilized to fight a "total" war, which meant that the number of industrial workers grew. In turn, this led to an increased membership of trade unions and the PSI, and both were increasingly militant by the end of the war.

ATL | **Research skills** ▶

Go to https://www.youtube.com/watch?v=GpZi84oVUrY, or go to criticalpast.com and search "Austro-Hungarian troops advancing...".

Watch Austro-Hungarian troops advancing after the Battle of Caporetto.

ATL | **Research and social skills**

In pairs or small groups, research in more depth the Italian front in the First World War. You should allow two hours for this task. You might want to focus on: specific battles or campaigns; the use of technology; the role of military leaders; conditions on the front lines; propaganda.

You need to review how to reference your sources and provide a list of works cited.

As a pair or in your group, give a 10-minute presentation on your research to the class.

What is Fascism?

Fascism did not have a clear founding doctrine, and it manifested itself differently in different countries. In general, Fascism promoted nationalism, a strong leader or dictator, one-party government, empire building and war. Nevertheless, it could be argued that it is easier to understand what Fascism was by considering what it stood against: it was anti-communist and against the class struggle, against internationalism, against multi-party liberal democracy and against pacifism.

Fascism's growth in Europe was fostered by the impact of the First World War. Mussolini set up his first Fascist units in March 1919, called *fascio di combattimento*.

Key features of Fascism

Nationalism
- View of the nation state, its culture and history, as a unifying force
- Desire to remove foreign influences
- Own nation seen as superior to other nations

Militarism
- Promotion of political violence and war as a method of revitalizing society
- Violence seen as necessary in order to progress
- Development of paramilitary organizations

Social Darwinism
- The belief that races have evolved as superior to other races
- "Survival of the fittest"

Social unity
- Opposes class-based divisions in society and promotes collective national society

Authoritarianism
- Totalitarian; the state has influence or control over all aspects of society
- The people are subservient to the state
- Mussolini: "obedience not discussion"

▲ Fascist symbol

Class discussion

Look at the characteristics of Fascism. In pairs or small groups, discuss what kind of foreign policy you would expect to see from a state following this ideology.

Fascio means "group" and would become associated with the bound sticks or *fasces* which Roman magistrates used as a symbol of office. Mussolini probably intended the symbolism to suggest strong bonds or ties between his men in the militia units.

Why did support for Fascism grow in Italy after the First World War?

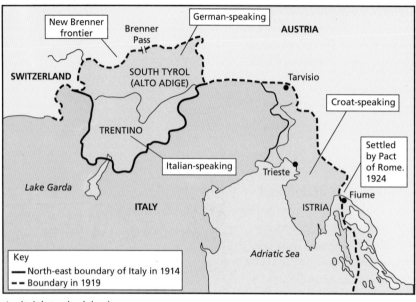

▲ Italy's territorial gains

Following the war, Italy entered into a period of political crisis. The liberal governments of 1918–22 began to lose control. As the franchise had been extended, the liberals fared badly in the elections of 1919 and gained fewer than half the seats in the chamber. Subsequently, none of the political parties were able to form a coherent coalition government. The result was short-term governments and this undermined the credibility of the democratic parliamentary system.

Moreover, support for the government declined further when it became clear that liberal Prime Minister Vittorio Emmanuelle Orlando had not obtained the territory Italy had claimed from the defeated Austro–Hungarian empire. Italy, having joined the war primarily for territorial gain, received, as promised, the province of Tyrol, the Istrian peninsular, the port of Trieste and the Dodecanese islands. It also got a port in, and the protectorate over, Albania.

However, although not clearly stated in the Treaty of London, Italy had also expected to gain the port of Fiume and Dalmatia.

Territory claimed by Italy	Territory promised at the Treaty of London, May 1915	Territory Italy received in the Treaty of St Germain in 1919
South Tyrol	*	*
Trentino	*	*
Istria	*	*
Fiume		
Dalmatia	*	
Colonies	*	

▲ Italy and the peace settlement

Prime Minister Orlando was accompanied to Versailles by his conservative foreign minister, Sydney Sonnino. Orlando had been willing to renounce Italian claims to Dalmatia in return for the port of

Fiume, but his foreign minister disagreed. In the end their differences were exploited by the other great powers and the Italians were not given either territory. Orlando was forced to resign.

There was widespread disgust in Italy at the outcome of the Versailles Settlement. As has been noted earlier, Italian casualties were more than 600,000 men killed and hundreds of thousands injured. The casualty rate for Italian forces was actually higher than the casualty rate for Britain: 39.1% of its forces were casualties compared to 35.8% for Britain. The Italian nationalist and poet, Gabriele D'Annunzio, deemed it a "mutilated victory".

The Fascist Party benefited from the post-war situation. As fascism was not based on a clear doctrine or theories it could appeal to a wide range of groups across the class divide. Italians embraced its demands for strict law and order after the violence on the streets following the First World War, and it gave its members the opportunity to regain a sense of national pride.

In the 1921 elections, 35 seats went to the Fascists (PNF), 108 to the Catholic Party and 138 seats to the Socialists and the Communists (newly founded in 1921). Italian politics was polarizing.

What was the impact of D'Annunzio and the Fiume affair on Fascism?

In September 1919, Gabriele D'Annunzio led 2,000 ex-soldiers to occupy Fiume by force in protest against the Italian government's agreement to hand the port over to Yugoslavia. The government proved too feeble to remove D'Annunzio until Giolitti was returned as prime minister in December 1920. The whole affair undermined the credibility of the Italian democratic system.

Source skills

Source A

Video clip of D'Annunzio and his forces in Fiume:

> http://www.britishpathe.com/video/dannunzio-at-fiume-aka-italian-army-review-at/query/AMERICAN+TROOPS+INSPECTION+ON+MARCH

The war left other major legacies. They included a thirst for justice ("land for the peasants") and a transformed economy. The war also produced tens of thousands of new officers, drunk with patriotism and greedy to command. They had won the war, and did not intend to let anyone forget it.

Source B

M. Clark. *Modern Italy 1871–1982* (1985).

> The Italians had been divided before, but by November 1919 they were more divided than ever: "combatants" against "shirkers", peasants against workers, patriots against defeatists. No conceivable form of government could suit them all.

Source C

Denis Mack Smith, a British historian who specialises in Italian history, in an academic book. *Modern Italy – A political history* (1997).

> Support for this escapade (the occupation of Fiume) was obtained from many patriots who had no intention of honouring Orlando's signature at Versailles, and D'Annunzio spoke for such people when in November he stated: "the Yugoslavs are excited by a savage spirit

of domination and we cannot avoid perpetual quarrel with them" ... The black-shirted arditi or shock troops were especially dangerous when demobilized, and in such circles there had been talk of a military coup détat ... The war had accustomed such people to the use of force. A continuation of the war under the respectable cloak of patriotism would be a godsend to them, and Fiume was the obvious place for it ... public opinion was encouraged by the government to solidify in favour of annexing Fiume and the possible international repercussions were completely disregarded ... [A] member of the royal family ... paid visits to D'Annunzio in Fiume ... [The Prime Minister Nitti] boasted of giving government money to help keep the artificial revolt alive ... apparently it meant nothing to him or the king that military indiscipline was unpunished and even rewarded.

D'Annunzio's "Regency of Carnaro" lasted for over a year. Although it was a petty and ridiculous affair, its example was an inspiration and a dress rehearsal for fascism ... The black shirts of the arditi were to be seen in Fiume as people shouted the future fascist war cry "A noi ... eja, eja, alala." Here, too, was seen the first sketch of the "corporate state". All this was later copied without acknowledgement by Mussolini.

First question, part a – 3 marks

What, according to Source B, was the impact of the First World War on Italy?

First question, part b – 2 marks

What is the message of the images from Pathé News in Source A?

Second question – 4 marks

With reference to its origin, purpose and content, analyse the values and limitations of Source C for historians studying Italy in the 1920s.

ATL Social skills

Share your response to the second question (above) with a partner. Peer assess each other's response to this question and award a mark out of 4. Discuss how and why you gave the marks awarded, and suggest how your partner might improve his or her response.

What was the impact of economic factors on the rise of Fascism?

The post-war economy was also an important factor in the rise of Fascism. High inflation hit both the fixed-wage workers and the middle classes with savings. Unemployment soared to 2 million by the end of 1919. This situation was exacerbated by new US restrictions on immigration that meant the southern poor could not emigrate to America to escape their poverty.

In addition, the Bolshevik revolution in Russia, in October 1917, had led to widespread fear of communism across Europe. Between 1919 and 1920 there was extensive unrest in Italy that became known as the "Two Red Years" (*Biennio Rosso*). During this time the socialists attempted to catalyse a Russian-style revolution. The Italian Communist Party (*Partito Comunista Italiano*) was formed on 21 January 1921; however, the strength of the left had already peaked and support passed to the Fascists who opposed the Communists. Mussolini and the Fascists gained support from the wealthy industrialists and landowners, as the Fascists offered not only ideological opposition but were also prepared to confront Socialists and Communists physically. Indeed, the conservatives initially believed that they could manipulate and use the Fascists to their own ends. There was complicity from the police and the army, who did not restrain the Blackshirts from their excesses.

Fascism was also supported by the Catholic Church which was a significant political force in Italy. Pope Pius XI backed Mussolini as he saw the Fascists as a means of improving the position of the Church and cementing church–state relations.

By 1922, therefore, there was a loss of faith in Italian state institutions that had failed to bring about a "victors" peace settlement, seemed unable to contain violence on the streets and had failed to establish a stable post-war economy.

Source skills

Source A

An extract from Mussolini's speech to the first meeting of the Milan *fascio* in March, 1919.

> I have the impression that the present regime in Italy has failed. It is clear to everyone that a crisis now exists. During the war all of us sensed the inadequacy of the government; today we know that our victory was due solely to the virtues of the Italian people, not to the intelligence and ability of its leaders.
>
> We must not be faint hearted, now that the future nature of the political system is to be determined. We must act fast. If the present regime is going to be superseded, we must be ready to take its place. For this reason, we are establishing the *fasci* as organs of creativity and agitation that will be ready to rush into the piazzas and cry out, "The right to the political succession belongs to us, because we are the ones who pushed the country into war and led it to victory!"

Cited in C.F. Delzell (ed). 1971. *Mediterranean Fascism, 1919–45: Selected documents*, page 10

Source B

Mark Robson. *Italy: Liberalism and Fascism 1870–45* (2004).

> It was not only over the issue of the supposed "socialist threat" that the right condemned the government. Nationalists who had always considered the Liberals weak and incompetent at running the war were now convinced that the government would fail to defend Italian interests at the peace conference. They demanded that Italy should receive not only those territories agreed with the Entente in 1915, (southern Tyrol, Trentino, Istria and parts of Dalmatia), but should also be given the city of Fiume on the border of Istria. When Britain and the United States of America refused to hand over Fiume, on the grounds that, despite its large Italian population, it was vital to the economy of the new Yugoslav state, the Nationalists blamed Liberal weakness. When, in addition, it became apparent that Italy would be denied Dalmatia because so few Italians lived there, and would not share in the division of German colonies in Africa, nationalists were outraged. To them, Italy had been cheated. Her sacrifices had won only a "mutilated victory", and Liberalism was the culprit!

First question, part a – 3 marks

What, according to Source A, is the problem with the existing Italian government?

First question, part a – 3 marks

Why, according to Source B, did Italians believe that they had been cheated after the war?

Second question – 4 marks

With reference to its origin, purpose and content, assess the values and limitations of Source A for historians studying Italy in the post war period.

Thinking, communication and social skills

In pairs or small groups, consider the following statement:

"Italians were justified in viewing the Versailles Settlement as a mutilated victory."

One student (or half your group) should prepare to argue for the assertion, the other (or other half of your group) against. Review the evidence presented on each side and together draw a conclusion based on the weight of your arguments.

How important was the March on Rome, October 1922?

A photograph of Mussolini with black-shirted Fascists before the March on Rome, 1922.

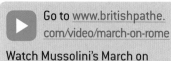

Go to www.britishpathe.com/video/march-on-rome

Watch Mussolini's March on Rome.

First question, part b – 2 marks

What is the message of this photograph?

By 1922, the liberal democratic government was weak and vulnerable; the Fascists believed that their time had come and that they were ready to take control in Italy. The key question was not whether they should lead Italy but how they would take power. The coalition government, led by the first Italian socialist prime minister, Ivanoe Bonomi, collapsed in February 1922. This was followed by a weak conservative coalition led by Luigi Facta that was unable to control the increasing violence.

In August 1922, the Socialists and Communists called a general strike, and the middle classes now believed that only Mussolini and his Fascists could restore law and order. Mussolini made it clear in a speech in September that he backed the monarchy, and he engaged in negotiations with conservative politicians to support his appointment as prime minister. Fascist squads had expelled Socialist councils in several towns and there had been widespread rumours that there would be a Fascist march on Rome. However, Mussolini wanted also to explore legal means, even though he was under increasing pressure from his own regional bosses, the Ras, to seize power.

In October 1922, talks continued with regard to the formation of a new government that would include Fascists. Although there was some willingness to offer Fascists cabinet posts, Mussolini would not

accept anything less than a major role. On 16 October, Mussolini met with leading Fascists in Milan and agreed that the time was right to seize power.

On 24 October, a Fascist congress was held in Naples. In imitation of the Italian unification leader, Garibaldi, 40,000 Black shirts chanted *A Roma* ("to Rome") and declared their intention to march on Rome. At three places, each 20 miles outside Rome, 10,000 of the planned 50,000 Fascists began to assemble. On the night of 27 October, Fascist squads attempted to seize control of government buildings in north and central Italy. This terrified local officials, who sent panicked reports back to Rome. The government resigned, but Prime Minister Facta, who had not taken firm action against the Fascists before 1922, was asked to stay. He asked the king to declare martial law so that the army could crush the Fascist revolt. At first the king agreed, but he then changed his mind and decided to side with Mussolini.

On 29 October, Mussolini received a telegram from the king:

> *Very urgent. Top priority, Mussolini, Milan. H.M. the King asks you to proceed immediately to Rome as he wishes to confer with you* — King Victor Emmanuel III, 1922

Mussolini, the leader of a party that had regularly participated in violence and had only 35 members of parliament, was offered the post of prime minister.

> *On 30th October, Mussolini arrived in Rome and Victor Emmanuel appointed him Prime Minister. The fascist leader was not satisfied with something so unspectacular as a royal appointment. He needed to develop the myth of a march on Rome by 300,000 armed fascists to enforce an 'ultimatum' he had given to the King, and eventually a legend was invented of Mussolini on horseback leading the legions across the Rubicon. In reality there were fewer than 30,000 fascist militiamen ready to march, many of whom had no arms at all and would have been quite unable to stand up to the garrison troops in Rome with their machine-guns and armoured cars: indeed, 400 policemen proved sufficient to hold up the fascist trains long before they reached Rome. Mussolini subsequently admitted this in private with amused satisfaction. His fascist squads did not arrive in Rome until twenty-four hours after he had asked to form a government and only after General Pugliese had orders to let them through. But the photographers were waiting to picture their arrival and the myth was launched of fascism winning power by an armed insurrection after a civil war and the loss of 3,000 men. These 3,000 fictitious "fascist martyrs" soon took their place in the government sponsored history books.* — Denis Mack Smith, 1983.

Self-management and social skills

In pairs or small groups, use the information in this chapter and in the source above to identify the key factors that led to Mussolini's appointment as prime minister in 1922.

Which of these factors do you consider were the most important?

How did Mussolini consolidate his power?

At first, the Fascists had to share power with other political parties. Mussolini was the prime minister of a coalition cabinet in which only 4 out of 12 ministers were Fascists. However, through a series of actions on the part of both Mussolini and other parties, Mussolini was able to move towards setting up a dictatorship:

- In November 1922, the new government won a vote of confidence and was able to vote in emergency powers to reform the administration and tax system.

- In February 1923, the Nationalists joined the Fascist Party.

- In July 1923, the Acerbo Law was passed, which stated that the party that won most votes in an election would automatically be given two-thirds of the seats in parliament to make strong government possible.

- In April 1924, the Fascists, after a campaign of intimidation and violence, were able to increase their representation in parliament from 7% to 66%.

- In May 1924, the liberal Giacomo Matteotti gave a speech in the Italian chamber of deputies condemning Fascist violence. He was murdered 11 days later by ex-squadristi Fascists.

- On 3 January 1925, following a wave of revulsion in Italy concerning Matteotti's death, Mussolini took responsibility for the violence of the Fascists. Most members of parliament withdrew in opposition. However, Mussolini now moved to establish himself as *Il Duce*.

- In December 1925, the Law on Powers of Head of Government gave Mussolini significant executive powers. Political parties and trade unions were banned. The press was now strictly controlled. Elected local officials were replaced by appointed government officials.

- Between November 1926 and January 1927 the Fascist Party increased repression and a new secret police was founded: the OVRA. The powers of arrest were increased, trial without jury was permitted and the scope of the death penalty was expanded to include action against the authorities.

Did Mussolini create a totalitarian state?

A totalitarian state is one in which the government has total control over all aspects of a citizen's life: political, economic, cultural and social. Under Mussolini, Italians had to conform to Fascist expectations and comply with the state's laws. There could be no overt opposition or criticism and this was enforced by the secret police and militia. Employees of the State had to swear an oath of loyalty to the regime and

the young were mobilized to join the Fascist youth movement. A form of cult developed around Mussolini. However, there were limitations to the totalitarian nature of the Fascist regime. The Fascists had compromised with powerful non-Fascists, such as the Vatican and the King.

Indeed, Mussolini could still be dismissed by the monarch while the Church retained considerable influence in Italy. In addition, Fascism never gained total control over the south where the Church and the landowning elites maintained their power. This contrasts with the more totalitarian nature of Hitler's Germany in the 1930s. Also, it was only in 1938 that anti-semitic racial laws were implemented and there was limited persecution of Jews until Italy became involved in the Second World War – and even then only after Hitler had urged Mussolini to impose them. Historian, Zara Steiner writes:

> *Mussolini was hardly a systematic thinker. He wrote no equivalent to* Mein Kampf. *He never developed the singular and all-embracing ideology that allowed Hitler to turn his fearsome doctrine of racial expansionism into political reality, nor did his programme of "domestic regeneration and radical revisionism" make the same impact on Italians that Hitler's doctrines made on the German people. There always remained competing claims and loyalties in Italy that Mussolini could not ignore, abolish, or totally destroy.* — Steiner, 2005

What factors influenced Mussolini's foreign policy?

To make Italy great, respected and feared. — Benito Mussolini

Unlike Hitler, Mussolini did not take power with a clear set of foreign policy goals already in place. However, after 1925, Mussolini developed a programme of action which included the following aims:

- increase national pride
- consolidate domestic support for the regime
- revise the post-war settlement of 1919–20
- dominate the Balkans
- dominate the Mediterranean
- build an Empire (gain *spazio vitale* or "living space"); expand its territories in Africa
- foster the spread of Fascism in other countries.

These aims were a product of various factors. The disappointment over the Versailles Settlement was key and helps to explain why Mussolini wanted to increase national pride and make Italy (and himself) a much more significant force in international politics.

Fascist ideology, with its expansionist aims, was also important. Linked to this was Mussolini's belief that Fascist Italy could be the second Roman Empire. Control of the Mediterranean Empire was key to his vision of Italy as "the heir of Rome".

Source skills

First question, part a – 3 marks

According to Steiner, how was Mussolini's ideology different to that of Hitler?

ATL Self-management and thinking skills

Review the factors identified on pages 84 that had an impact on Mussolini's foreign policy. Add to your spider diagram any evidence from pages 84 onwards to support the impact of these factors.

Domestic considerations were important, too. Mussolini needed to consolidate support for his regime and he also needed to address the economic needs of Italy. These factors influenced his goals of controlling the Mediterranean and setting up an empire with living space for the Italians.

What impact did economic issues have on Italian foreign policy?

In a speech in December 1925, Mussolini said:

> *I consider the Italian nation to be in a permanent state of war … To live, for me, means struggle, risk, tenacity … not submitting to fate, not even to … our so-called deficiency in raw materials.*

Mussolini's foreign policy ambitions were reliant on strengthening the economy. His economic policies therefore aimed not only to consolidate his political control and the Fascist system, but also to make Italy self-sufficient (known as "achieving autarky") and to have an economy capable of supporting a militarist state. These aims were difficult to achieve, however, as Italy had limited raw materials and the south was far less industrialized than the north. The Italians also had a low literacy rate compared to people in other industrialized European nations.

In order to address the economic weaknesses of Italy, Mussolini promoted "productivism", a vague term that merely described the intent to increase productivity. Heavy industry was favoured at the cost of consumer goods and there was also high taxation to fund the development of this area, which was a burden on the working classes.

However, Mussolini's big idea was the "Corporate State". This was supposed to be a new way of organizing the economy, an alternative to capitalism and socialism. Fascists believed that in their system neither the capitalist employers nor the workers would lose. They envisaged a society in which all people involved in the economy would work together for the national good. This system would be based on a system of corporations, and would have the advantages of capitalism and socialism but without their disadvantages. In sum, it would serve the national interest, the economy would be regulated, all interests would be protected and class conflict would cease. The idea of the Corporate State probably helped to keep divergent forces from causing political problems, but in practice labour was exploited and the system has been called an "elaborate fraud".

To help achieve economic greatness, Mussolini also launched three key initiatives: the Battle for Grain in 1925; the Battle for the Lira in 1926; and the "Mussolini Law" in 1928, which set out a programme of land reclamation.

These policies had little success. The Battle for Grain did lead to an increase in grain production and imports fell by 75%, but this improvement in output came at the cost of other key crops, such as olives. The area that saw the most negative impact was the south, where

▲ Mussolini carries an armful of grain as he helps with the harvesting on a farm near Rome

the soil was not suitable for growing wheat. The state also failed to challenge the big landowners to redress the poverty in the south. When Mussolini increased the value of the lira from 154 lira to 90 lira to the British pound, exports fell and there was not a corresponding benefit to consumers as they had to pay more for imported goods due to tariffs. The government also cut wages in 1927 by 10%. In general the land reclamation was also an expensive failure.

Overall, the pursuit of an assertive fascist foreign policy was hampered by the continued weakness of Mussolini's economy.

Source skills

Source A

Antonio Cippico, Italian politician and writer, in his book of lectures, *Italy: The central problem of the Mediterranean* (1926).

During 1920 there took place in Italy 1,881 industrial strikes and 189 agricultural strikes ... During 1923, the first year of the Fascist régime, industrial strikes were reduced to 200 …

In December, 1921, there were 541,000 unemployed; in October 1924, this had fallen to 117,000…

The new Fascist government had the task of restoring order where the maddest anarchy reigned; of giving back to the citizens security for life and property of governments, of parliaments, and sometimes of magistrates …

A really immense undertaking which Fascism, in the two and a half years that it has been in power, has almost accomplished. It is rare in the history of civilized nations, and has never before occurred in that of Italy, that a government has achieved so much in so short a time.

First question, part a – 3 marks

What, according to Source A, are the achievements of Mussolini's economic policies?

Second question – 4 marks

With reference to its origin, purpose and content, analyse the value and limitations of Source A for historians studying Mussolini's Italy in the 1920s.

> **Examiner's hint:** *Refer to page 107 for ideas on how to answer this question..*

Source B

Robert Mallet. *Mussolini and the Origins of the Second World War* (1983).

Italy's unenviable weak financial and industrial position acted as a further serious impediment to Mussolini's projected drive towards the Mediterranean and Red Sea supremacy. Despite the dictator's conclusion of a war-debt agreement with Great Britain in 1926, an agreement that allowed Rome greater access to foreign capital, and, as a consequence, permitted greater spending on armaments, Italy remained heavily reliant on imported staple raw materials like coal and petroleum …

First question, part a – 3 marks

What, according to Source B, are the key issues for Mussolini's foreign policy?

Source C

Thomas Meakin. "Mussolini's Fascism: What extent Italian Fascism represented a triumph of style over substance". *History Review*, number 59 (2007).

In an effort to adapt the Italian economy to the needs of a future war, the Fascist Party attempted to reduce Italian dependence on imports. The Battle for Grain, launched in 1925, imposed high tariffs on imported foreign cereal goods, whilst government subsidies were made available to assist in the purchasing of machinery and fertilisers. In the decade from 1925 wheat imports fell by 75 per cent, and by 1940 the country almost achieved complete self-sufficiency in cereals. However, these economic gains came at a great price, as exports fell and the importation of fertilisers failed to keep pace.

The propaganda and agricultural benefits of the Battle for Grain were soon outweighed by a decline in the quality of the Italian diet, and a further reduction in standards of living, especially in the poorer south.

The third of Mussolini's economic battles was the Battle of the Marshes, designed to increase the availability of agricultural land, demonstrate Fascist dynamism, and provide employment. The scheme was introduced in 1923. Huge swaths of previously uninhabitable and malarial marsh land in areas such as the Pontine Marshes were drained, whilst the newly created cities of Aprilla, Latina and Sabaudia won the regime international praise. "Fascist land reclamation is not only defence against malaria," proclaimed a Fascist textbook in 1938, "it is the new duty of the state". In reality, however, the scheme had only mixed success. Only 80,000 hectares were reclaimed, not one-sixth the area of Italy, as the government insisted.

In total, the Fascist intervention in the economy resulted in some gains… However, the propaganda victories did not reflect the dire economic situation brought about by unwise, unplanned, and disorganised forays into economics from 1925 onwards.

ATL Thinking skills

In pairs discuss the points made in Source C regarding Mussolini's economic policies.

Class discussion

Which aspects of Mussolini's economic policies affected his foreign policy aims? Following on from your class discussion, add more information to your spider diagram (page. 84) on the factors influencing foreign policy.

How successful was Mussolini's foreign policy in the 1920s?

Many of the foreign policy aims outlined on page 97 were similar to the aims of previous Italian administrations. Indeed, Mussolini initially had to work with many ministers and bureaucrats who had remained in place after he was appointed prime minister. However, Mussolini used foreign policy in the 1920s to consolidate his domestic control in Italy, and by the 1930s Italy's foreign policy would become more Fascist in character. Mussolini appeared to have a contradictory approach to European cooperation. On the one hand, he seemed to work with the other powers to promote peace; on the other hand, he acted, at times, to undermine attempts at cooperation.

Ambitions in the Balkans

The aspiration of gaining influence in the Eastern Mediterranean and in Africa was an aim held by many Italian nationalists. In 1923, Mussolini invaded the Greek island of Corfu after an Italian official was killed on the Greek border with Albania. The League of Nations condemned this action and demanded that the Italians withdraw. Only when Britain threatened to use its navy did Mussolini agree to withdraw, but he also demanded payment of 50 million lire of compensation from the Greeks. Although the "Corfu Affair" was seen as a great success in

Italy, Mussolini had learned that he could only bully smaller states; he could not intimidate more powerful states such as Britain. In fact, Mussolini went on to develop a good relationship with the British Foreign Minister Austen Chamberlain.

The following year, in 1924, Mussolini had a foreign policy victory when he gained control of the disputed port of Fiume, having sent a military commander to rule over it. In the Pact of Rome, the Yugoslavs gave in and the port was ceded to Italy. Mussolini's success in the Balkans led him to believe he could intimidate the Yugoslavs and undermine French influence there. He tried to destabilize the country by funding ethnic groups who wanted independence, such as the Croats.

Also in 1924, an Italian-backed leader, Ahmed Zog, took power in Albania, on Yugoslavia's border. Mussolini invested in Zog's regime and helped to train the Albanian army. This led to an official treaty of friendship between the two states in 1926, through which Albania became an Italian protectorate.

Relations with Western European powers

Mussolini's actions in Yugoslavia clearly undermined France's position, as France had backed the Little Entente alliance of Yugoslavia, Romania and Czechoslovakia. Indeed, Mussolini was hostile to France for several reasons:

- Italy had claims over the French territories of Corsica, Nice and Sardinia

- Mussolini was jealous of French North Africa and he supported opposition movements to French control in Tunisia and Morocco

- Mussolini aimed to replace French influence in the Balkans and the territory around the Adriatic.

However, although his actions had been aggressive in the Balkans, Mussolini still wanted to present himself as a force for moderation in Western Europe. In October 1925, Mussolini met with leaders from Britain, Germany, Belgium and France at Locarno in Switzerland. The seven agreements that resulted aimed to secure the post-war settlement and normalize relations with Germany. The agreements confirmed Germany's western borders with France and Belgium, but left its eastern border open for future negotiation. The Rhineland Pact was also signed to prevent future conflict between the Germany, France and Belgium.

Although Mussolini failed to get the Italian border with Austria included in the Locarno Treaties, he had played a key part in the meetings. The Locarno Treaties ushered in a new period of cooperation and hope for future peace, known as the "Locarno Spirit". This culminated in the

Source skills

Source A

A cartoon by David Low published in the UK newspaper, *The Star*, in August 1923.

"Come Inside!"

First question, part b – 2 marks

What is the message of the cartoonist in Source A?

Kellogg–Briand Pact of 1928, which denounced the use of war as a means to resolve disputes. Italy was one of more than 60 signatories to the declaration, which had been drawn up by US Secretary of State Frank Kellogg and the French Foreign Minister Aristide Briand. Mussolini has been quoted as saying that the Kellogg–Briand Pact was "*so sublime that it should be called transcendental*".

Nevertheless, in direct breach of the Treaty of Versailles, Mussolini not only funded right-wing groups in Germany but he also secretly trained German pilots in Italy.

In addition, Mussolini pursued his aims to expand Italy's empire in Africa. He continued to support independence movements against the French in Morocco. His violent methods were highlighted when he brutally crushed a revolt in Libya in 1922–28. In 1928, the "pacification" campaign had become a full-scale war, and was only put down with the use of massive force and mass executions. In a cynical move, Mussolini also signed a treaty of "friendship" with Abyssinia in 1928, despite his long-term ambitions of conquest there.

By the end of the 1920s, Mussolini was becoming frustrated with the failure of traditional diplomacy, but had to support the disarmament efforts of the League of Nations due to the weaknesses of the Italian armed forces. In 1927, he ominously informed the Italian Parliament that he would expand the Italian air force until it could "blot out the sun".

In the 1930s, once the failing of his corporate state had become apparent, and after Hitler had come to power in Germany, Mussolini's foreign policy became more assertive. He looked for opportunities to demonstrate that Italy was a major power. He then argued that the future lay with new virile states such as Germany and not with the old, liberal and decadent British and French empires.

Relations with the Soviet Union

Italy had broken off formal diplomatic relations with the Soviet Union when the Bolsheviks seized power in October 1917. However, along with other European powers, Mussolini's government adopted a pragmatic approach once it was clear that Lenin's regime was not going to fall. In 1921, Italy "recognized" the new government in the Soviet Union when it negotiated two trade agreements with Moscow. Mussolini wanted to develop commercial arrangements and, in 1924, Italy formally recognized the Soviet Union. Mussolini saw that the Soviet Union could be a useful tool in gaining diplomatic leverage over other powers. The Soviets were also interested in fostering better relations with Italy. Germany and Bolshevik Russia had signed the

Rapallo Treaty in 1922, in which they renounced all territorial and financial claims following the First World War and the Soviet Union wanted to draw Italy into the Rapallo alignment. After all, Italy was also dissatisfied with the post-war settlement.

Fascist Italy and communist Russia remained on good terms throughout the 1920s. Even when the Italian socialist leader Matteotti was murdered, the Soviets did not cancel the dinner they were holding for Mussolini at the Soviet embassy.

Communication skills

Patricia Knight. 2003. *Mussolini and Fascism*, page 82. Routledge. London, UK

… Mussolini's style and methods were quite different from those of his predecessors. Ignoring Italy's economic and military weaknesses, he was impulsive, inconsistent and erratic. He valued prestige more than anything else and was never satisfied unless he was in the limelight playing a leading role. He was to become increasingly fond of making grandiloquent statements such as "better to live one day as a lion than a thousand years as a lamb", and declaring that war was not only inevitable

but also desirable, adding "the character of the Italian people must be moulded by fighting". With a "tendency to view European diplomacy through the eyes of a newspaper editor", he aimed at spectacular gestures without much thought for consequences, resulting in a foreign policy that has been described as "by turn ambivalent, futile and malignant".

In pairs, discuss the descriptions in this source of Mussolini's style and methods with regard to his foreign policy in the 1920s. Can you find examples from this chapter to support the assertions made in this source?

Thinking and self-management skills

1. Look back at Mussolini's broad foreign policy aims on page 97. Discuss the extent to which he had achieved these aims by 1929.

2. Put the following events under the appropriate heading, either "Cooperation" or "Aggression":

   Locarno, 1925

   Corfu, 1923

   Fiume ,1924

   Albania, 1926

   The Kellogg-Briand Pact, 1928

   The crushing of the Libyan revolt, 1922–28

   The Treaty of Friendship with Abyssinia, 1928

3. How far do you agree with Mack Smith in Source B on the next page that in foreign policy in the 1920s Mussolini "was concerned less to reduce international animosities than to foster them"?

4. What long-term view of fascism does Mussolini express in Source A on the next page?

Source A

Benito Mussolini in his autobiography *My Rise and Fall* (1998).

I am strict with my most faithful followers. I always intervene where excesses and intemperance are revealed. I am near to the heart of the masses and listen to its beats. I read its aspiration and interests.

I know the virtue of the race. I probe it in its purity and soundness. I will fight vice and degeneracy and will put them down. The so-called "Liberal institutions" created at other times because of a fallacious appearance of protection are destroyed and divested of their phrases and false idealism by the new forces of Fascism with its idealism planted on realities.

Air and light, strength and energy, shine and vibrate in the infinite sky of Italy! The loftiest civic and national vision today leads this people to its goal, this people which is living in its great new springtime. It animates my long labors. I am forty-five and I feel the vigor of my work and my thought. I have annihilated in myself all self interest: I, like the most devoted of citizens, place upon myself and on every beat of my heart, service to the Italian people. I proclaim myself their servant. I feel that all Italians understand and love me; I know that only he is loved who leads without weakness, without deviation, and with disinterestedness and full faith.

Therefore, going over what I have already done I know that Fascism, being a creation of the Italian race, has met and will meet historical necessities, and so, unconquerable, is destined to make an indelible impression on twentieth century history.

Da Capo Press. New York, USA (combined volume incorporating Mussolini, B. 1928. *My Autobiography* Curtis Publishing, New York, USA; and Mussolini, B. 1948.)

Source B

Denis Mack Smith. *Mussolini* (1983).

Despite his outward pretence that fascism was not for export, Mussolini set considerable store on spreading the message abroad, using Italian embassies as well as unofficial channels, for instance setting up bogus trade companies which used their profits for propaganda. Soon he spoke openly of his mission to extend fascism "everywhere" and his propagandists began to talk about sweeping away the "Protestant civilization" of northern Europe. By April 1925 it was estimated that fascist parties existed in forty different countries, and a consignment of black shirts was sent as far away as Hyderabad. Already the possibility of forming an international anti-communist movement was being discussed.

Mussolini's style abroad, as at home, was that of the bully rather than the negotiator and here too he firmly believed that in politics it was more advantageous to be feared than liked. In foreign policy he was concerned less to reduce international animosities than to foster them…

First question, part a – 3 marks

What, according to Source B, did Mussolini do to export fascism?

Second question – 4 marks

With reference to the origins, purpose and content, assess the value and limitations of Source A for historians studying Italy under Mussolini.

Source help and hints

Source C

(See page 92.)

Second question – 4 marks

With reference to its origin, purpose and content, assess the values and limitations of Source C for historians studying Italy in the 1920s.

> **Examiner's hint:** *When reviewing a historian's work, make sure you look carefully at the date of publication and the title of the work as these will help you to work out the possible values and limitations.*

Values

- A value of the origin is that Mack Smith is a professional historian and an expert on Mussolini.

- The date of publication and access to recent sources holds value as the author had the benefit of hindsight.

- The title of the book suggests that the work focuses on the political history of Italy and would offer insight into the political context of fascism in Italy.

- A value of the content is that it seems to be an academic analysis of the situation in the 1920s.

Limitations

- As a British historian, it is possible that he may not have a full insight into the Italian perspective of events

- There may also be a limitation in that the book is a broad study that considers the political history of the whole modern era in Italy. There may be a lack of focus on Mussolini's Italy in the 1920s.

Source A

(See page 94)

A photograph of Mussolini with black-shirted Fascists before the march on Rome, 1922.

First question, part b – 2 marks

What is the message of Source A?

> **Examiner's hint:** *Look carefully at Mussolini: his pose and position in this photo are key to working out the message of the photograph. Remember to look also at the people surrounding him. Refer to the details of the photograph to support your points.*

Example answer

The overall message of this photograph is that Mussolini is in control and is leading these men, who are looking to him for leadership. We can see this by his confident and defiant pose, and the fact that he is in the middle of the photo with everyone looking at him. Another message is that he has a lot of supporters, and that many of these supporters are war heroes as they are wearing medals.

Work in pairs on the following questions. These sources relate to Mussolini's foreign policy in the 1920s.

Source A

Martin Blinkhorn. *Mussolini and Fascist Italy* **(1984).**

A combination of boldness and negotiation enabled him [Mussolini] to… achieve Fiume's incorporation in Italy; the terms of Mussolini's agreement with Yugoslavia consigned Fiume to isolation from its hinterland and consequent economic stagnation, but Italian patriots were ecstatic… Less successful was Mussolini's impetuous occupation of the Greek island of Corfu, which international and especially British pressure forced him to evacuate. Having learned that he could not yet defy those more powerful than himself, Mussolini for almost a decade trod more warily, seeking to strengthen Italy's position through maintaining good relations with Britain while working to undermine France's alliance system in south-eastern Europe. Crucial to this strategy was his friendly relationship with Austen Chamberlain*, one of the many European conservatives who admired the Duce's anti-Bolshevism and imposition of internal "order". Chamberlain's benevolence ensured British acquiescence in the establishment of an Italian protectorate over Albania in 1926 and made possible the cession to Italy of two small pieces of African territory.

Austen Chamberlain was the British Foreign Minister from 1924–29. He was the half-brother of Neville Chamberlain, who became prime minister of Great Britain in 1937.

First question, part a – 3 marks

What, according to Source A, were the key features of Italy's relations with Britain up to 1926?

In pairs, read through Source A and draft a response to the first question, part a. Check your response with the examiner's tips below. Do you have three clear points? How many marks would you have been awarded?

> **Examiner's hint:**
>
> - British pressure forced Mussolini to pull out of Corfu.
>
> - Britain was more powerful than Italy, so Mussolini had to comply with Britain's wishes.
>
> - Italy wanted to maintain good relations with Britain while undermining the French alliance system.
>
> - Mussolini's special relationship with Austen Chamberlain was key.

Source B

A cartoon by David Low published in the UK newspaper, the *Evening Standard*, on 29 November 1927.

CAMERA MAN: "GET CLOSER TOGETHER, BOYS, IF YOU WANT A GOOD PICTURE."

First question, part b – 2 marks

What is the message of the cartoonist in Source B?

Look at Source B and draft a response to the first question, part b. Check your response with the examiner's tips on the right. Do you have two clear points? How many marks would you have been awarded? Are there points that you had not noticed?

Examiner's hint:

- Mussolini (or Italy) was out of control or misbehaving.

- Italy does not take participation at conferences seriously; childish behaviour is shown.

- France is turning away from Italy and appears concerned by its behaviour.

- The USA is ignoring Italy's behaviour.

Source C

Antonio Cippico, Italian politician and writer, in his book of lectures, *Italy: The central problem of the Mediterranean* (1926).

This enormous work of internal renovation has been accomplished in only two and a half years. Mussolini's foreign policy is no less worthy of mention. In proof of its attachment to peace the Italian Government has signed eight commercial treaties and other exemplary agreements based on arbitration with a large number of states. She, alone, amongst the European Powers, has signed twelve out of the seventeen conventions submitted by the International Labor Bureau of Geneva. (She is the only European nation that desired that both houses should legally sanction the obligation of the eight-hour day.). By the episode of the bombardment of Corfu she gave the world the proof, beside that of her will to be respected in all parts of the world, of her great moderation. During the long and tedious treaties with Yugoslavia she has given ample proof of her good will. In her relations with the League of Nations the Fascist government wished to display the high consideration in which she holds it, when, less than a year ago, she gave me the honourable change of announcing at the General Assembly of the League at Geneva the offer of founding an Institute for the unification of private law, to be established at Rome at Italy's expense under the auspices of the League.

Second question – 4 marks

With reference to its origin, purpose and content, assess the values and limitations of Source C for historians studying Italy in the 1920s.

Examiner's hint: *Review Chapter 1 of this book and also look at the examples given of how to answer second questions. Draft a response to this question. Check your response with the tips below – do you have clear points on the value of the origin, purpose and content of the source? How many marks would you have been awarded? Are there points in the mark scheme that you had not noticed?*

Example answer

Values

- A value of the origin is that the author was Italian and therefore may have experienced Mussolini's Italy first hand.

- It was written in 1926 which means it provides an insight into a view from the time of Mussolini's rule.

- The content suggests that the author played a key role in Italian foreign policy as a representative at Geneva; therefore a value would be his knowledge and understanding of Italian policies and conditions in the 1920s.

- A value of the purpose is that it is an assessment of the issues in the Mediterranean at the time and may put events into a broader context.

Limitations

- Source C was written in 1926, which means that the author lacks hindsight on events. It was written at an early stage of Mussolini's rule over Italy.

- Mussolini's perspective may have changed over time, particularly when his policies shifted in the 1930s.

- The content seems focused on presenting a positive view of Mussolini's regime, both in terms of its use of language and selection of supporting evidence.

- The author's previous role representing Mussolini's government at Geneva may mean the source is too one-sided in favour of the regime, or may be justifying the author's support or compliance with it.

Source D

Denis Mack Smith. *Mussolini* (1983).

The League of Nations could not much appeal to someone bent on upsetting the world community. Sometimes he condemned it as "a holy alliance of the plutocratic nations" against smaller and poorer countries such as Italy. Later, when many of those smaller countries expressed outrage at his bullying over Corfu, he used the almost opposite argument that too many small and "semi-barbarian nations" claimed an equal voice in it, whereas they should learn to keep their place and not interfere with their more civilized neighbours. Though he went on telling foreigners he would do all in his power to support the League, his representative at Geneva was actively sabotaging its work, and Italy remained a member only because he realized that international conflicts would otherwise be resolved without an Italian voice being heard.

Third question – 6 marks

Compare and contrast the views expressed regarding Italian foreign policy in Sources C and D.

Example answer

Comparisons

- Both Sources discuss Italy's relationship with the League of Nations.

- Both Sources discuss Italy's actions in Corfu.

- Both Sources suggest that Italy openly stated its support for Geneva.

Contrasts

- Source C claims that Italy pursued peace through the League, whereas Source D suggests that Italy's actions upset the international community.

- Source C suggests that Italy was behaving like a bully over Corfu, whereas Source D suggests Italy showed moderation over Corfu.

- Source C claims that Italy held the League in the highest regard and supported its work while Source D suggests that Italy was sabotaging its work.

Fourth question – 9 marks

Work on your own. Read through all four sources again and write a full response to the following question (in the style of a fourth question). You have 25 minutes.

Using the sources and your own knowledge, to what extent do you agree with the statement: *"Mussolini pursued an aggressive foreign policy in the 1920s"*?

Here are some points to help you.

- Source A: This suggests the use of force, but also some degree of negotiation and compromise with the British. Mussolini worked to undermine the French and acted aggressively over Fiume and Corfu.

- Source B: Mussolini's actions were chaotic and out of line with the actions of other powers. His policies were causing alarm to the French.

- Source C: Mussolini acted in the interests of the international community and worked with the League. He had shown moderation over issues such as Corfu.

- Source D: Mussolini used and manipulated the League of Nations and pursued aggressive policies that showed he was intent on sabotaging the League's work.

These are some points you could bring in from your own knowledge.

- Mussolini had worked with the international community at Locarno in 1925, and had signed up to the Kellogg–Briand Pact, which renounced war as a tool of diplomacy in 1928.

- However, Mussolini had used force to gain the port of Fiume from Yugoslavia in 1924, and he had previously demanded compensation when met with British opposition over his occupation of Corfu in 1923.

- Mussolini had provoked the French by promoting independence movements in Morocco and destabilizing its alliance partner, Yugoslavia.

- Mussolini's aggression was most marked in his actions in Africa, in the brutal crushing of the Libyan revolt up to 1928.

References

Carocci, G. 1974. *Italian Fascism*. Penguin. Harmondsworth, UK

Cippico, A. 1926. *Italy: The Central Problem of the Mediterranean*. Yale University Press. New Haven, CT, USA

Clark, M. 1985. *Modern Italy 1871–1982*. Longman. London, UK

Delzell, C. (ed). 1971. *Mediterranean Fascism, 1919–45: Selected Documents*. Macmillan. London, UK

Knight, P. 2003. *Mussolini and Fascism*. Routledge. London, UK

Mack Smith, D. 1983. *Mussolini*. Paladin Books. London, UK

Mack Smith, D. 1997. *Modern Italy – A Political History*. Yale University Press. New Haven, CT, USA

Mallet, R. 1983. *Mussolini and the Origins of the Second World War, 1933–40*. Palgrave Macmillan. London, UK

Meakin, T. 2007. "Mussolini's Fascism: What extent Italian Fascism represented a triumph of style over substance". St Hugh's College, Oxford, in association with *History Review*, number 59

Mussolini, B. 1998. *My Rise and Fall*. Da Capo Press. New York, USA (combined volume incorporating Mussolini, B. 1928. *My Autobiography*. Curtis Publishing. New York, USA; and Mussolini, B. 1948. *The Fall of Mussolini: His Own Story*. Farrar, Straus and Giroux. New York, USA

Robson, M. 2004. *Italy: Liberalism and Fascism 1870–45*. Hodder and Stoughton. Oxford, UK

Steiner, Z. 2005. *The Lights that Failed*. Oxford University Press. Oxford, UK

2.2 The impact of Nazism on German foreign policy: the origins, 1918–1933

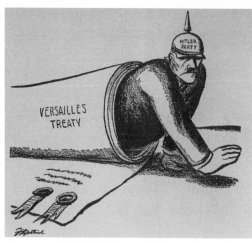

▲ Cartoon by Daniel Fitzpatrick, St. Louis Post-dispatch, October 19th, 1930

Conceptual understanding

Key concepts

→ Causation

→ Perspectives

→ Continuity

Key questions

→ Examine the reasons for the growth in support for Nazism after the First World War.

→ To what extent did Hitler have clear foreign policy objectives before he came to power?

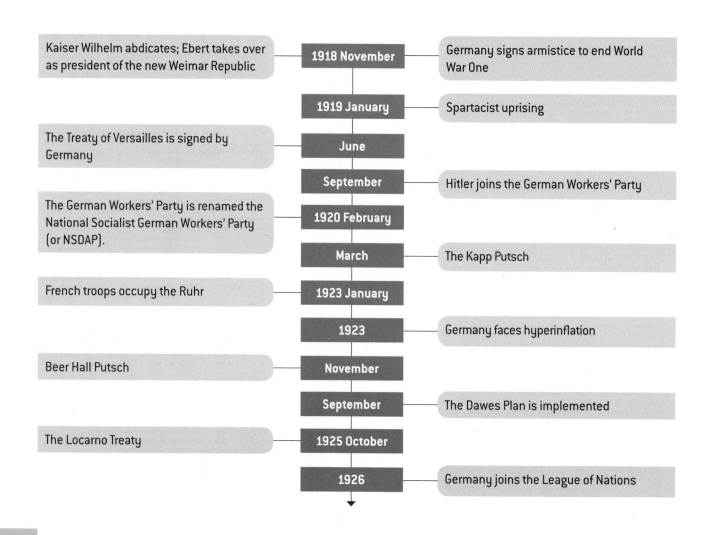

Kaiser Wilhelm abdicates; Ebert takes over as president of the new Weimar Republic — **1918 November** — Germany signs armistice to end World War One

1919 January — Spartacist uprising

The Treaty of Versailles is signed by Germany — **June**

September — Hitler joins the German Workers' Party

The German Workers' Party is renamed the National Socialist German Workers' Party (or NSDAP). — **1920 February**

March — The Kapp Putsch

French troops occupy the Ruhr — **1923 January**

1923 — Germany faces hyperinflation

Beer Hall Putsch — **November**

September — The Dawes Plan is implemented

The Locarno Treaty — **1925 October**

1926 — Germany joins the League of Nations

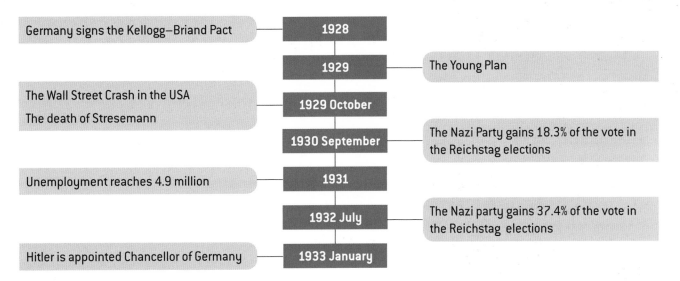

Germany signs the Kellogg–Briand Pact	**1928**	
	1929	The Young Plan
The Wall Street Crash in the USA The death of Stresemann	**1929 October**	
	1930 September	The Nazi Party gains 18.3% of the vote in the Reichstag elections
Unemployment reaches 4.9 million	**1931**	
	1932 July	The Nazi party gains 37.4% of the vote in the Reichstag elections
Hitler is appointed Chancellor of Germany	**1933 January**	

Nazism refers to the policies of the Nazi or National Socialist Party that took power, with Adolf Hitler as its leader, in Germany in 1933. Hitler's rise to power and indeed his views on German foreign policy had their roots in the circumstances of Germany's defeat in the First World War, the Armistice that was signed in November 1918 and the Treaty of Versailles of 1919. However, it was the Wall Street Crash of 1929 and the ensuing Great Depression which allowed Hitler to attain popularity and thus achieve enough of the German vote to become a force in German politics. Once Chancellor, Hitler was able to take total control of Germany and thus put into action his foreign policy aims.

What was the impact of the First World War and defeat on Germany?

Kaiser Wilhelm II had taken Germany into the First World War in 1914 expecting it to be short and victorious. However, the failure of the German Schlieffen Plan, by which Germany had intended to achieve a swift victory over France before attacking Russia, ended this expectation. Germany ended up in a war of attrition on the Western Front, in trenches facing the Allies. At the same time, it was involved in an equally bloody conflict with Russia on the Eastern Front.

However, in 1917, victory finally seemed in sight for Germany. On the Eastern Front, the Bolsheviks, following the Russian Revolution of October 1917, sued for peace. In the Treaty of Brest Litovsk, Germany secured substantial territorial gains from Russia. On the Western Front, the German General Ludendorff, who was managing the German war effort, then launched an offensive (supported by the German troops that had been freed up from the Eastern Front) which pushed the Alllies back to near Paris. The German population expected victory. Even when this

▲ Kaiser Wilhelm II

111

Kaiser Wilhelm II

Germany was ruled by Kaiser Wilhelm II. The political system was authoritarian, with power held by the Kaiser and his chancellor. The power of the German parliament, the Reichstag, was limited. Germany had only become unified in 1871, the work of the German Chancellor Otto von Bismarck, who fought a war against Austria and a war against France (1870) to achieve this. In the war of 1914–18, Germany fought with Austria–Hungary against the Allies: Britain, France and Russia. France hoped to gain revenge for its defeat in the war of 1870–71.

hope was crushed as the Allies pushed back, German defeat was not certain. By November 1918, the Allies had not invaded German territory. In fact, at this point, Germany still controlled most of Belgium and large areas of Eastern Europe (see the map below).

Nevertheless, Germany had lost its best troops in the 1918 offensive; morale was low as they retreated, and this was not helped by an outbreak of the deadly Spanish Influenza. Ludendorff was convinced that the German army could not carry on fighting and that Germany would be defeated in the spring of 1919. He also hoped that Germany would receive less severe terms if the government asked US President Woodrow Wilson for a cease fire based on Wilson's 14-point programme (see next page). Asking for an armistice before Germany was invaded would also preserve the army's reputation.

Believing that better terms could be gained from a civilian government, Ludendorff handed over power to a government led by Prince Max of Baden. Negotiations over the armistice then lasted for several weeks, with Wilson demanding the Kaiser be removed from power before an armistice could be signed.

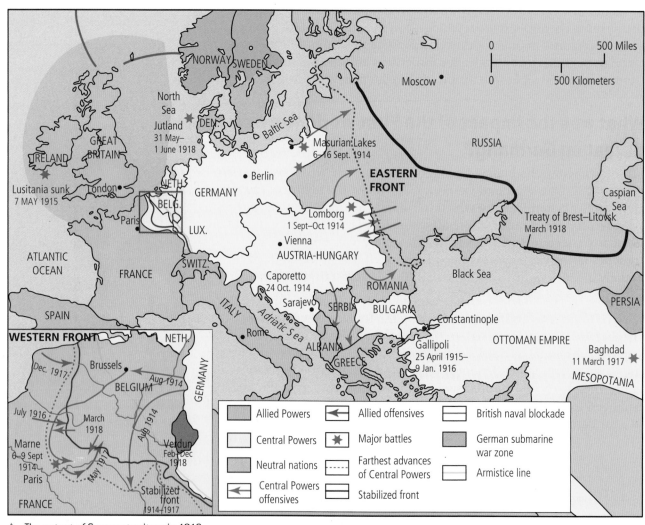

▲ The extent of German territory in 1918

At this point Germany also faced severe domestic problems: strikes, political unrest, a mutiny from sailors at Kiel, and the impact of the Allied blockade which was causing drastic food shortages. Thus, with civil war imminent in Germany, the Kaiser abdicated and, on 11 November, a new German socialist government agreed to the terms of the armistice.

For the many Germans who thought they were winning the war, the armistice was a shock. This was to give rise to the idea that the German army had in fact never lost the war. The *Dolchstosslegende* or "stab in the back" theory developed, which explained Germany's defeat by blaming the socialists of the new government for agreeing to an armistice just when Germany had been on the point of winning the war.

ATL Thinking skills

Study the source below showing Wilson's 14 points.

1 What do you consider to have been Wilson's overriding aims for a European peace settlement?

2 Based on these points, what kind of agreement do you think Germany was hoping to obtain?

Wilson's 14 points

1 No more secret agreements ("open covenants openly arrived at")

2 Free navigation of all seas

3 Removal of economic barriers between countries

4 Reduction in armaments, "to the lowest points consistent with domestic safety"

5 Colonial problems to be settled with reference to the interests of colonial peoples

6 The German army to be evacuated from Russia

7 Evacuation of Belgium

8 France should be fully liberated and allowed to recover Alsace–Lorraine

9 All Italians to be allowed to live in Italy. Italy's borders to be "along clearly recognisable lines of nationality"

10 Self-determination for all those living in Austria–Hungary

11 Self-determination and guarantees of independence should be allowed for the Balkan states

12 The Turkish people should be governed by the Turkish government. Non-Turks in the old Turkish Empire should govern themselves

13 Creation of an independent Poland, which should have access to the sea

14 Establishment of a League of Nations to guarantee the political and territorial independence of all states

What was the impact of the Treaty of Versailles?

The armistice was followed up with a peace treaty, signed in 1919. This was drawn up at the Palace of Versailles outside Paris and was mainly the work of three men: Prime Minister Clemenceau of France, Prime Minister Lloyd George of Britain, and President Woodrow Wilson from the USA. The aims of these statesmen were very different, particularly the aims of Clemenceau and Wilson. As you have seen from his 14 points, Wilson aimed to set up a lasting and just system of international relations that could be held in place by an international body, the League of Nations.

Thinking and social skills

In pairs, study Source A and Source B below. Discuss the following questions.

1 Which aspects of the Treaty of Versailles were most likely to anger Germans?

2 On what evidence do you think Steiner bases her argument that Germany "remained a great power"?

However, Clemenceau wished to make Germany pay for the damage it had caused France, and also to ensure that Germany was weakened sufficiently to prevent it from threatening France again. Britain was anxious to preserve Britain's naval supremacy and hoped to enlarge the empire. Lloyd George was more inclined to leniency than Clemenceau but had to take on board the anti-German feeling in Britain.

Given these different aims, along with the multiplicity of problems the peacemakers faced and the speed at which it was drawn up, it is perhaps not surprising that, as the historian Zara Steiner writes, "*[the Treaty of Versailles] failed to solve the problem of both punishing and conciliating a country that remained a great power despite the four years of fighting and its military defeat … it was a bundle of compromises that fully satisfied none of the three peace makers*" (Steiner, 2011).

Source skills

Source A

Key articles of the Treaty of Versailles, 1919.

Article number	Description
1–26	The Covenant of the League of Nations was established; Germany was not allowed to join.
42	The Rhineland was demilitarized; the German army was not allowed to go there. The Allies were to keep an army of occupation in the Rhineland for 15 years.
45	The Saar, with its rich coalfields, was given to France for 15 years.
51	Alsace–Lorraine was returned to France.
80	Germany was forbidden to unite with Austria.
87	Lands in eastern Germany, the rich farmlands of Posen and the Polish Corridor between Germany and East Prussia, were given to Poland.
100	Danzig was made a Free City under League of Nations control.
119	All Germany's colonies were taken and given to France and Britain as "mandates".
160	The German army was restricted to 100,000 men.
181	The German navy was restricted to six battleships and no submarines.
198	Germany was not allowed to have an air force (though the military inspectorate that oversaw the military clauses was withdrawn in 1927).
231	Germany was responsible for causing all the loss and damage caused by the war. This was known as the War Guilt Clause.
232	Germany would have to pay reparations, to be decided later. It was eventually set at 132 billion gold marks in 1921. (However, in reality, only a trivial amount of this sum was actually paid.)

Source B

Map showing the territorial losses of Germany after World War One

Territorial losses of Germany amounted to the loss of approximately 13% of the country's economic production capacity and about 10% of its population. However, Germany was still left intact, with a population which was almost double the population of France.

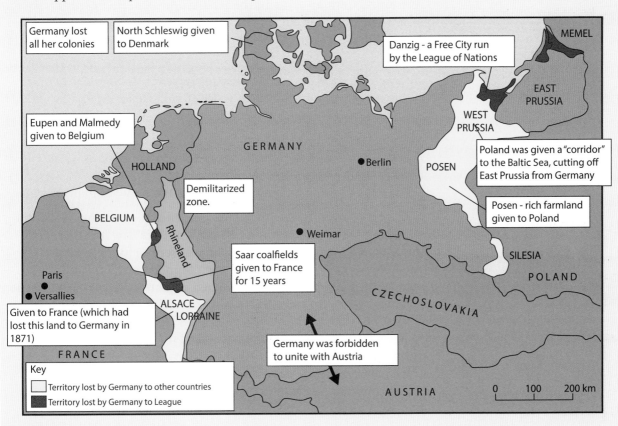

Germany lost all her colonies

North Schleswig given to Denmark

Danzig - a Free City run by the League of Nations

MEMEL

EAST PRUSSIA

Eupen and Malmedy given to Belgium

GERMANY

WEST PRUSSIA

HOLLAND

• Berlin

POSEN

Poland was given a "corridor" to the Baltic Sea, cutting off East Prussia from Germany

Demilitarized zone.

BELGIUM

Posen - rich farmland given to Poland

Rhineland

• Weimar

SILESIA

POLAND

Paris

Saar coalfields given to France for 15 years

• Versallies

C Z E C H O S L O V A K I A

Given to France (which had lost this land to Germany in 1871)

ALSACE LORRAINE

Germany was forbidden to unite with Austria

FRANCE

AUSTRIA

0   100   200 km

Key

☐ Territory lost by Germany to other countries

■ Territory lost by Germany to League

Source skills

Ruth Henig. *The Origins of the Second World War*, pages 4–5, (1985).

Here was the first major post-war problem: Germany had lost the First World War, but large and important sections of post-war Germany did not accept that defeat and the peace settlement which followed it as a fair or final outcome. No German government in the 1920s could readily agree to allied treaty demands without incurring widespread public hostility. Enduring nationalist themes included "the shame of Versailles", the "war guilt lie", and "the November criminals". These were alleged to have "stabbed Germany in the back" by fermenting demonstrations and strikes in German industrial areas, thus preventing her army from winning the glorious victory so nearly within its grasp. The Social Democratic Party, which shouldered the responsibility of signing the peace *diktat* and which tried to advocate some measure of compliance with its terms, lost electoral support as a result … It is significant that the new states of Poland, Czechoslovakia and Romania were referred to in Germany as *Saisonsstaaten* – states born to die within a single season: annuals rather than perennials like Germany or France.

First question, part a – 3 marks

What, according to this source, was the attitude of the German population towards the Treaty of Versailles?

What was the impact of the First World War on Hitler's foreign policy?

The defeat of Germany and the impact of the Treaty of Versailles that followed the end of the war in 1919 were key in the development of Hitler's foreign policy objectives. Hitler was Austrian by birth and had fought in the German army in the First World War. He heard the news of the German surrender while recovering from an injury he had received in the war, and was horrified, writing:

> So it had all been in vain. In vain all the sacrifices. In vain the hours in which, with mortal fear clutching at our hearts we did our duty. In vain the death of two millions. Had they died for this, so that a gang of wretched criminals could lay hands on the fatherland?

Hitler fully embraced the ideas held by nationalist and conservative groups that the Treaty of Versailles was a *diktat*, imposed on Germany at the end of the war with no consultation, and that it had been signed by "the November criminals" – the socialists of the new Weimar Republic.

Hitler's disgust with the treaty helped influence his decision to become involved in politics after the First World War. Working for the army authorities as an intelligence agent, he was sent to investigate the German Worker's Party which had been founded in January 1919 by Anton Drexler, and which was suspected of plotting left-wing revolution. In fact, it was an extreme nationalist party which was attempting to win over working-class support. Hitler accepted Drexler's invitation to join, soon becoming its leading member. He had the party renamed to become the National Socialist German Workers' Party and gave it the swastika as a new symbol. The *Sturmabteilung* (SA), or "Stormtroopers", (see page 120) was established as a paramilitary group led by Ernst Röhm, who recruited thousands of ex-soldiers into its ranks. The party was based on similar extreme ideas as Mussolini's Fascist Party, with the same strands of nationalism, militarism, Social Darwinism, authoritarianism, and a hatred of communism, socialism and trade unions. However, some historians, such as Klaus Hildebrand, would argue that it was so dominated by Hitler's personal ideas that it cannot be fitted into the overall category of European Fascism.

ATL Thinking and communication skills

Study the source below. Make bullet point notes answering the following questions:

1   On what grounds did Hitler condemn the Treaty of Versailles?

2   What other foreign policy aims can be seen in Hitler's speech that are unrelated to the Treaty of Versailles?

Source skills

A speech by Adolf Hitler on the Treaty of Versailles, 17 April 1923.

With the armistice begins the humiliation of Germany. If the Republic on the day of its foundation had appealed to the country: Germans, stand together! Up and resist the foe! The Fatherland, the Republic expects of you that you fight to your last breath, then millions who are now enemies of the Republic would be fanatical Republicans. Today they are the foes of the Republic not because it is a Republic but because this Republic was founded at the moment when Germany was humiliated, because it so discredited the new flag that men's eyes must turn regretfully toward the old flag.

So long as this Treaty stands there can be no resurrection of the German people; no social reform of any kind is possible! The Treaty was made in order to bring 20 million Germans to their deaths and to ruin the German nation. But those who made the Treaty cannot set it aside. At its foundation our Movement formulated three demands:

1   Setting aside of the Peace Treaty.

2   Unification of all Germans.

3   Land and soil [*Grund und Boden*] to feed our nation.

Our movement could formulate these demands, since it was not our Movement which caused the War, it has not made the Republic, it did not sign the Peace Treaty.

There is thus one thing which is the first task of this Movement: it desires to make the German once more National, that his Fatherland shall stand for him above everything else. It desires to teach our people to understand afresh the truth of the old saying: He who will not be a hammer must be an anvil.

An anvil we are today, and that anvil will be beaten until out of the anvil we fashion once more a hammer, a German sword!

First question, part b – 2 marks

Refer back to the cartoon at the start of this chapter on page 110. What is the message of this cartoon concerning the Treaty of Versailles?

Second question – 4 marks

With reference to its origin, purpose and content, assess the value and limitations of using this source as evidence of Hitler's foreign policy aims.

Third question – 6 marks

Compare and contrast the points made by Henig on page 115 regarding the Treaty of Versailles to those made by Hitler in this speech.

The speech above was given by Hitler in 1923. Also in 1923, while in prison (see page 120), Hitler wrote a book called *Mein Kampf*. This set out his ideas on a wide range of issues; German unity, nationalism, anti-Semitism. However, the bulk of the book was on foreign policy. His desire to overturn the Treaty of Versailles was stressed, but other important ideas were also put forward in *Mein Kampf*, indicating that, unlike Mussolini, Hitler had clear foreign policy aims well before actually attaining power.

1. A "Gross Deutschland"

Also known as Pan-Germanism, the idea of creating a *Gross Deutschland* had been an important aim of German nationalists in the 19th century. For Hitler, this foreign policy aim would mean the unification not only of Austrian Germans with Germany (which was forbidden by the Treaty of Versailles), but also the unification of Germany with German minorities that were now under the rule of other states, notably Czechoslovakia and Poland.

2. Race and living space

Linked to the last point was the issue of race; in fact, all of Hitler's political ideas were defined in terms of race. A new Greater Germany would include only "pure" Germans who were of the superior Aryan race, which combined "robust muscular power with first class intellect". Such views on the existence of a hierarchy of races had become popular towards the end of the 19th century with the belief in Social Darwinism.

The Third Reich

The Third Reich was a term used by Adolf Hitler in the 1920s to describe the 1,000-year empire he intended to create. The First Reich (or Empire) was the Holy Roman Empire which had existed from the time of Charlemagne to 1806. The Second Reich was the German Empire of 1871–1918 created by Otto von Bismarck.

This held that human life, like animal life, was subject to the natural laws of selection and only the fittest would survive. Hitler developed this theory in *Mein Kampf*. He further argued that the Aryan race would need more space (*Lebensraum*) and that this should come from the East, as far as the Ural mountains. This would involve dispossessing the Slavs, Russians, Ukrainians, Poles and other "inferior" nations or *untermenschen*.

The most "inferior" people, according to Hitler, were the Jews. Here Hitler was reflecting the anti-Semitic views which had been prevalent in Europe for hundreds of years, but his rhetoric and actions towards the Jews were to reach new and hitherto unimagined extremes of violence. His view was that if Jewish influence was left unchecked, it would result in "national race tuberculosis". This meant that the German race must be protected against contact with inferior blood, such as that of the Jews, if it was to become the dominant force in Europe.

Once the living space for the Germans had been secured, the foundations would have been laid for the "Third Reich".

Source skills

An extract from *Mein Kampf*, written by Hitler in 1923.

Germany has an annual increase in population of nearly 900,000. The difficulty of feeding this army of new citizens must increase from year to year and ultimately end in catastrophe unless ways and means are found … Nature knows no boundaries … she confers the master's right on her favourite child, the strongest in courage and industry … Only a sufficiently large space on this earth can ensure the independent existence of a nation … As members of the highest species of humanity on this earth, we have a[n] obligation … [to] … fulfil … The acquisition of land and soil [must be] the objective of our foreign policy … The demand for the restoration of the frontiers of 1914 is a political absurdity … We … are turning our eyes towards the land in the East … The colossal empire in the East is ripe for dissolution. And the end of the Jewish domination in Russia will also be the end of Russia as a state … Today we are struggling to achieve a position as a world power; we must fight for the existence of our fatherland, for the unity of our nation and the daily bread of our children. If we look around for allies from this point of view, only two states remain; England and Italy.

First question, part a – 3 marks

According to Hitler, why must Germany expand to the east?

3. Natural enemies and allies

As you can see from the source, Hitler saw Russia as a natural enemy of Germany. There were many Jews in Russia and it was also a communist country led by the Bolsheviks. Hitler loathed communism and was, in fact, convinced that all Bolsheviks were Jews.

In addition, France was a natural enemy because of what had happened in the First World War, and because of France's role in the drawing up of the Treaty of Versailles. In a speech in 1923, Hitler said, "France does not want reparations; it wants the destruction of Germany, the fulfilment of an age-old dream; a Europe dominated by France."

Britain, however, was seen as a potential ally, especially after it opposed France's occupation of the Ruhr in 1923 (see page 120). In fact, Hitler had great admiration for the British, partly because he saw them as being similar racially, but also because he admired their empire and

the way in which a small nation had been able to control so much of the world. Italy was also seen as an ally because of the ideologically sympathetic nature of Mussolini's government.

Source skills

An extract from *Mein Kampf*, pages 564–66, written by Hitler in 1923.

Anyone who undertakes an examination of the present alliance possibilities for Germany … must arrive at the conclusion that the last practicable tie remains with England … we must not close our eyes to the fact that a necessary interest on the part of England in the annihilation of Germany no longer exists today; that, on the contrary, England's policy from year to year must be directed more and more to an obstruction of France's unlimited drive for hegemony …

And Italy, too, cannot and will not desire a further reinforcement of the French position of superior power in Europe.

First question, part a – 3 marks

According to Hitler, why would Britain and Italy want an alliance with Germany?

Second question – 4 marks

With reference to its origin, purpose and content, assess the value and limitations of using this extract of *Mein Kampf* to identify Hitler's foreign policy aims.

Why did support for Nazism grow after the First World War?

The Weimar Republic: Years of crisis

The National Socialist German Workers' Party (NSDAP) was one of many extreme political groups in the new Weimar Republic. These were years of political unrest and crisis, and the Weimar Republic faced challenges internally from both left and right, from French occupation, as well as from a severe economic crisis:

- In 1919, a communist party called the Spartacists, led by Rosa Luxembourg and Karl Liebknecht, launched a rebellion. President Ebert called in the army and the Freikorps to put the rebellion down. Left-wing uprisings in other parts of Germany were also crushed by the Freikorps who were paramilitary groups made up of ex-soldiers.

- In March 1920, some members of the Freikorps attempted to overthrow the government. Its leader, Wolfgang Kapp, claimed that he would make Germany strong again after the detested Treaty of Versailles. However, when workers in Berlin went on strike in support of the government, Kapp fled and the *putsch* collapsed.

- Although Freikorps units were then disbanded, right-wing extremists continued their attack against left-wing politicians via assassinations. Between 1919 and 1922 there were 376 political assassinations. Of these, 354 were by right-wing assassins and 326 went unpunished – evidence of the sympathy that these right-wing assassins got from the conservative judges. Walther Rathenau, the German foreign minister, was one of the left-wing politicians who was assassinated. Many conservatives, including many members of the civil service and judiciary, still looked to the army to replace the democratic system.

- In January 1923, French and Belgian troops invaded the industrial heartland of Germany, the Ruhr, to force Germany to pay reparations owed to them. In response, the German government ordered "passive resistance" and strikes, thus denying the French various German goods and raw materials. The German government continued to pay the workers and to be able to do this they printed huge quantities of money, which exacerbated the inflation that already existed into hyperinflation. In 1920, the mark was worth 10% of its 1914 value, but by January 1923 one pre-1914 mark was worth 2,500 paper marks. This affected the middle classes and those on fixed incomes in particular. Many had their savings and pensions wiped out, which further alienated them from the Weimar Republic.

Source skills

Mary Fulbrook. *The Fontana History of Germany: 1918–1990*, **page 34 (1991).**

> The savings, hopes, plans and assumptions and aspirations of huge numbers of people were swept away in a chaotic whirlwind … Even when the worst material impact was over, the psychological shock of the experience was to have longer lasting effects,

confirming a deep-seated dislike of democracy, which was thereafter equated with economic distress, and a heightened fear of the possibility of economic instability.

First question, part a – 3 marks

According to Fulbrook, what was the impact of the hyperinflation of 1923?

The SA and the SS

The SA (*Sturmabteilung* or "Brown Shirts") was the paramilitary wing of the Nazi Party. Initially, it was made up largely from the Freikorps and ex-soldiers. They wore brown uniforms, following the lead of Mussolini's Fascist Blackshirts in Italy. The SA protected party meetings, marched in Nazi rallies, and physically assaulted political opponents, thus playing a key role in Hitler's rise to power in the 1920s and 1930s.

The *Schutzstaffel* (or SS) was formed in April 1925 as a section of the SA and functioned as a personal bodyguard for the NSDAP leader, Hitler. The SS was considered to be an elite force and membership was restricted to those who were pure Aryan Germans. Under Himmler's leadership, the SS was used to carry out the killings on the "Night of the Long Knives". It ultimately became one of the largest and most powerful organizations in the Third Reich.

What was the impact of the Munich Putsch of 1923 on the success of Nazism?

With this backdrop of political unrest, French occupation and economic catastrophe, Hitler launched his own bid to take over the government. By 1923 he had become the political leader of the *Kampfbund*, which was an association of militant right-wing groups created to coordinate tactics against the Republic. This involvement pushed Hitler into looking for a military solution to taking power; he was also impressed by Mussolini's successful March on Rome in 1922. War hero General Ludendorff gave his support to a plan that involved winning control of Bavaria and then marching on Berlin. Gustav Ritter von Kahr, the Bavarian leader, had indicated that he would support the attempted takeover, but then, at the last minute, he backed down. Despite having no support from the Bavarian government, police or army, Hitler decided to go ahead anyway and, with about 600 SA men, tried to take over government buildings. The result was disastrous; armed police opened fire and killed 16 Stormtroopers. Hitler was arrested and, along with Ludendorff, tried for treason.

However, the publicity of the trial turned Hitler into a national figure and provided the Nazis with free publicity. Hitler claimed that he was acting as a patriotic German and, although he was found guilty, he received the lightest sentence: five years' imprisonment. Moreover, he served less than a year of this sentence and was released in December 1924. It was during this time in prison that he wrote *Mein Kampf*.

What was the impact of Stresemann?

Following his release from prison, Hitler decided to use legal and constitutional means to take power in Germany. The Nazi Party was relaunched in 1925 with Hitler as overall leader or Führer, although he did not secure total control over the party until 1926. The party was also reorganized; youth and women's groups were established and the *Schutzstaffel* (or SS) was created. Modern propaganda techniques were employed as Hitler aimed to spread Nazi ideas to a wider audience.

Economic recovery in the 1920s

However, in the years following Hitler's release from prison, Germany experienced an economic recovery which meant that electoral support for the Nazi party was limited. Under Gustav Stresemann, who acted first as chancellor and then foreign minister during 1924–29, the hyperinflation was halted. The currency was stabilized with the introduction of the Renten mark, and the Dawes Plan was negotiated with the USA. This plan froze German reparation payments for two years, scaled down the level of German repayments demanded by the Treaty of Versailles and also set up loans for Germany from the USA. These were important in helping to regenerate the German economy. This was followed up in 1929 with the Young Plan, by which the USA, agreed to give further loans to Germany. A much-reduced scheme of repayments for reparations was established to spread over the next 50 years.

The changing international situation

Stresemann brought Germany back into the international community in other ways. In fact, Stresemann's foreign policy aims to restore Germany's position in Europe and to revise the Treaty of Versailles were not dissimilar to Hitler's. However, Stresemann was a pragmatic nationalist who believed that cooperation with Britain and France was the best way to achieve these aims. Germany joined the League of Nations in 1926 and signed the Kellogg–Briand Pact, which outlawed war, in 1928. Meanwhile, in the Locarno Treaties of 1925, Germany agreed to uphold the western borders with France and Belgium that had been established in the Treaty of Versailles. Locarno was key to bringing about a degree of rapprochement between Germany and France and it ushered in a period of hope for European cooperation known as the Locarno Spring.

Given the economic recovery and the new international standing of their country, many Germans were not interested in extreme politics and the Nazi Party was unable to make any electoral breakthrough. Although Nazi support grew in rural and protestant areas in the 1920s, it seems that it did not pose a substantial threat to the Weimar government.

What was the impact of the Great Depression on the Nazi Party?

The dependence of Weimar on US loans made its recovery dependent on US stability, and the Wall Street Crash of 1929 had a catastrophic impact on Germany. This would be key to explaining German support for Hitler's foreign and domestic policies.

▲ Gustav Stresemann, who was foreign minister between 1924 and 1929

The Rapallo Treaty

Another key treaty that Germany signed in the 1920s was the Rapallo Treaty. This was signed on 16 April 1922 by representatives of the governments of Germany and the Soviet Union at a world economic conference at Genoa in Italy. The treaty re-established diplomatic relations, renounced the financial claims that each country had on the other and pledged future cooperation. Secret clauses to the treaty allowed Germany to manufacture aeroplanes and ammunition forbidden by the Treaty of Versailles in the Soviet Union; German officers also trained in Russia.

The USA called in its loans and all financial support to Europe was stopped. Unemployment in Germany, which was already 2.8 million in 1929, grew to 5 million by February 1931 and to 6 million a year later. Chancellor Heinrich Brüning pursued deflationary policies, which included government expenditure cuts. This resulted in wage cuts and more job losses. Agriculture also suffered; food prices fell and small farmers in particular were badly affected. Banks also began to fold and industrial production dropped by over 50%.

This extreme economic situation led to a polarization in German politics. Germans turned to the more extreme parties: the Communists on the far-left and the parties on the far-right, including the National Socialists. Hitler portrayed the Nazi Party as the party that would provide food and jobs in the economic crisis. He also stepped up his attacks on the Weimar Republic, restating the myth that Germany had been "stabbed in the back" by the "November criminals" who still dominated the Weimar government. Along with other right-wing parties, Hitler also criticized Stresemann's policies of friendship and collaboration with the West. It was believed by those on the right that Stresemann's policies amounted to acceptance of the Treaty of Versailles. They believed that the Locarno Treaties only benefited the French and that Germany should not join the League of Nations, which was responsible for enforcing the Treaty of Versailles. Meanwhile, the Dawes Plan and the Young Plan were opposed because these agreements accepted the fact that Germany should be paying reparations.

Hitler's foreign policy aims did not change as a result of the Depression that followed the crash of 1929. However, the acute economic crisis made Hitler's promises, both domestic and foreign, more attractive to the German people.

Source skills

Stephen Lee. *The European Dictatorships 1918–1945*, **page 153 (1987).**

Taking advantage of the unpopularity of the Versailles Settlement, Hitler was able to implant upon the national consciousness terms like "November Criminals" and the "stab in the back". He also slammed the policy of détente pursued by Stresemann: "our people must be delivered from the hopeless confusion of international convictions and educated consciously and systematically to fanatical Nationalism." Another mainline policy, guaranteed to be taken seriously across most of the political spectrum, was anti-Communism. Finally, he made effective use of the deep undercurrent of anti-Semitism in Germany making the Jews a scapegoat for all of Germany's evils.

First question, part a – 3 marks

According to Stephen Lee, how did Hitler gain support in his election campaign?

Class discussion

In pairs, discuss the links between economic prosperity and political stability, and economic crisis and political radicalization.

1 What conclusions can you draw from your discussion?

2 What examples can you find from Japan, Italy and Germany to support your conclusions?

ATL **Self-management skills**

	Japan	Italy	Germany
League of Nations (date of entry/departure)			
Washington Conference 1921–22			
Rapallo Treaty, 1922			
Dawes Plan, 1924			
Locarno Conference, 1925			
Kellogg–Briand Pact, 1928			
Young Plan, 1929			

Japan, Italy and Germany all signed up to international agreements that supported international cooperation in the 1920s. Compare their involvement by copying and completing the table to the left. Identify which country or countries signed each treaty and state their involvement in each case.

What factors allowed Hitler to become a dictator?

When Brüning decided to call for unscheduled elections in 1930, this gave the Nazis a chance to break into mainstream policies. They increased their seats from 12 to 107, winning almost 6 million votes. In the 1932 presidential elections, Hitler stood for the Nazis against General Paul Von Hindenberg and gained 11 million votes (30% of the vote) in the first round and 13 million votes (36%) in the final round.

Hitler's electoral following impressed army leaders and right-wing nationalist politicians who wanted to form a strong government. Hitler was summoned by leading members of the German government, including army leader Kurt von Schleicher and nobleman Franz von Papen, to be Chancellor of Germany in 1933. They believed that it would be useful to have Hitler and his party on their side; they also believed that they would be able to control him. In the hope of creating a stable government, President Hindenburg agreed to the plan. However, the idea that Hitler could be, as Von Papen put it, "framed in", was a serious misjudgment. In the position of chancellor, with only two other Nazi party members in the cabinet, Hitler was able to secure his position as dictator of Germany.

Steps to dictatorship

1   Hitler called a new election, hoping to gain a Nazi majority in the Reichstag. On 27 February 1933, the Reichstag building was burnt down. A communist called Van der Lubbe was found inside the Reichstag and the Nazis claimed it was a communist plot. As a result, a decree was passed suspending freedom of the press, of speech and of association. Leading communists and socialist politicians were imprisoned. The Nazis won 43.9% of the vote.

2   Hitler then passed the Enabling Act, which gave him the power to pass laws without the Reichstag's consent. This change in the constitution, for which Hitler needed two-thirds of the vote, was achieved by preventing the communists from taking their seats, and by winning Centre Party support.

TOK

Consider the factors that fostered support for the ideas of the National Socialist Party in Germany. Investigate radical political parties and movements in your region today. Why do some people support these ideas? Are there any similarities or differences between the factors that led people to support radical parties in the past and the reasons people are attracted to these groups today? Feedback to the class. Discuss the extent to which studying History helps you to better understand the present.

ATL **Thinking skills**

Research further the actions of von Papen, von Schleicher and President Hindenberg 1932–1933. To what extent can it be argued that Hitler's position of power by 1933 was caused by *"the scheming and intrigue of unscrupulous careerists and extreme right-wing sympathizers"* (Henig, 1997)?

3   The rest of the political system was Nazified: state parliaments were abolished, trade unions were shut down, and the Socialist Party and Communist Party were banned. Other parties dissolved themselves. By July 1933, Germany was a one-party state.

4   In 1934, Hitler moved against the SA, which, under Ernst Röhm, was becoming a potential threat and an embarrassment. Röhm wanted to join the SA and the army together and keep both under his control. This was alarming both to Hitler and also the army leaders. Hitler did not want any challenge to the regular army as he needed its support for both internal security and expansion abroad. During the Night of the Long Knives, some 200 people were killed as Hitler used the SS to purge the leaders of the SA and to get rid of other enemies.

5   When the President of the Weimar Republic, General Paul von Hindenberg, died in 1934, Hitler merged the offices of chancellor and president, becoming the Führer of Germany, and in August 1934 all German armed forces took a personal oath of loyalty to Hitler.

As early as 1933, the first concentration camp had been established at Dachau to deal with political enemies. The category of political enemies soon extended to include Jews, Roma, homosexuals and Jehovah's Witnesses. Meanwhile, in the Nuremberg Laws of 1935, pure Aryan Germans were forbidden from having any relationship with Jews. Only those of Aryan blood could become German citizens with full political rights.

Thus, Hitler was in total control of Germany by 1934 and was enforcing Nazi doctrines and ideology in all aspects of life. Hitler's position was unassailable and he was in a strong position to carry out his foreign policy aims, though whether he had a clear plan of how to achieve these is less clear (as discussed on page 126).

Source skills

Source A

German unemployment and the Nazi vote share.

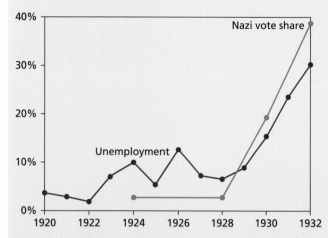

First question, part b – 2 marks

What is the message of Source A?

Source B

Nazi election poster of 1932: "Our last hope: Hitler".

First question, part b – 2 marks

What is the message of Source B?

Source C

Summary of Hitler's election promises as appeared in the *Sydney Morning Herald*, 1932.

… Herr Hitler is the last hope of a people from whom everything has been taken. The only thing that remains is the belief that he alone can restore their honour, their freedom, and their bread. Herr Hitler denotes salvation, and fulfils fearlessly the last will of the 2,000,000 German dead, who did not die in the war for the present slow destruction of Germany, but for a better German future. Herr Hitler is the people's man, because he understands them and fights for them. He represents the stern will of German youth, striving for a new form of life. Herr Hitler is the flaming torch of those wanting a new future for Germany.

Source D

Adolf Hitler's "Appeal to the German People", a radio address made on 31 January 1933.

Over fourteen years have passed since that unhappy day when the German people, blinded by promises made by those at home and abroad, forgot the highest values of our past, of the Reich, of its honour and its freedom, and thereby lost everything. Since those days of treason, the Almighty has withdrawn his blessing from our nation. Discord and hatred have moved in. Filled with the deepest distress, millions of the best German men and women from all walks of life see the unity of the nation disintegrating in a welter of egotistical political opinions, economic interests, and ideological conflicts.

… But the misery of our people is terrible! The starving industrial proletariat have become unemployed in their millions, while the whole middle and artisan class have been made paupers. If the German farmer also is involved in this collapse we shall be faced with a catastrophe of vast proportions. For in that case, there will collapse not only a Reich, but also a 2000-year-old inheritance of the highest works of human culture and civilization.

All around us are symptoms portending this breakdown. With an unparalleled effort of will and of brute force the Communist method of madness is trying as a last resort to poison and undermine an inwardly shaken and uprooted nation.

The task before us is the most difficult which has faced German statesmen in living memory. But we all have unbounded confidence, for we believe in our nation and in its eternal values. Farmers, workers, and the middle class must unite to contribute the bricks wherewith to build the new Reich.

Third question – 6 marks

Compare and contrast Sources C and D regarding Hitler's promises to the German people.

Fourth question – 9 marks

Draft a response to this question:

Using the sources and your own knowledge, examine the reasons why Hitler's foreign policy aims were popular with the German people.

Examiner's hint: *For the third and fourth questions above, use the markbands on pages 10 and 11 to assess a partner's work. Share your feedback with your partner.*

1 How could your partner improve his or her responses?

2 How could you have improved yours?

The historical debate: Did Hitler have a clear plan for achieving his foreign policy goals when he took power in 1933?

Hitler's overall foreign policy aims, as laid out in *Mein Kampf* and in the *Zweites Buch* (written in 1928 but unpublished in his lifetime), seem very clear, and he returned to them again and again in speeches between 1928 and 1933. He also continued to make references to them in briefings and in letters after he took power, indicating that his views became fixed at an early stage and never really altered.

However, did he actually have a clear plan as to how he was to achieve these aims when he took power in 1933?

Historians are divided over this issue. Some, such as AJP Taylor and Hans Mommsen, have argued that Hitler did **not** have a blueprint of how to achieve his objectives. Rather, his actions were usually determined by economic pressures and demands from within the Nazi Party, and he seized each opportunity that was presented to him.

Historians of the intentionalist school, such as Andreas Hillgruber and Klaus Hildebrand, argue that Hitler had a definite programme of expansion and conquest with clear phases. The first phase would be the ending of the Treaty of Versailles and the formation of an alliance with Britain and Italy. The second phase would be the defeat of France. The third and final phase would be the conquest of Russia. Intentionalists such as Hildebrand and Hauner, known as globalists, go further and argue that Hitler's ultimate aim was to take over the USA and thus achieve world domination.

Another area of debate regarding Hitler's foreign policy is whether it was a continuation of earlier German foreign policy, or a radical break from the past. Following the Second World War, historians argued the latter. However, the German historian Fritz Fischer claimed in the late 1960s that Hitler's aims were similar to those of Kaiser Wilhelm II in the First World War; in other words, hegemony over much of Europe, the creation of a Greater Germany and rule over a fragmented Russia. Other historians have stressed the continuity between the Weimar Republic's foreign policy aims and those of Hitler with regard to his revision of the Treaty of Versailles. However, Stephen Lee clearly refutes this latter argument:

> *In retrospect, however, it is obvious that the continuity between the diplomacy of the Weimar Republic and the Third Reich can be misleading. The crucial point which showed that Nazi foreign policy was as revolutionary as its domestic counterpart was that Hitler saw revisionism merely as a step towards projects which were well beyond the ambitions of the Republic's statesmen. Although the Republic's politicians had a strong element of opportunism, even ruthlessness, they did not share Hitler's Social Darwinism and racialist vision. They also respected the traditions of European diplomacy and, under Stresemann, contributed much to international co-operation. One of Hitler's aims was to smash the multinational agreements, like the Locarno Pact, which had been carefully built up during the 1920s.* — Lee, 1987

Source help and hints

Second question – 4 marks

(See page 117)

With reference to its origin, purpose and content, consider the value and limitations of using this source as evidence of Hitler's foreign policy aims.

> **Examiner's hint:** *Some points that you could consider are listed below.*

Values

- A value of the origin is that it is from Hitler himself explaining his aims regarding foreign policy.

- A value of the date (1923) is that it shows us that Hitler had these aims 10 years before he took power.

- Regarding content, Hitler refers to several aims, such as getting rid of the Treaty of Versailles, unifying all Germans and getting more land and soil, so it is a comprehensive overview of what he wanted to achieve.

Limitations

- With regard to origin, Hitler made these comments in 1923 (before he took power) and he could have amended his aims by 1933.

- A limitation of the purpose is that it is a speech through which he is trying to win support for his ideas and so could be exaggerating certain aspects of his ideas.

- The point above can also be seen in the content: the language is very strong and exaggerated, e.g. using the imagery of the hammer and the anvil.

First question, part b, 2 marks

(See page 124)

What is the message of Source B?

▲ Nazi election poster of 1932: "Our last hope, Hitler"

> **Examiner's hint:** *As with all visual sources, posters need to be studied carefully for details that will help you understand the message. Posters were a key part of the Nazi propaganda machine, which was run by Josef Goebbels; they are usually quite simple, but very clever and effective.*
>
> *Your contextual knowledge is important for helping you to get the main point. Here, the impact of the Great Depression on Germany is key. For this poster, consider:*
>
> - *the way that the German people are portrayed in the background, including their expressions and the way they are standing*
>
> - *the message, "Our last hope"*
>
> - *the choice of colour to reinforce the message*
>
> - *the size of the font for "Hitler".*

Third question – 6 marks

(See page 125)

Compare and contrast Sources C and D regarding Hitler's promises to the German people.

Comparisons

- Both talk about Germany being in a desperate state.

- Both say that Hitler is the only hope for Germany.

- Both say that Hitler will create a new Germany.

Contrasts

- Source D is much more specific as to the causes of Germany's distress, talking about "treason" and mentioning communists as being responsible, whereas Source C is more general.

- Source D is also much more specific as to the problems facing Germany at that time, particularly the economic problems, whereas Source C focuses on the past problems of losing the war.

- Source D discusses the terrible situation Germany is in without the promise of recovery, whereas Source C focuses on the future and the hope that Hitler brings.

References

Fulbrook, M. 1991. *The Fontana History of Germany: 1918–1990.* Fontana. London, UK

Henig, R. 1985. *The Origins of the Second World War.* Routledge. London, UK

Hitler, A. 1925. *Mein Kampf.* Eher Verlag. Berlin, Germany

Lee, S. 1987. *The European Dictatorships 1918–1945.* Methuen. London, UK

Rogers, P. *Aspects of Western Civilization, Volume II: Problems and source in history.* Prentice Hall. New York, USA

Steiner, Z. 2011. *The Triumph of the Dark: European International History 1933–1999.* Oxford University Press. New York, USA

2.3 Italian expansion, 1933–1940

Conceptual understanding

Key concepts
→ Change
→ Continuity
→ Perspective

Key questions
→ Examine the reasons for Italy pursuing a more expansionist foreign policy in the 1930s.
→ To what extent was there continuity in Italian foreign policy in the 1930s?
→ Discuss the consequences of foreign policy in the 1930s for Italy.

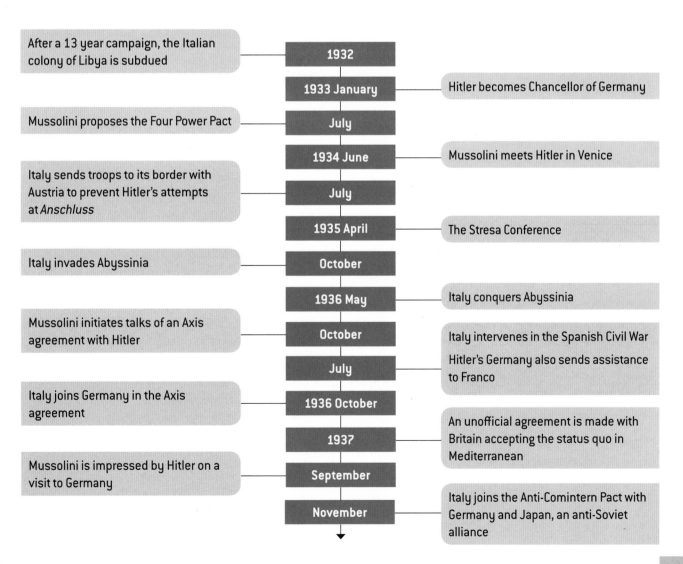

After a 13 year campaign, the Italian colony of Libya is subdued — **1932**

1933 January — Hitler becomes Chancellor of Germany

Mussolini proposes the Four Power Pact — **July**

1934 June — Mussolini meets Hitler in Venice

Italy sends troops to its border with Austria to prevent Hitler's attempts at *Anschluss* — **July**

1935 April — The Stresa Conference

Italy invades Abyssinia — **October**

1936 May — Italy conquers Abyssinia

Mussolini initiates talks of an Axis agreement with Hitler — **October**

July — Italy intervenes in the Spanish Civil War. Hitler's Germany also sends assistance to Franco

Italy joins Germany in the Axis agreement — **1936 October**

1937 — An unofficial agreement is made with Britain accepting the status quo in Mediterranean

Mussolini is impressed by Hitler on a visit to Germany — **September**

November — Italy joins the Anti-Comintern Pact with Germany and Japan, an anti-Soviet alliance

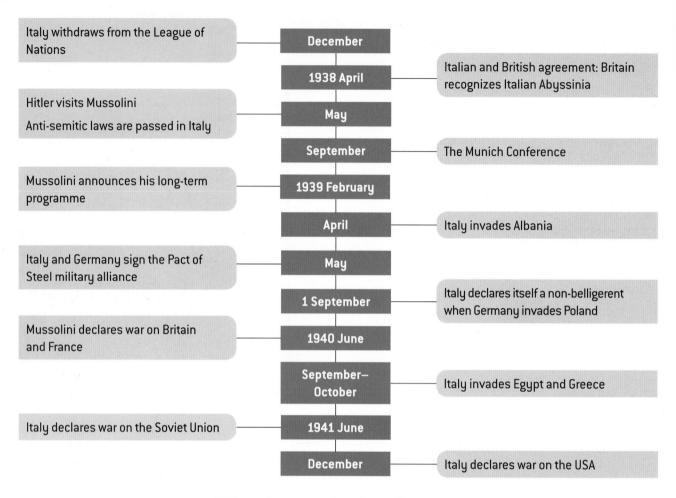

Italy withdraws from the League of Nations	**December**	
	1938 April	Italian and British agreement: Britain recognizes Italian Abyssinia
Hitler visits Mussolini Anti-semitic laws are passed in Italy	**May**	
	September	The Munich Conference
Mussolini announces his long-term programme	**1939 February**	
	April	Italy invades Albania
Italy and Germany sign the Pact of Steel military alliance	**May**	
	1 September	Italy declares itself a non-belligerent when Germany invades Poland
Mussolini declares war on Britain and France	**1940 June**	
	September–October	Italy invades Egypt and Greece
Italy declares war on the Soviet Union	**1941 June**	
	December	Italy declares war on the USA

What factors had an impact on Italy's foreign policy in the 1930s?

1. The impact of fascism

The character of the Italian people must be moulded by fighting.
— Mussolini

In the 1930s, Italian foreign policy continued to be influenced by the factors identified on page 84. However, historians generally agree that Italian foreign policy was directed by Mussolini during this period and that he pursued a more clearly Fascist foreign policy from the mid-1930s: glorification of war for its own sake, pursuit of imperial expansion, and a move away from diplomacy and cooperation.

During this period, Mussolini's methods became more assertive and he was more aggresive diplomatically. He continued to assert anti-French territorial claims, but he moved away from his relatively good relationship with the British, instead fostering closer ties to Hitler's Germany. This led to a series of Italo–German agreements including the Rome–Berlin Axis and the Pact of Steel. Mussolini also engaged in wars in Abyssinia, Spain and Albania.

ATL · Self-management and thinking skills

Refer back to the diagram on page 89 which identifies the key characteristics of Fascism. As you read through this chapter, identify where Fascist ideology appears to have shaped Mussolini's foreign policy.

The road Mussolini embarked on in the 1930s would ultimately lead to the Italian entry into the Second World War in 1940 as an ally of Germany.

2. The impact of domestic economic isues

As with the other European countries and Japan, Italy was also affected by the Great Depression. The economic problems caused by overvaluing the lira were exacerbated by this worldwide crisis. Investment from the USA was withdrawn, and Italian farmers were also badly affected by the collapse in grain prices. Industry declined and unemployment grew to 2 million. The government responded with more intervention, including bailouts for the industrialists. The Bank of Italy was on the brink of collapse when the government set up the *Istituto Mobiliare Italiano* in 1931, which gave financial support to banks and industries. The allocation of raw materials was brought under government control and direct control of major industries increased. The *Istituto per la Ricostruzione Industriale* was set up in 1933 and took over shares of companies and banks. As a result, Italy developed the largest public sector in Europe, excluding the Soviet Union. Indeed, by the end of the 1930s, the government controlled 20% of the capital of key companies. Wages that had already fallen before the depression were cut further.

There were some measures that provided relief from the impact of the Great Depression, such as public works programmes and the removal of the ban on emigration. Indeed, Mussolini managed to prevent the social and political upheaval that the depression precipitated elsewhere in Europe and he retained power. Nevertheless, the economic crisis meant that Mussolini needed to distract the Italian public from Italy's internal economic problems by fostering the "revolutionary" spirit that he and fascism espoused. Foreign policy would now need to be more dynamic and inspirational.

The result of this, however, was that from 1936 the Italian economy was further undermined by Mussolini's emphasis on autarky, and the costs of *Il Duce's* wars. Thus, domestic economic factors may have been a factor in Mussolini's decision to invade Abyssinia and intervene in the Spanish Civil War; nonetheless, these wars came at a high price for the Italian economy. Even though taxes were increased, the wars led to an annual budget deficit of 28 billion lire by 1939. This ultimately had a negative political impact and undermined support for the regime from the elites.

TOK

Discuss in pairs the extent to which economic forces are the main driving force for historical change. You should consider the first case study on Japan in the 1920s and 1930s as well as considering this case study on Italy. Make notes from your conversation and add to these as you read through this chapter.

Autarky
Economic independence, or self-sufficiency.

Who controlled Italian foreign policy in the 1930s?

When he came to power in 1922, Mussolini wanted to control Italian foreign policy himself. In 1929, once his authority seemed secure, he appointed Dino Grandi as foreign minister. Grandi was a committed Fascist who favoured a "strong" foreign policy. He wanted to move away from Anglophile policies and demonstrate Italian strength, and ultimately ready the armed forces for the "coming war". Grandi believed that Italy should not trust the League of Nations. Nevertheless, Mussolini still directed foreign policy and in July 1932 he moved Grandi to the position of ambassador in Britain.

In 1936, Mussolini appointed his son-in-law, Count Galeazzo Ciano to work on foreign policy. Ciano had initially supported closer links with Germany. However, Ciano then became disillusioned with Hitler and argued against the Pact of Steel, signed in May 1939. Ciano advised Mussolini to create a buffer zone in the Balkans against Germany and he supported the invasion of Albania. Ciano lost favour with Mussolini for his anti-German stance when Hitler swept victoriously across Europe. Ciano ultimately relented and supported Italy joining the war with Germany in June 1940.

Source skills

J. Calvitt Clarke and C. Foust. *Russia and Italy against Hitler: The Bolshevik–Fascist Rapprochement of the 1930s* **(1991).**

In the mid-1930s, Italy received 86 percent of its imports by sea, and of these, 13 percent passed through the Dardanelles, 17 percent through Suez, and 70 percent through Gibraltar. Hence the fascist conviction that Italy must either dominate or be the prisoner of its Nostro Mare, the Mediterranean. Nor could Italy willingly concede to any other power hegemony in the Mediterranean's hinterland – the Danubian (including Austria and Hungary) and Balkan areas.

First question, part a – 3 marks

What key points are made in this Source regarding Italian economic needs and their influence on Italian foreign policy in the 1930s?

Examiner's hint: *In pairs, identify three of the following points. Highlight them in the source.*

- *Italy was dependent on imports from the sea.*
- *The majority of imports came through Gibraltar.*
- *Italy had to dominate the Mediterranean.*
- *Italy could not allow another power to dominate the area.*

3. Changing diplomatic alignments in Europe after 1933

Extract from Dino Grandi's diary, 1932

I have asked myself why the Boss is so taken with Hitler. [Mussolini] has searched breathlessly for the last ten years or so, wherever they might be found, for "allies" for a revolutionary foreign policy destined to create a "new order" in Europe, a new order of which He considers himself supreme Pontiff not only in the spiritual but also in the material sense … An international action founded exclusively on the Party, on the Regime, on a revolutionary ideology.

Social skills

Discuss the following question with a partner.

What does the quote from Grandi's diary (above) suggest Mussolini wanted to gain from potential "allies"?

To demonstrate Italy's central role in European diplomacy, Mussolini held a meeting in Rome in 1933. Mussolini's intention was to develop an alternative to the League of Nations for European diplomacy. The Four Power Pact, or Quadripartite Pact, was signed on 15 July 1933 in Rome. It set out that smaller nations should have less say in "Great Power" relations, unlike their role at the League of Nations. Britain, France, Germany and Italy signed the agreement, although the French parliament never ratified it. The signatories agreed to adhere to the League's covenant, the Locarno Treaties and the Kellogg–Briand Pact.

The resulting Four Power Pact allowed for further "Great Power" cooperation, though in reality this pact had little meaning and was dismissed by the other powers. In Italy, however, it was heralded as a success for Mussolini.

Nevertheless, in 1934, Mussolini's actions *were* seen as significant, not only domestically, but also by the other European powers. Italy had promoted an independent Austria since the end of the First World War and so Mussolini opposed *Anschluss* (the name given to Austria's unification with Germany, which was one of Hitler's aims). When, on the 25 July 1934, Austrian Nazi supporters murdered the Austrian Chancellor Engelbert Dolfuss, Mussolini immediately mobilized his troops to the border to deter any attempt by Hitler to achieve *Anschluss*. This action was sufficient to deter Germany and Hitler did not intervene.

In addition, because by 1935 Hitler's rearmament was alarming the rest of Europe, Italy was now perceived to be key to guaranteeing the status quo in Europe. In response to Hitler's policies, Italy, Britain and France met in the Italian town of Stresa in April 1935. The "Final Declaration of the Stresa Conference", signed on 14 April 1935, aimed to reaffirm the Locarno Treaties and to confirm the independence of Austria. The three powers also agreed to resist further attempts to breach the Treaty of Versailles. Together, they protested against Hitler's violation of the Treaty of Versailles. This "Stresa Front" agreed to work to prevent any future changes to the European settlement. (See also pages 214–215.)

However, the agreement was vague and did not even specifically name Germany. No methods to uphold their aims were agreed. In fact, Italy had been keener than Britain to adopt a firm stance regarding Germany; Britain was more concerned not to offend Hitler. None of the signatories would sanction an actual invasion of Germany.

Nevertheless, Mussolini knew that a resurgent Germany would frighten Britain and France, and that this could lead them to be more accommodating towards Italian territorial demands. The Stresa Front also gave Italy more protection from *Anschluss*. Most significantly, Mussolini got the impression during the Stresa talks that, in working with Britain and France, he had gained their consent to expand Italian control in Abyssinia.

Only two months later, in June 1935, Britain apparently broke the principles agreed at Stresa when it signed the Anglo–German Naval Agreement with Hitler's Germany (see page 214). By signing this agreement, Britain had condoned German naval rearmament and had done so without consulting its Stresa Front allies. Mussolini believed that this action ended the Stresa agreement.

Class discussion

Discuss Mussolini's attitude towards Hitler's new government in Germany up to 1935. Why might Italy be seen by the Western democracies as key to containing an expansionist Germany?

Source skills

Robert Mallet, a British historian and academic, in an academic book *Mussolini and the Origins of the Second World War, 1933–40*, (1983).

> In the long-term … Hitler's avowed determination to overturn the Versailles settlement offered fascist Italy, if allied to Germany, clear possibilities for the creation of Mussolini's long anticipated Balkans, Mediterranean and Red Sea empire. As Mussolini stressed to Hungarian prime minister, Gyualia Gömbös, that same spring,

he did not intend Ethiopia to be the limit of an Italian expansionist drive. On the contrary, after taking Ethiopia he would also conquer the British-controlled territories of Egypt and the Sudan, thereby linking Italian north Africa possessions with those to the east of the continent. Italy's empire would stretch uninterrupted from the Mediterranean to the Indian Ocean.

But in the immediate short term Mussolini continued to face domestic anxiety over his plans for Ethiopia. The fear that Hitler might well attempt a coup against Austria once Italy had deployed large numbers of troops to East Africa remained widespread, and Mussolini could not move without quelling Italian anxieties which, by mid 1935, were mounting. The foreign ministry, although having given support to Mussolini's Africa policy, remained emphatic in its demands that Austria should remain an independent state. A detailed report on the current European situation of 2nd April concluded that Austria amounted to Italy's own "demilitarised zone", and that Italian defence

policy should consider its future defence from German incursions to be an absolute priority. Meanwhile the Italian military continued to express their own reservations to the wisdom of Mussolini's enterprise … In actual fact, Mussolini had already elected to give orthodox diplomacy one last try. Amid rumours that the German and Austrian general staffs had recently held conversations, the dictator requested a meeting of British, French and Italian statesmen that April at Stresa, in northern Italy … If Mussolini had wanted to sow anxiety within official German circles, he had succeeded.

First question, part a – 3 marks

According to this source, what were Mussolini's key motives for engaging in the Stresa Front agreements?

Second question – 4 marks

With reference to the origin, purpose and content of this source, assess its values and limitations for historians studying Mussolini's foreign policy in the 1920s.

Examiner's hint: *Remember that, as this is a "to what extent" question, you should identify points that agree and points that disagree with the assertion that Mussolini's foreign policy had only limited success up to 1935.*

ATL Self-management, social and thinking skills

In pairs, discuss and make bullet point notes on the following question.

"Mussolini's foreign policy had only limited success up to 1935." To what extent do you agree with this statement?

Italian foreign policy, 1935–39

Mussolini's Italy was at war continuously between 1935 and 1939. The key turning point in Italian foreign policy was the invasion of Abyssinia in 1935–36, which would take Italy's foreign policy on a new course. This action was condemned by the League of Nations and limited sanctions were imposed. Although its aggression had a negative impact on its relations with the Western democracies, the invasion was received positively in Italy. The conquest of Abyssinia led to a surge of nationalist feeling and this in turn encouraged Mussolini to further acts of aggression.

What were the domestic influences on Italian foreign policy in 1935–39?

There was a lack of support from the political elites, including the King, for a shift in Italian foreign policy that had traditionally supported Britain. These groups were generally hostile to the Germans. The economic situation also influenced foreign policy. Italian industry and agriculture had not fulfilled Mussolini's goal of autarky and the economy would not be able to sustain a general war. The limited war in Abyssinia and the intervention in Spain would be a drain on Italian resources. These factors had to be borne in mind while Mussolini still aspired to control the Mediterranean and maintain the momentum of "Fascistization" that had followed the war in East Africa.

Why did Mussolini invade Abyssinia in October 1935?

Source skills

Source A

A speech Mussolini made to the Italian public the day before the Italian invasion of Abyssinia, October 1935.

It is not only our army that marches to its objective, 44 million Italians march with that army, all united and alert. Let others try to commit the blackest injustice, taking away Italy's place in the sun. When, in 1915, Italy united her fate with the Allies, how many promises were made? To fight the common victory Italy brought her supreme contribution of 670,000 dead, 480,000 disabled and more than one million wounded. When we went to the table of that odious peace they gave us only the crumbs of colonial booty.

First question, part a – 3 marks

What, according to Source A, were the reasons for the invasion of Abyssinia?

Second question – 4 marks

With reference to the origin, purpose and content of Source A, assess its values and limitations for historians studying the Italian invasion of Abyssinia.

Source B

Patricia Knight. *Mussolini and Fascism* (2003).

The invasion of Abyssinia was undertaken primarily to demonstrate Italy's great power status and, in doing so, avenge Adowa, the scene of the disastrous defeat of Italian troops in 1896. One of the more frustrating aspects of Versailles had been Italy's failure to acquire any new colonies and Mussolini now intended to recreate the glories of the Roman Empire and achieve a "place in the sun" to rival Britain and France. Further motives were the prospect of economic gains in the form of oil, coal and gold and of African recruits for the Italian army. Mussolini also thought of East Africa as a fertile area for Italian settlement, given the expected increase in population from the Battle for Births. Abyssinia was in any case the only remaining uncolonized African territory and seemed an easy target, given Italy's military superiority and its presence in neighbouring Eritrea and Somaliland.

Examiner's hint: *Read the provenance of Source A again. In response to the second question, consider the values and limitations given below.*

- *Would you have found the same values and limitations?*
- *Which ones had you not thought of?*
- *Do you have any comments to add?*

Values

- *A value of the origin is that it is a speech made by the dictator of Italy himself, and Mussolini directed foreign policy. The author had planned and ordered for the invasion of Abyssinia.*

- *A value of the purpose is that it offers insight into how the invasion was presented at the time to the Italian public. As it is a speech, it will give the reasons that Mussolini used to justify the invasion.*

- *A value of the content is that it reveals what the Italian government believed to be the key reasons for the invasion and what the Italian public would have related to at the time. It offers an insight into what Italians saw as important in October 1935.*

Limitations

- *Mussolini needed to justify his policies publicly and may not be representing the wider views held in Italy at the time.*

- *The date of the speech may be a limitation, as it is the day before the invasion and Mussolini needs to rally support. Indeed, as this is a speech, it is probably propaganda. Other motives for the invasion, such as to rally public support for his personal dictatorship, would not be revealed.*

- *The speech lacks hindsight as it was given on the eve of the invasion.*

- *The content focuses on the justifications, mainly historical, for Italian expansion. It presents a highly one-sided perspective of Italy's position and does not elaborate on the specific aims of* Il Duce.

2

ATL Thinking skills

Refer back to the terms of the Treaty of London on page 87, and the gains Italy attained from the Paris Peace Settlement on page 90. In pairs or small groups, discuss the validity of Mussolini's claim that Italy had been given *"only the crumbs of colonial booty"* (Source A page 135).

ATL Communication skills

Draw a mind map that summarizes the reasons for Mussolini's invasion of Abyssinia.

ATL Thinking skills

In pairs, discuss the following questions.

1 What key factors motivated the Italian invasion of Abyssinia according to Source B on page 135?

2 Attempt to find evidence from the sources and this chapter that support:

- economic motives for the invasion
- ideological motives for the invasion
- changing diplomatic alignments in Europe as a factor in the invasion.

Mussolini's foreign policy objectives in invading Abyssinia, which had not yet been colonized, originated in the longer-term Italian nationalist ambitions to build an empire and to become a great imperial power like Britain and France. He also aspired to an empire akin to the classical Roman Empire, which had controlled large swathes of African territory.

The political reason for the invasion was to consolidate Mussolini's personality cult (*Il Duce*) and to rally support behind the regime. War for its own sake was also an element of the Fascist ideal, and this war would give Mussolini an easy victory as Abyssinia was not modernized. It would also be revenge for Italy's ignoble defeat to the Abyssinians in 1896. In addition, Mussolini would be able to bolster his own military forces by drawing on colonial troops. However, there were also economic reasons for conquering Abyssinia. Mussolini needed to divert attention from the failings of the corporate state and the impact of the Great Depression. Abyssinia was targeted in order to gain territory for emigration and to provide an export market for Italian goods. Mussolini also hoped to find oil.

When Hitler announced German rearmament, Mussolini briefly hesitated in his invasion plans as he did not want to leave himself too exposed in Europe when he was at war in Africa. However, the Stresa Conference led him to think he had nothing to fear; the meetings had convinced him that Britain and France would not object strongly to an expansion of Italian control in the territory. Mussolini also wanted to demonstrate Italy's power to Germany. Nevertheless, Mussolini did not make his plans clear to Britain and France as he did not want to provoke them in an area where they, too, had colonial possessions (see map).

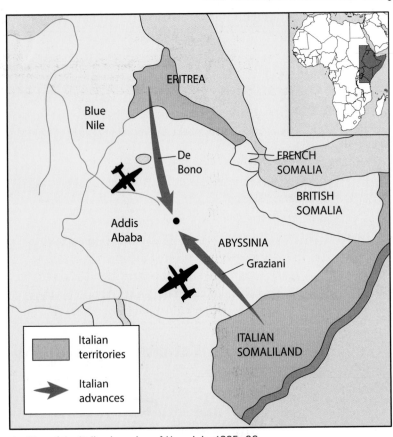

▲ Map of the Italian invasion of Abyssinia, 1935–36

The events – What happened?

As you see from the map on the previous page, Italy had already acquired colonial territory on the border of Abyssinia. The border itself lacked clarity, and this lack of clarity gave Mussolini the opportunity to manufacture an incident that would lead to war.

It was Italy that had backed Abyssinia's entry into the League of Nations in 1923 and (as you read on page 102) the two countries had signed a treaty of friendship in 1928. However, Italy drew up a plan to annex Abyssinia in 1929 and an invasion plan in 1932. Then, in December 1934, Italian forces clashed with Abyssinians at the disputed Wal Wal oasis, which resulted in the death of 30 Italians. Mussolini demanded an apology and considerable compensation; the Emperor of Abyssinia, Haile Selassie, requested an investigation by the League of Nations. However, Mussolini would not entertain the idea of a League investigation, and in a secret order instructed his forces to attain "total conquest" of Abyssinia. *Il Duce* made a huge commitment to the war, sending an army with support personnel totalling 500,000 to East Africa. The Abyssinians, without modern weapons, were soon in retreat.

In September 1935, the League resolved that neither side could be held responsible for the Wal Wal incident as the area had been disputed. On 3 October, Italy launched its full-scale invasion, and then on 6 October, Italian forces captured Adowa. This had historic importance to Italy as its forces had been defeated there in 1896. The League of Nations condemned Italy as the aggressor on 7 October and, four days later, the League of Nations' Assembly voted to impose sanctions. On the 18 November, these sanctions, although limited, were put into effect.

During the war, tensions between Italy and Britain reached crisis point in the Mediterranean, where Britain had two large naval bases. However, Britain and France wanted to retain good relations with Italy and to maintain the Stresa Front to contain Hitler's Germany. In December 1935, the British and French foreign ministers, Samuel Hoare and Pierre Laval respectively, drew up a secret pact which would offer Italy half of Abyssinia to bring about a swift resolution to the crisis. However, this plan was leaked to the press, and Britain and France were pressured by public opinion to withdraw the deal (see Chapter 2.6).

Italy continued its war and, on 6 April 1936, the Abyssinian army was defeated at Lake Ashangi. Italian forces finally took the capital, Addis Ababa, on 5 May 1936, and Emperor Haile Selassie fled to Britain. On 9 May, Abyssinia was formerly annexed by Italy. It became part of Italian East Africa with Eritrea and Somaliland.

Mussolini had his great conquest. The war had the desired impact domestically, with a surge in nationalist sentiment that was further encouraged by the League's condemnation and economic sanctions. Even the Italian Queen Mother had supported the war effort, and participated in the call to fund the war by donating her gold wedding ring to the government.

ATL Communication skills

Go to www.youtube.com/watch?v=op-dD3oUMh0, or search for "The Abyssnia Crisis, 1935–6".

This clip from "The Road to War: Italy" shows the Italians' motives and actions in Abyssinia.

Class discussion

Why was the conquest of Abyssinia important to Mussolini? Consider the role of ideology as well as other factors such as economics and the impact of events outside Italy.

ATL Self-management skills

Summarize Mussolini's actions in Abyssinia on a detailed timeline. Place Mussolini's actions above the timeline. After reading Chapter 2.6, you can add the actions of Britain and France below the timeline.

Source A

R. Overy and A. Wheatcroft. *The Road to War: The Origins of World War II*, pages 220–21 (2009).

The threat of sanctions united public opinion behind Mussolini. There developed a strong anti-British sentiment. In cafes, zuppa inglese was re-christened *zuppa imperiale*. The war was popular at home. Women exchanged their gold wedding rings for iron substitutes to swell the national bullion reserves. The Queen was the first of 250,000 Roman women to offer her ring in a ceremony held at the War Memorial in Rome. A total of ten million were collected nationwide. When the war began to go Italy's way in February 1936, the new commander, Marshal Pietro Badoglio, became a national hero. But the victory was won only with a massive war effort, using all the modern weapons of war against Ethiopian tribesmen armed with rifles and spears. By May 1936 there were over 400,000 Italian and native troops in Ethiopia, and a war that was supposed to cost 1.5 to 2 billion lire in total ended by costing 1 billion lire every month. To speed up occupation the Italian air force used gas bombs on Ethiopian soldiers, both mustard gas and phosgene, a total of 1521 canisters, which killed and maimed an unknown number of soldiers and civilians. In May the whole of Ethiopia was annexed and on the 9th King Victor Emmanuel was declared Emperor. The King received the news, Mussolini recorded, with "tears in his eyes". The Pope presented the new Empress of Ethiopia with a Golden Rose.

Mussolini now enjoyed a new role as conqueror and imperialist; his reputation in Italy reached its highest point.

Source B

Extracts from Mussolini's telegrams to a commander in Abyssinia, 1936–37.

5 June 1936

All rebels made prisoner are to be shot.

8 June 1936 [SECRET]

To finish off rebels as at Ancober use gas.

8 July 1936

I repeat my authorization to initiate and systematically conduct policy of terror and extermination against rebels and populations in complicity with them. Without the law of ten eyes for one we cannot heal this wound in good time.

21 February 1937

Agreed that male population of Goggetti over 18 years of age to be shot and village destroyed.

Questions

In pairs or as a class, discuss what the telegrams in Source B suggest about the nature of the Italian war in Abyssinia. In what ways do these telegrams support the points made by Richard Overy in Source A?

What were the results of the Abyssinian War?

Speech by Mussolini, May 1936

Italy has her empire at last; a Fascist empire because it bears the indestructible tokens of the will and of the power of the Roman lictors … An empire of civilisation and humanity for all the populations of Abyssinia. That is the tradition of Rome, who, after victory, associated the peoples with their destiny.

— Lowe, C and Marzari, F. 1975.

The results of the Abyssinian War for Italy

By May 1936, Italy had won the war. Mussolini had succeeded in creating an Italian East African empire. The war had been won relatively quickly and had cost only 1,000 Italian casualties. Mussolini had demonstrated Italian military might and he had expanded the Italian empire. This was to be the peak of his foreign policy success. Giovanni Gentile, a Fascist philosopher, claimed: "*Mussolini … has not just founded an empire in Ethiopia. He has made something more. He has created a new Italy*".

Nevertheless, the assault on Abyssinia had initiated a "Mediterranean scare" and the Naval Chief of Staff Admiral Domenico Cavagnari warned Mussolini against raising tension with Britain. Indeed, the Italian navy was incomplete due to unfinished building and modernization programmes and it could not take on the British Royal Navy. A naval war between Italy and France, and their ally Yugoslavia, was possible, but Cavagnari cautioned that a naval war with Britain would mean certain defeat.

In addition, although the League of Nations lifted sanctions in July, the Italian victory had come at a high economic price. The budget deficit had risen from 2.5 billion to 16 billion lire during the war, and there was the continued cost of maintaining 250,000 occupying troops. In October 1936, the lira was devalued by 40%, which hit the middle classes hard. Italian trade had to shift to Germany due to the sanctions imposed by the League.

The ferocity and atrocities perpetrated by Italian forces gave them a reputation for great brutality. Finally, for Italy, the war did not really end in 1936. The Italians were forced to fight a drawn-out guerrilla war in Abyssinia until it fell to the British in 1941.

The results of the war for collective security

The war had once again exposed the weakness of the League of Nations, which had been utterly ineffective in its response to Italian aggression. It also caused Italy to move away from good relations with Britain and France, and closer to Germany. Indeed, it is significant that, during the war, on 6 January 1936, Mussolini told the German ambassador that he no longer had objections to Austria becoming a German satellite. He stressed, however, that it must remain independent. Then, on 22 February 1936, Mussolini agreed to the German rearmament of the Rhineland; this meant Italy would no longer uphold its Locarno obligations. (See page 162 for further discussion of the impact of Mussolini's actions on Germany.)

Source skills

Source A

An Italian poster from May 1936, "Italy finally has its Empire".

L'ITALIA HA FINALMENTE IL SUO IMPERO

Source B

A cartoon by David Low published in the UK newspaper, the *Evening Standard*, on 15 February 1935.

First question, part b – 2 marks for each source

What is the message of the artists in Sources A and B?

Second question – 4 marks

With reference to its origin, purpose and content, assess the values and limitations of Source B for historians studying the Italian war with Abyssinia.

ATL Thinking skills

1   Discuss, in pairs or small groups, the key differences in how Source A and B each get their 'message' across to the viewer. Which source is more effective in achieving this?

2   In what ways could the Abyssinian crisis be seen as a turning point in international relations?

Source skills

Fourth question – 9 marks

Here are some examples of the style of question you could expect for the Fourth question on a Paper 1 set on the Italian expansion in Abyssinia:

a   Using the sources and your own knowledge, examine the reasons for the Italian invasion of Abyssinia in 1936.

b   Using the sources and your own knowledge, discuss the results of the Italian invasion of Abyssinia in 1936.

c   Using the sources and your own knowledge, to what extent do you agree that "Mussolini's foreign policy was wholly successful up to 1936".

Why did Italy intervene in the Spanish Civil War in 1936–39?

Mussolini's success in Abyssinia encouraged him to look for further military greatness and, when civil war broke out in Spain in 1936, he quickly decided to intervene. Taking military action was in line with Fascist ideals regarding the central role of war and society. Mussolini hoped to gain naval bases in the Balearic Islands from General Franco in return for his assistance, and had aspirations to re-establish the Mediterranean Roman Empire.

Nevertheless, Italian intervention in the Spanish Civil War was also motivated by ideology; Mussolini responded to requests for assistance from the militarist rebels to help fight against liberal democracy and socialism. Mussolini had made, as he had done in Germany, close connections to right-wing groups in Spain since the installation of a new Spanish Republic in 1931. He wanted to stop communism spreading in Spain and to prevent communists from attaining a strategically important position at the mouth of the Mediterranean. Indeed, he presented the rationale for intervention to the Italian public as part of the continuing struggle against Marxism. Finally, he also intended to weaken France, part of his wider foreign policy objectives, as France had close links with the left Popular Front government that Franco and the generals were attempting to overthrow. Thus, Mussolini would prevent France from gaining influence in a left-wing Spain, and would strengthen his own strategic position in the Mediterranean.

Zara Steiner highlights another reason:

> *Mussolini saw in the Spanish War an opportunity to fashion the "new Italy" and "the new Italian". "There is only one way to create a warlike people", the Duce claimed, "to have ever greater masses who have waged war and ever greater masses who want to go to war".* — Steiner, 2011

However, unlike during his invasion of Abyssinia, Mussolini did not have a clear plan when he sent his forces to Spain; nor were there clear "nationalist" goals that could appeal to the wider Italian population. Italy sent more assistance, including 70,000 troops, to Franco than any other country and the war raged on far longer than he had anticipated.

TOK

Spend 30 minutes reviewing the primary sources in the case studies you have covered thus far. With a partner discuss how far you agree with the following statement:

"Sources from the time are always biased and give an incomplete picture of events." Follow up on your discussion by considering how the limitations of sources pose a challenge for historians. Feedback to the class.

The Spanish Civil War 1936–39

The Spanish Civil War was a war fought between Spanish Republican forces, who supported the democratically elected left-wing coalition Popular Front government and Spanish Nationalist forces who supported conservative and right-wing groups. These included fascists, supporters of the church, the military and the royal family. The Nationalists, led by General Franco, had attempted to seize power in a coup in July 1936. A civil war developed, when the Nationalist forces failed to take the capital, Madrid, and half the army remained loyal to the government.

What were the results of intervention in the Spanish Civil War?

Although the intervention was supported by the Church as Franco's forces had aligned themselves with the Roman Catholic Church in Spain, it was not generally popular with Italians. Indeed, the consequences were mainly negative for Italy:

- The economic cost had been high; the lira was devalued and it lost half its foreign currency reserves. The total cost of the war amounted to around 14 billion lire and it led to Italy increasing its trade with Germany.

- One third of Italy's arms stocks were consumed by the war. Although Italy had helped secure a right-wing regime in Europe, and was on the winning side, Italy's military weakness had been exposed. For example, Italian forces were roundly defeated by the International Brigades fighting for the Republic at the Battle of Guadalajara in March 1937.

- Italian submarine attacks on supply ships led to increased tension between Italy and France and Britain.

- General Franco maintained his independence and Spain did not become an Italian satellite state.

- Italy drew closer to Germany.

ATL Thinking skills

1 What does the extract below from the historian Richard Overy suggest about:

- the economic impact that Mussolini's wars in Abyssinia and Spain had on Italy

- the impact of domestic economic weaknesses on Italian foreign policy?

War had become an addiction for Mussolini. His conversation had always been spiced with a vocabulary of conflict, but after Ethiopia and Spain, he came to see himself as a great war leader. In March, 1938, jealous of the King's position as formal head of the armed forces, he appointed himself and his monarch as "First Marshals of the Empire" to create a spurious equality between them. Yet without expanding and modernizing Italy's armed forces, future warfare was in jeopardy … The limited effort in Ethiopia and Spain forced Italy to spend almost as much of her national income on armaments as richer, industrialized Germany, and twice as much as Britain or France. From 1937 onward Mussolini, who now bore sole responsibility for the three service departments in the Italian government, began to authorize substantial new programmes of rearmament … The great weakness of the Italian strategic position was the economy. Italy was heavily reliant on foreign sources of raw materials, particularly coal, oil and iron ore, and was very vulnerable to blockade … She lacked the real means to play the part of a great power. Mussolini declared the need for a policy of self-sufficiency … To ensure that the strategy worked, the state extended controls over the economy like in Germany, on trade, investment, and labour utilization. By 1939 the state owned 80% of the country's arms capacity. Italy was transformed into a war economy in peacetime.

Overy, R and Wheatcroft, A. 2009. *The Road to War: The origins of World War II*, pages 222–23. Random House. London, UK

Changing diplomatic alignments in Europe after 1936

The new relationship between Fascist Italy and Nazi Germany

One of the key results of the Spanish Civil War for Mussolini was that he now committed himself to a formal alliance with Germany by signing the Rome–Berlin Axis Alliance on 25 October 1936. This coalition agreement between Italy and Germany was drawn up by Italian Foreign Minister Galeazzo Ciano.

Source skills

A public speech announcing the Rome–Berlin Axis by Benito Mussolini, 1 November 1936.

This vertical line between Rome and Berlin is an axis around which all the European states animated by the will for collaboration and peace can collaborate. It is not a matter of surprise that today we hoist the flag of anti-Bolshevism …

We have in common many elements of our Weltanschauung [world view]. Not only have National Socialism and Fascism everywhere the same enemies, in the service of the same master, the Third International, but they have many conceptions of life and history in common. Both believe in will as the determining power in the life of nations and the driving force of their history … Both are based on young people, whom we train in discipline, courage, resistance, love of the fatherland, and contempt for easy living … Germany and Italy follow the same goal in the sphere of economic autarky. Without economic independence the political independence of a nation is doubtful.

First question, part a – 3 marks

According to this source, what key factors do Mussolini's Italy and Hitler's Germany have in common?

The end of Italian participation in Collective Security

Italy joined the Anti-Comintern Pact in November 1937, with Germany and Japan. The Pact was directed against the Communist International, and stated that in the case of an attack by the Soviet Union the signatories would consult on measures to "safeguard their common interests". By joining the Pact, the member states now formed the group that would become the Axis Powers. Although Italy had drawn closer to Germany during the mid-1930s, the Axis Pact is seen by some historians as a key turning point for Italian foreign policy. Indeed, in December 1937 Italy left the League of Nations.

Italy's new relationship with Germany was most starkly apparent with regard to Austria. As you have already read, Mussolini had promoted and protected Austrian independence since the end of the First World War. Indeed, he had successfully warned Hitler off *Anschluss* in 1934. However, in 1936 Mussolini told the Austrian government to deal directly with Germany, thus implying that Italy would no longer protect it, and in 1938 he accepted *Anchluss* when Hitler invaded Austria. This represented a major shift in the Italian position on Austria. The creation of Austria had been a key strategic gain for Italy at Versailles, and Mussolini's shift in policy was not popular domestically.

> **Third International**
> This was also known as the Communist International or Comintern. It was an association of national Communist Parties founded in 1919.

143

Source skills

Source A

Denis Mack Smith. *Mussolini* **(1983).**

After the Nazis won power in January 1933, Mussolini had ideological as well as pragmatic reasons for closer ties with Germany. "The victory of Hitler is also our victory" was his immediate comment: a victory he had helped with arms and money and which raised the possibility of creating a new Rome-Berlin axis. Hitler sent him messages of homage and admiration, and other Germans were ready with positive encouragement for Italy to replace France as the dominant power in North Africa and the Mediterranean. If this encouragement was sincere, here was a basis for agreement. Tentative feelers were therefore put out to see whether the Germans would agree to confine their ambitions to Poland and the Baltic, leaving Italy free in the Mediterranean and the Balkans … One obstacle to such an axis was Hitler's ideas about racial inequality … A more serious obstacle to an entente with Germany was the Nazi ambition to annex Austria, whereas Mussolini had confidently promised to defend his country against "Prussian barbarism" … Three times in 1933, Dollfuss was brought to Italy and given a clear promise that, if both the Nazi and socialist parties in Austria were suppressed, Italian military support could be relied upon to prevent a German invasion.

Source B

The German Ambassador to Italy reports back to the German Foreign Ministry his conversation with Mussolini in January 1936.

[Mussolini] thought it would now be possible to achieve a fundamental improvement in German-Italian relations and to dispose of the only dispute, namely, the Austrian problem … The simplest method would be for Berlin and Vienna themselves to settle their relations … in the form of a treaty of friendship … which would in practice bring Austria into Germany's wake, so that she could pursue no other foreign policy than one parallel with that of Germany. If Austria, as a formally quite independent state, were thus in practice to become a German satellite, he would raise no objection.

Source C

A cartoon by David Low, "European clothes-line", published in the UK newspaper, the *Evening Standard* **on 9 May 1933.**

EUROPEAN CLOTHES-LINE.

First question, part a – 3 marks

According to Source A, what were the key areas of dispute between Italy and Germany?

First question, part b – 2 marks

What is the message of Source C?

Second question – 4 marks

With reference to the origin, purpose and content of Source B, assess the values and limitations of this source for a historian studying Mussolini's position on Austria in the 1930s.

ATL **Thinking and self-management skills**

1   In pairs, discuss the reasons for the change in Mussolini's position towards Austria by 1938.

2   How far was the alliance between Mussolini and Hitler an alliance of equals?

What was Italy's role during the Sudetenland crisis in September 1938?

See page 178 for a full account of the Sudetenland Crisis.

During the Munich crisis in September 1938, Mussolini assumed a high profile. He wanted to be seen as a great broker of peace, helping to avert a general war. Following Chamberlain's failure to gain a peace, deal over the Sudetenland after two meetings in Germany, Mussolini stepped in as a "peacemaker" at Munich. He was hailed in Europe as the architect of peace.

However, it was clear by this time that Mussolini was now subservient to Hitler; in fact, he had simply put forward Hitler's own plan for the Sudetenland. In March 1939, Hitler broke the Munich Agreement and invaded the rest of Czechoslovakia.

The Munich Agreement highlighted the weakness of Britain and France, and Mussolini was now determined to take advantage of this. In November 1938, he instructed the Italian parliament to demand the annexation of Corsica, Nice and Tunis from France. Mussolini believed that he could win a war against France, and do so with German support. Britain had shown itself desperate to prevent a war, at almost any price.

Source skills

Source A

Mussolini's speech to the Fascist Grand Council, February 1939.

Italy is surrounded by an inland sea which is connected to the oceans by the Suez Canal … and by the straits of Gibraltar, dominated by the guns of Great Britain.

Italy therefore does not have free access to the oceans; Italy therefore is actually a prisoner in the Mediterranean and the more populated and powerful she becomes the more she will suffer from her imprisonment.

The bars of the prison are Corsica, Tunisia, Malta, Cyprus; the guards of this prison are Gibraltar and Suez. Corsica is a pistol pointed at the heart of Italy; while Malta and Cyprus are a threat to all our positions in the central and western Mediterranean. Greece, Turkey, Egypt are all states ready to link up with Great Britain and complete the political and military encirclement of Italy …

… From this situation, you can draw the following conclusions:

1. The task of Italian policy, which cannot and does not have territorial aims in continental Europe except for Albania, is initially to break the bars of the prison.

2. Once the bars have been broken, Italian policy has only one direction: to march to the ocean.

Which ocean? The Indian Ocean, connecting Libya to Ethiopia through the Sudan, or the Atlantic Ocean through French North Africa.

In both cases, we come up against Anglo-French opposition. It is stupid to try to resolve this problem without covering our backs on the Continent. The policy of the Rome-Berlin Axis thus caters for this fundamentally important historical question.

Source B

Richard Overy and Andrew Wheatcroft, British professors of history, in an academic book *The Road to War: The Origins of World War II* (2009).

After Munich Mussolini's options became narrower still. The German success fed his desire to share with Hitler the opportunity presented by Western weakness to "change the map of the world", to make Italian policy genuinely independent of the approval of the West. But at the same time he knew that Italy was not yet strong enough to risk war with a major state. Tied down militarily in Africa and Spain, with a weakened economy, Italy did not pose the same threat as Germany. Chamberlain confessed that if he could get a German settlement he would not "give a rap for Musso". On the other hand Mussolini was aware that Britain and France were not the powers they had been in the 1920s. His analysis of the old empires as decadent and spineless, first formulated in 1935, seemed truer after Munich.

First question, part a – 3 marks

What, according to Source A, are key foreign policy aims for Mussolini's Italy?

Second question – 4 marks

With reference to its origin, purpose and content, assess the values and limitations of Source B for historians studying Mussolini's foreign policy in the 1930s.

Class discussion

Read Source A again.

Discuss the following questions:

1 What continuity was there in Mussolini's foreign policy in the 1930s?

2 What changes had occurred by 1939 in Mussolini's foreign policy objectives?

Why did Italy invade Albania in April 1939?

Hitler broke the terms of the Munich Agreement in March 1939 when he invaded the rest of Czechoslovakia. Nazi Germany had now gone beyond revision of the Treaty of Versailles and had seized control of a sovereign state. Mussolini had not been consulted by Hitler. He was only informed of the conquest after the fact. Mussolini now wanted to regain the initiative and emulate Hitler's success.

On 7 April 1939, Italy made a punitive assault on Albania. The invasion of Albania was rather meaningless as the country had been for some time a satellite state (see page 101). However, Mussolini wanted to assert Italian strength in order to imitate Hitler's successful expansion, intimidate Yugoslavia, and pursue his ambition of dominating the Adriatic. Dino Grandi claimed that the conquest of Albania would *"open the ancient paths of the Roman conquests in the east to the Italy of Mussolini"* and threaten Britain *"with the loss of its naval bases, and our complete domination of the Eastern Mediterranean"*.

▲ Italian forces landing at Durazzo, Albania

How did Italy take over Albania?

King Zog of Albania had attempted to assert some independence from Italy when in 1934 he signed trade agreements with Greece and Yugoslavia. He had also refused to be intimidated when Mussolini sent warships to the region. When, on 25 March, Mussolini sent an ultimatum to the capital, Tirana, demanding agreement to the Italian occupation of Albania, King Zog refused.

Zog had attempted to keep the Italian ultimatum secret. However, the news was leaked and even the distraction of the birth of a royal baby, his heir, on 5 April did not prevent widespread anti-Italian demonstrations on 6 April. Mussolini sent 100 planes to fly over Tirana dropping leaflets telling the Albanians to submit but the demonstrators demanded weapons to fight the Italians. Then, although a mobilization of the Albanian reserves was issued, many Albanian officers and government officials fled the country. Nevertheless, King Zog broadcast a public address to his people stating he would resist Italian occupation.

Source skills

Source A

G. Bruce Strang. *On the Fiery March: Mussolini prepares for war* **(2003).**

Ciano had been considering annexing Albania. The Anschluss, while disquieting for Italy, also threatened Yugoslavia. He mused that [Yugoslav Prime Minister] Stoyadinovic's need for Italian friendship might mean that the Yugoslavian prime minister would be prepared to sacrifice Albania's independence in order to secure an Italo-Yugoslav alliance. Mussolini later agreed, saying that he was prepared to face a war, "as long as we get Albania". Ciano's tour of Albania, preceding Hitler's visit to Italy, had represented a kind of reconnaissance mission; Mussolini and Ciano needed better information to determine whether or not their project was desirable or feasible. Upon his return, Ciano submitted a report that encouraged Mussolini's expansionist desire. Albania had excellent agricultural potential, Ciano wrote, and had very extensive deposits of coal, though no one had yet completed a full list of Albania's potential mineral wealth. On the strategic side, there were several advantages. In the wake of Anschluss, German economic, cultural, and political tentacles would reach into the former Austrian sphere of influence. A firm warning from Italy and subsequent annexation of Albania would prevent any further German penetration there.

Source B

Robert Mallet. *Mussolini and the Origins of the Second World War* **(1983).**

Less than a month after Hitler took Prague, the regime in Rome ordered the invasion of Albania. The idea of an outright annexation of the Balkan state had been under consideration by Mussolini since the time of Hitler's visit to Rome. It had also been the subject of some discussion by the naval staff and the chiefs of staff as a whole. As we have already seen, Cavagnari had urged Bagoglio to give the Italian strategic position in the Adriatic greater focus from his very first days in charge of the navy. Subsequently, the naval staff had demanded, in the immediate aftermath of the Mediterranean crisis of 1935, that

consideration be given to an outright invasion of Albania as a means of securing Italian domination of the Adriatic. Determined to secure some form of immediate gain from their developing, if tricky, relationship with Berlin, Mussolini and Ciano ordered the operation to go ahead in early April. The invasion, which included a naval bombardment of the port of Durazzo, brought widespread condemnation, and precipitated yet another crisis in Whitehall. It also poured scorn on Mussolini's declaration of peaceful Italian intentions during his meeting with Chamberlain in January.

Third question – 6 marks

Compare and contrast the views expressed in Source A and Source B regarding Italian motives for invading Albania in April 1939.

> **Examiner's hint:** *Take a copy of the above sources. Using different coloured pens to underline or highlight the text, identify the following comparisons and contrasts.*
>
> **Comparisons**
>
> - *Mussolini had been considering annexing Albania for some time.*
>
> - *There were strategic reasons for annexing Albania.*
>
> - *The Italian relationship with Germany influenced Italy's decision to invade.*
>
> **Contrasts**
>
> - *Source A highlights the role of the Italian Foreign Minister Ciano in the decision to invade, whereas Source B highlights the role of the Italian Navy.*
>
> - *Source B focuses on the motive of dominating the Adriatic, whereas Source A focuses on the economic gains to be made in Albania.*
>
> - *Source A suggests the invasion was to prevent Germany increasing influence in the area, whereas Source B suggests that it was motivated by Italy attempting to gain from its developing relationship with Germany.*
>
> - *Source A only considers the reasons for the invasion, whereas Source B also considers the results, specifically the impact on relations with Britain.*

On 7 April, led by General Alfredo Guzzoni, Italy invaded Albania with a force of 100,000 men and 600 aircraft. The Albanian army that faced them had only 15,000 badly equipped troops which had been trained by the Italians. King Zog had hoped to fight a war of resistance in the mountains, but Italian agents sabotaged the Albanians' limited equipment. By the afternoon of the very first day of fighting, all ports were in Italian hands. The King and his family fled to Greece.

On 8 April, Italian forces entered Tirana and seized control of all government buildings. Then, on 12 April, the Albanian parliament deposed King Zog in absentia and voted to unite with Italy in "personal union".

Albania withdrew from the League of Nations on 15 April 1939. The Italians then set up a Fascist government under Shefqet Verlaci. The Albanian foreign office was merged with the Italian foreign ministry and the Albanian army was put under Italian command. Mussolini declared the official creation of the Italian Empire and King Victor Emmanuel, already Emperor of Ethiopia, was crowned King of Albania.

Mussolini would later use Albania as a base from which to launch an invasion of Greece on 28 October 1940.

Italy and the Second World War

Changing diplomatic alignments in Europe after 1939

The Pact of Steel, or Pact of Friendship and Alliance, was signed between Italy and Germany on 22 May 1939. The Pact comprised two sections: the first was a declaration of trust and cooperation between the two nations; the second, a secret protocol, fostered a union of military and economic policies. The original intention had been to include Japan in the Pact but Japan had wanted the focus to be anti-Soviet, whereas Italy and Germany wanted the agreement aimed at Britain and France. (See pages 181–182 for more discussion of the Pact of Steel.)

Despite the Pact of Steel's apparent show of unity, Hitler and his foreign minister, Ribbentrop, negotiated the Nazi–Soviet Pact in August 1939 between the Soviet Union and Germany (see page 183). Mussolini was only told about the agreement two days before it was signed.

> **Class discussion**
>
> In small groups, discuss the impact of Fascism on Italian foreign policy up to April 1939. Does everyone in your group agree on the impact of fascism on foreign policy?
>
> What conclusions can be drawn from your discussions?

Source skills

Richard Overy and Andrew Wheatcroft. *The Road to War: The Origins of World War II* **(2009).**

Now that Mussolini had restored his prestige in Albania by matching German with Italian "dynamism", he began to contemplate a unilateral approach to Germany with the offer of an alliance which he was to call the "Pact of Blood". There was strong resistance to such an idea inside Italy, even from the ranks of senior Fascists. The generals were hostile to further dangerous commitments; public opinion was strongly anti-German. Secret police reports showed a growing wave of opposition to war, economic crisis and the link to Germany … Mussolini knew that he was increasingly on his own and resented the humiliating evidence of anti-German sentiment. No doubt honour had something to do with his decision … In May he sent Ciano to Berlin with authority to sign an immediate agreement with Hitler pledging full military assistance in the event of German involvement in war. On 22nd May the agreement was signed; Mussolini changed its name to the more teutonic "Pact of Steel". German leaders were surprised and suspicious at Mussolini's move, though pleased enough that Italian promises might neutralize the threat from the West over Poland.

First question, part a – 3 marks

According to Overy and Wheatcroft, why was there resistance in Italy to the idea of a Pact of Steel with Germany?

Why did Italy remain a non-belligerent in 1939?

When Hitler invaded Poland on 1 September 1939, he unleashed a general European War. During negotiations over the Pact of Steel, Mussolini had suggested that Italy would not be ready for a general war until 1943. Thus, when Hitler ignited war over Poland, Mussolini declared Italy a non-belligerent.

It would seem that Mussolini's response to the outbreak of war in Europe in September 1939 was against his aims of creating a "warlike" militarized society and his view that war strengthened a nation. It was also against the terms of the Pact of Steel with Hitler. Some historians have argued that from 1936 Mussolini had sealed the fate of Italy, and from then on he was on a path directed by Nazi Germany. However, the Italian historian Renzo De Felice asserts that this was not the case and that Mussolini had continued to consider an alliance with Britain and France against Germany until 1940. (De Felice has been criticized by left-wing historians in Italy, such as Paolo Alatri, for being too sympathetic to Mussolini and an apologist for fascism.) However, it could be argued that Mussolini was being realistic in not joining the war. Italy had been waging war for several years, in Africa and in Europe, and the country was war weary and could not afford to join a general European conflict.

Why did Italy join the war in June 1940?

Despite having declared Italy non-belligerent, it was difficult for Mussolini to keep Italy out of the war for several reasons:

- Not to join the war was something of an embarrassment for the Fascist leader; it was contrary to his Fascist doctrine and at odds with his portrayal of confident and decisive leadership as *Il Duce*.
- Mussolini did not want Italy to become a lesser rank power by staying neutral; he did not want to be "another Switzerland". In April 1940, he said: "*To make a people great [the country] must be sent into battle*".
- The war could give Mussolini the opportunity to radicalize the regime and to remove the influence of conservatives and the Church.
- If Italy remained neutral and Germany won the war, Europe would be dominated by a Germany that would be hostile towards Italy because it had remained neutral.
- The war could bring territorial gains and perhaps control over the Mediterranean.

However, in the end, the Italian motives for joining the Second World War in June 1940 were predominantly economic. Germany had been a principal buyer of Italy's food and textiles, and by August 1939 it owed Italy US $40 million. Italy received German coal in return and became dependent on it. This German coal – two thirds of the Italian supply – had to be delivered by sea. In March 1940, Britain blockaded all German coal ports.

In June 1940, Mussolini declared war on Britain and France.

Source skills

Source A

Mussolini's declaration of war on Britain and France, June 1940.

After having solved the problem of our land frontiers, we are taking up arms in establishing our sea frontiers. We want to break the territorial and military chains that are strangling us in our own sea. A nation of 45 million souls is not truly free unless it has free access to the ocean.

This gigantic struggle is only one phase of the logical development of our revolution … it is the struggle of young and fertile peoples against sterile ones who stand on the verge of decline; it is the struggle between centuries and two ideas.

Delzell, C. 1971.

First question, part a – 3 marks

What are the key points made by Mussolini in Source A?

First question, part b – 2 marks

What is the message conveyed by Source B?

Source B

A 1941 poster showing Italian, Japanese, German and Italian soldiers attacking. The text reads "Victory! For the new social order, for civilization".

PER IL NUOVO ORDINE SOCIALE, PER LA CIVILTÀ

Perspectives

Italian historiography

In general, "left-wing" historians in Italy assert that Mussolini had an overtly aggressive foreign policy and expansionist aims. The "right-wing" historians, such as Renzo De Felice (Mussolini's Italian biographer), argue that Italy did not have large-scale expansionist plans. De Felice views Mussolini's foreign policy in the context of the policies pursued before 1914 by the liberal Italian government. He argues that, from the 1920s up to at least 1935, Mussolini wanted to get France's agreement to establish Italy as a great power with an expanded empire in North Africa. To this end, he was advised to pursue the "policy of the pendulum" or, in other words, to be the decisive weight in European relations. In addition, the right-wing historians generally claim that the alliance with Hitler's Germany was not sealed in order to pursue imperialist objectives. Britain's pressure on France to follow sanctions over Abyssinia may have fostered a new course. Felice suggests that Mussolini remained equivocal about Hitler, and hoped to attain his objectives by making one side and then the other pay for his support. Mussolini continued to follow this plan until his decision to enter the Second World War in June 1940.

The British historian AJP Taylor

Taylor suggests that Mussolini had expansionist goals, but that there was a lot of conflict between the foreign policies of Hitler and Mussolini. He argues, however, that Mussolini thought Hitler would agree to leave Austria independent and that Italy could then play France and Germany off against each other while gaining concessions from both. The problem was that Hitler intended to achieve *Anschluss*.

The German historian Gerhard Schreiber

Schreiber sees Mussolini's foreign policy as dependent on socio-economic domestic policy. In his view, foreign policy was used for propaganda purposes, and its real aim was to gain domestic consensus and limited imperial expansion. He claims that Mussolini had no clear strategy aligned to Nazi Germany, and was more a victim of his own public promises to his people that he would create a Fascist empire. By the summer of 1940 he therefore had no choice but to join Germany in a general European war.

Mussolini's actions in the war up to 1941

Following Mussolini's declaration of war, there were some limited air raids and skirmishes between Italy and France before an armistice came into effect on 25th June 1940.

Mussolini expanded the war in Europe in the Mediterranean and into North Africa. Italian forces invaded Egypt from the Italian colony of Libya, whilst another Italian force invaded Greece from Albania. However, both of these Italian offensives failed due to the British response. Mussolini's failures meant Hitler's forces were drawn into both the Balkans and North Africa. German forces took Yugoslavia and Greece in April 1941, and forced an evacuation of British forces. Hitler's forces, under General Rommel, had pushed the British back and advanced as far as El Alamein in Egypt by June 1942.

ATL Self-management skills

Consider Mussolini's foreign policy aims:

- increase national pride
- consolidate domestic support for his regime
- revise the settlement of 1919–20
- dominate the Balkans
- dominate the Mediterranean
- build an empire, gain *spazio vitale* (living space), and expand territories in Africa
- foster the spread of Fascism.

For each of these aims, identify the extent to which it had been achieved by 1941 and give evidence for your conclusions.

Full document question: Italy's invasion of Abyssinia

Source A

La domenica del Corriere, weekend supplement of the Italian newspaper *Corriere della Sera,* depicting Italian Blackshirts in action against Abyssinian forces, January 1936.

Le Camicie Nere al passo di Uarieu. I militi della Divisione XXVIII Ottobre, dopo aver resistito per due giorni agli assalti delle truppe scelte dei ras Cassa e Sejum, attaccano alla baionetta sbaragliando definitivamente gli assalitori. (Disegno di A. Beltrame).

Source B

Memorandum from Marshal Badoglio, Chief of General Staff to Mussolini, December 1934.

The problem of Italian-Abyssinian relations has very recently shifted from a diplomatic plane to one which can be solved by force alone ... The object ... is nothing more or less then the complete destruction of the Abyssinian army and the total conquest of Abyssinia. In no other way can we build the Empire ... The speedier our action the less likely will be the danger of diplomatic complications. In the Japanese fashion there will be no need whatsoever officially for a declaration of war and in any case we must always emphasise the purely defensive character of operations. No one in Europe would raise any difficulties provided the prosecution of operations resulted rapidly in an accomplished fact. It would suffice to declare to England and France that their interests would be recognised.

Source C

Ruth Henig. *The Origins of the Second World War 1933–41* (1985).

Since his ascension to power in 1922, the Fascist leader had made no secret of his ambition to raise Italy's status as a European power by increasing its influence around the Mediterranean and by expanding its empire. Unlike Japan, however, Mussolini lacked a strong economic base and well-equipped, effective military forces, and the onset of the Depression made it even harder for him to secure them. Thus he aimed in the short term to seek glorious expansion on the cheap, possibly in Africa at the expense of Abyssinia, but for that he needed the agreement, or at least tacit consent, of Britain and France ... Mussolini was inclined more and more towards the prospect of a glorious, short, triumphant war of conquest.

Source D

Martin Blinkhorn. *Mussolini and Fascist Italy,* (1984).

The conquest of Ethiopia represented Mussolini's accomplishment of what had been an Italian nationalist dream for half a century. Neither the problems of the depression nor the African interests of certain industrial pressure groups were sufficient to dictate it. Existing colonies were failing to attract the millions of potential emigrants beloved of fascist propaganda, and were proving unrewarding to the few thousand who actually settled there; moreover, their administration, policing and economic infrastructures constituted a considerable drain on the Italian treasury. The explanation for the attack on Ethiopia thus lies in fascism and its Duce. The fascist need for excitement, conflict and dramatic success was perfectly personified in Mussolini himself and sanctified by the puerile *machismo* of the Duce cult. Other dictators such as Franco in Spain and Salazar in Portugal constructed personal cults on the appeal of stability and lack of excitement. Neither Mussolini's personality nor the psychology of fascism rendered such a thing conceivable.

First question, part a – 3 marks

According to Source B how should an Italian invasion of Abyssinia be executed?

First question, part b – 2 marks

What is the message of the artist in Source A?

Second question – 4 marks

With reference to its origin, purpose and content, assess the values and limitations of Source B for historians studying the Italian invasion of Abyssinia.

Third question – 6 marks

Compare and contrast the views expressed in Source B and Source C regarding Mussolini's motives for invading Abyssinia.

Fourth question – 9 marks

Using the sources and your own knowledge, analyse the reasons for the Italian invasion of Abyssinia.

Class discussion

Source B was written in 1934. Which events does it refer to when it says: "in the Japanese fashion there will be no need for a declaration of war…" What links are suggested here between events in Asia and Japanese expansionism and Italian expansionist plans?

References

Blinkhorn, M. 1984. *Mussolini and Fascist Italy*. Methuen. London, UK

Calvitt Clarke, J and Foust, C. 1991. *Russia and Italy against Hitler: The Bolshevik-Fascist Rapprochement of the 1930s*. Greenwood Press. New York, USA

De Felice, R. 1981. *Mussolini il duce: Lo Stato totalitario (1936–40)*. Einaudi. Turin, Italy

Delzell, C. 1971. *Mediterranean Fascism, 1919–45: Selected Documents*. Macmillan. London, UK

Henig, R. 1985. *The Origins of the Second World War 1933–41*. Routledge. London, UK

Knight, P. 2003. *Mussolini and Fascism*. Routledge. London, UK

Lowe, C and Marzari, F. 1975. *Italian Foreign Policy, 1870–1940*. Routledge. London, UK

Mack Smith, D. 1983. *Mussolini*, page 210. Paladin Books. London, UK

Mallet, R. 1983. *Mussolini and the Origins of the Second World War, 1933–40*. Palgrave Macmillan. London, UK

Overy, R and Wheatcroft, A. 2009. *The Road to War: The Origins of World War II*. Random House. London, UK

Steiner, Z. 2011. *The Triumph of the Dark: European International History 1933–1999*. Oxford University Press. New York, USA

Strang, G. 2003. *On the Fiery March: Mussolini Prepares for War*. Praeger. Westport, CT, USA

2.4 German expansion, 1933–1938

Conceptual understanding

Key concepts

→ Causation

→ Consequence

→ Continuity

Key questions

→ Examine the ways in which Hitler challenged the post-war settlement.

→ Discuss the consequences of Hitler's actions for the international situation.

▲ Adolf Hitler, taken in 1933

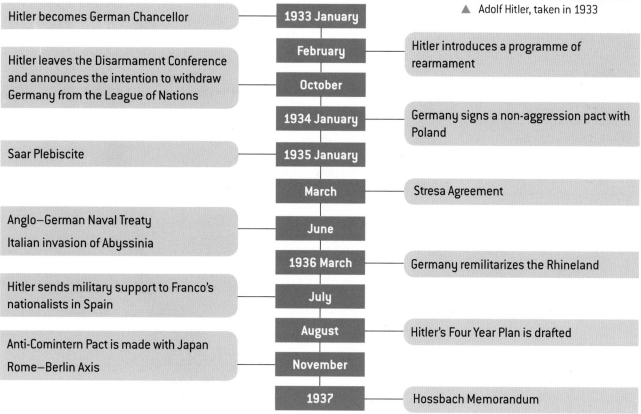

Hitler becomes German Chancellor	**1933 January**	
	February	Hitler introduces a programme of rearmament
Hitler leaves the Disarmament Conference and announces the intention to withdraw Germany from the League of Nations	**October**	
	1934 January	Germany signs a non-aggression pact with Poland
Saar Plebiscite	**1935 January**	
	March	Stresa Agreement
Anglo–German Naval Treaty Italian invasion of Abyssinia	**June**	
	1936 March	Germany remilitarizes the Rhineland
Hitler sends military support to Franco's nationalists in Spain	**July**	
	August	Hitler's Four Year Plan is drafted
Anti-Comintern Pact is made with Japan Rome–Berlin Axis	**November**	
	1937	Hossbach Memorandum

As we have seen, Hitler's main foreign policy aim after achieving power was to destroy the Versailles Peace Settlement, which had to be carried out alongside rearmament. This was achieved between 1933 and 1938 and, in the process, the stage was set for further territorial claims and the outbreak of general war in Europe in 1939.

Changing diplomatic alignments in Europe after 1933

The response of Britain and France to his actions after 1933 would be key for Hitler and his goal of overturning the Treaty of Versailles; Germany's position in Europe was still vulnerable and it remained under the constraints of the Treaty of Versailles. Fortunately for Hitler, the international situation after 1933 worked to his advantage.

Britain

Britain was pre-occupied not only with the economic crisis but also by events in the Far East, where it was worried about Japanese expansion. Its resources were already overstretched, with its main priority being the safety of the British Empire. Many British politicians also considered the Treaty of Versailles to be unfair and supported some redress of "legitimate grievances". Many right-wing politicians in Britain were also afraid of the communist dictator, Stalin, and had sympathy with Hitler, who they also saw as a buffer to the spread of communism from the East.

France

France was very concerned by the possible German threat but was too weak to act on its own, especially after the failure of its 1923 intervention in the Ruhr. It was also politically divided, following a series of weak governments, and had major economic problems. Lacking support from the USA or Britain in the task of preserving the Versailles settlement, it built a defensive line of fortresses along the Maginot Line between 1929 and 1938. It also developed alliances with countries on Germany's eastern borders: Poland and "The Little Entente" countries – Czechoslovakia, Romania and Yugoslavia.

> **The Little Entente**
>
> This was a series of treaties between Romania, Czechoslovakia and Yugoslavia, which were concluded from 1920 to 1921, and aimed to prevent Austria and Hungary from regaining territory lost after the First World War.

The USA

The economic depression meant that the USA was focused on domestic concerns and was unlikely to change its isolationist stance.

Other factors also worked in Hitler's favour:

- The international economic situation was encouraging national insularity rather than collective security.

- The memories of the First World War were still acute, and the horror of this war made many determined to take any measures necessary to prevent another war.

- The need to avoid another war was reinforced by the military weakness of Britain and France at this time.

- Britain and France were unable to agree on a common policy for dealing with Hitler.

- The League of Nation's perceived failure to deal effectively with Japanese expansion in Manchuria was a blow to both the Washington System and to the League itself.

- The revision of the Treaty of Versailles had already begun; Britain and France evacuated the Rhineland in 1929–30 and German reparation payments were effectively cancelled at the Lausanne Conference of 1932.

However, as the historian Zara Steiner writes,

even allowing for the breakdown of the international regime, Hitler moved with a speed and ultimate purpose that clearly distinguished him from his predecessors — Steiner, 2011: 95

Germany's challenges to the post-war settlements, 1933–38

Although the international situation favoured Hitler's aims, he still had to be careful to avoid an international backlash. He thus followed a cautious policy. Publicly, Hitler claimed that he desired only peace, and he worked carefully to defuse any potential opposition. However, his actions over the next five years undermined collective security: he worked to withdraw Germany from multilateral commitments that might limit his action, he isolated France by undermining existing alliances, and, at the same time, he negotiated alliances with Britain and Italy. Alongside these actions, Hitler was able to effectively challenge the Treaty of Versailles and to increase the prestige and power of his own dictatorship and of Germany within Europe.

Challenging the Treaty of Versailles: Withdrawal from the Disarmament Conference

Article 8 of the Covenant of the League of Nations had demanded that national armaments be "reduced to the lowest point consistent with national safety". However, the difficulties in implementing an international disarmament policy meant that it took until 1932 for an international conference to be organized.

When the Disarmament Conference finally convened in Geneva in 1933, there was still little consensus on how disarmament could be achieved. France, in particular, was unwilling to disarm with the new threat of Nazism on its borders. The events unfolding at the same time in Manchuria were also not conducive to thinking about disarmament.

Furthermore, it was clear that Britain and France did not agree about the way that Germany should be treated, with Britain indicating that it was prepared to make concessions to Germany.

German governments prior to Hitler had requested parity of armaments, arguing that Germany would participate only if other countries reduced their armaments to Germany's level, or allowed Germany to rearm to theirs. When France refused this at the Disarmament Conference in 1933, Hitler pulled out of both the Conference and the League of Nations, claiming that these organizations were part of a French conspiracy to keep Germany weak and incapable of self-defence. In November 1933, a plebiscite gave Hitler 95% approval for his actions, with Germans rejoicing that Germany had at last stood up to the "victors". Hitler's withdrawal from the talks and the League gave him the freedom he needed to launch an assault on the rest of the Treaty of Versailles.

Source skills

Source A

A speech by Hitler, broadcast on 14 October 1933.

Germany cannot tolerate the deliberate degradation of the nation by the perpetuation of a discrimination which consists in withholding the rights which are granted as a matter of course to other nations … The men who are at present the leaders of Germany have nothing in common with the traitors of November 1918. Like every decent Englishman and every decent Frenchman, we all had our duty to our Fatherland and placed our lives at its service. We are not responsible for the war but we feel responsible for what every honest man must do in the time of his country's distress and for what we have done. We have such infinite love for our people that we desire wholeheartedly an understanding with other nations … but, as men of honour, it is impossible for us to be members of institutions under conditions which are only bearable to those devoid of a sense of honour …

Since it has been made clear to us from the declarations of certain Great Powers that they were not prepared to consider real equality of rights of Germany at present, we have decided that it is impossible, in view of the indignity of her position, for Germany to continue to force her company upon other nations.

Source B

Gordon A. Craig, writing in an academic book *Germany 1866–1945* (1978).

It was necessary to avoid appearing the villain of the piece. When the rupture came, [Hitler's] foreign minister told Nadolny later in the month, "the lack of an intention to disarm on France's part must be seen to be the cause".

In the end, Hitler effected his purpose by using tactics that foreshadowed those he would employ in the Sudeten affair five years later: he made demands at Geneva that he was reasonably sure that the other powers would not accept. He insisted that equality of status was not enough and that, since the other powers were reluctant to reduce their forces to Germany's level, all controls must be lifted so that it could seek actual equality in its own way. To this kind of intransigence the French, supported by the British government, refused to yield, insisting on a waiting period in which Germany could prove its good faith and give some indication of what its intentions were. This gave Hitler the excuse he needed and, brushing aside an Italian attempt to find a compromise, he announced on 14 October 1933 that Germany was ending both its participation in the conference and its membership of the League of Nations, an institution that he had always regarded as a symbol of Germany's second class status and for whose members, including the German ones, he privately felt contempt.

First question, part a – 3 marks

What, according to Source A, is Germany's attitude towards international cooperation?

Third question – 6 marks

Compare and contrast the views expressed in Source A and Source B regarding Hitler and the Disarmament Conference.

Examiner's hint: *Highlight the comparisons and contrasts in the sources as shown below. Then write two full paragraphs showing clear linkage between the sources and giving brief quotes to support your points.*

Similarities

- *In Source A, Hitler talks about degradation and "perpetuation of a discrimination" and Source B refers to Germany seeing itself as a "second class" member of the League of Nations.*

- *Source A talks about "equality of rights" for Germany. Source B also says that Germany was looking for "equality".*

- *Source A blames "certain great powers" for not allowing Germany to be on an equal footing and Source B specifically names France as a country that "refused to yield".*

- *Source B talks of the "contempt" that Hitler had for the League of Nations and this tone is present*

in Source A, where the language "deliberate degradation", "indignity", "devoid of a sense of honour" shows Hitler's feelings for Germany's treatment.

Contrasts

- *Source A blames "certain great powers" for the failure of the Disarmament Conference, but Source B says that Germany was doing this only so that it would not appear to be "the villain of the piece".*

- *Source A claims that Germany is the victim of other countries' actions, whereas Source B talks of the "intransigence" of Germany and claims that Hitler was looking for an "excuse" to leave the League of Nations.*

- *In Source A, Hitler says he wants "an understanding with other nations", whereas Source B implies that he did not want an understanding but was putting forward demands "that the other powers would not accept".*

Undermining collective security: The Non-Aggression Pact with Poland

Germany's withdrawal from the League was a setback for the concept of collective security. Poland, on Germany's eastern border, was particularly vulnerable and, alarmed at the West's failure to stop Germany rearming, entered into a 10-year Non-Aggression Pact with the German government in January, 1934.

The Non-Aggression Pact took the world by surprise. The clauses of the Versailles Treaty that had given German land to recreate Poland were particularly resented in Germany; at Locarno, Stresemann had been unwilling to guarantee the eastern borders of Germany even though he had accepted the western border with France as part of the 1925 Locarno Treaty. For the moment, however, this pact suited Hitler. He was unable to take any action against Poland at this stage and, by signing the pact, he was securing his eastern frontier. It also weakened France's security system in Eastern Europe. France had signed an alliance with Poland in 1921 and had hoped that this would keep pressure on Germany's eastern borders. Germany had now broken out of the diplomatic encirclement that the French had attempted to impose on it. The pact also ended any chance of rapprochement between Czechoslovakia and Poland, thus further undermining the collective security system. Moreover, as this was an unpopular move in Germany, the Non-Aggression Pact looked to the international community like an act of statesmanship; it could be used to convince Britain and others that Germany was a peaceful nation.

Of course, Hitler had no intention of keeping to this agreement. Hitler preferred bilateral agreements to collective security agreements, as these could more easily be broken. He declared privately that "All our agreements with Poland have a temporary significance".

> **Class discussion**
>
> What do Hitler's actions in the years 1933–34 over disarmament and Poland reveal about his tactics for achieving his foreign policy objectives in these years?

159

Changing diplomatic alignments: Mussolini and Austria

In June 1934, Hitler and Mussolini met. However, the meeting was not a success; Mussolini was unimpressed by Hitler and would not agree to Hitler's position on Austria. *Anschluss*, the unification of Germany and Austria, had always been an important part of Hitler's foreign policy aims, and Hitler tried to persuade Mussolini that Austria should become a "satellite" of Germany. Mussolini rejected this, however, as he wanted to keep Austria as a buffer state between Germany and Italy. He was also aware that South Tyrol, which had been gained by Italy as part of the Versailles Settlement, had a substantial German minority.

Meanwhile, in Austria, Hitler was supporting the Austrian Nazi Party led by Alfred Eduard Frauenfeld. The Austrian Nazis organized a campaign of intimidation and terrorism, which culminated in the assassination of the Austrian Chancellor Englebert Dollfuss. This was intended to be the first step of a *coup d'état* that would force the union with Germany.

The attempted coup caused international concern. Mussolini immediately mobilized 100,000 troops and moved them to the Brenner pass, Italy's border with Germany, in a show of strength in July, 1934. Hitler was forced to back down and to disown the actions of the Austrian Nazis. The right-wing politician Kurt von Schuschnigg took over and stabilized the Austrian regime.

At this point, therefore, Hitler was forced to play a waiting game regarding unification with Austria. He did not want to alienate Mussolini, whose support he would need against the Western democracies, and he reassured Mussolini that Austria would not be annexed.

The growing strength of Germany: The Saar plebiscite, January 1935

In accordance with the Treaty of Versailles, the Saar, a small coal-rich territory, held a plebiscite in 1935. This area of Germany had been under French control since 1919 and was now given the opportunity to return to Germany. The result of the plebiscite was an overwhelming agreement (90.9% of the vote) that the Saar should return to Germany. This was a triumph for Hitler. The voting was supervised by the League and so done fairly, and the result was not surprising given that the entire population of the territory was German. It was nevertheless a great opportunity for Nazi propaganda to reinforce the growing power and strength of Germany and the popularity of the Nazi regime. Historian Gordon Craig writes:

This success, with which the other Powers made no attempt to interfere, marked the beginning of a new phase in his policy. He had survived the period of extreme vulnerability unscathed, and, thanks to the distractions and differences of the other Powers, his own tactical skill, and a good deal of luck, had been able in the course of two years to free himself from the restraints of the European security system. — Craig, 1978

▲ Hitler and Mussolini meet in Venice in 1934

Coup d'état
This is a sudden and violent take over of government, usually by a small group of people. A putsch is another word for a coup (for example, Hitler's attempted Munich putsch in 1923)

Source skills

A poster from 1934, in the lead up to the Saar plebiscite. The words at the foot read *"To Germany"*.

First question, part b – 2 marks

What is the message of this poster?

Communication skills

Go to http://www.britishpathe.com/video/hitler-acclaimed-in-saar-news-in-a-nutshell.

Watch the Pathé News clip showing Hitler's arrival in the Saar. How does Hitler use this event to show his growing power?

Thinking and self-management skills

Look back at Craig's assessment of Hitler's situation by the end of 1935. He identifies several reasons for Hitler's success:

- Hitler's tactical skill
- luck
- the distractions and differences of the other powers.

Find examples from the period 1933–35 to support each of these factors.

Which of these factors do you consider to be the most significant in explaining Hitler's success? (You may want to review your answer to the question on page 159, identifying the different tactics that Hitler used.)

Challenging the Treaty of Versailles: Rearmament

As early as February 1933, Hitler told his generals that rearmament was the most pressing priority: *"the next five years must be devoted to the defence capacity of the Germany people"*. In fact, Germany had always ignored the rearmament clauses of the Treaty of Versailles. With the cooperation of the Soviet Union under the Rapallo Treaty (see page 121), Germany had continued to build aircraft and to train and expand its army. In this sense, Hitler was continuing what had already been started by previous German governments. However, he now increased the pace of rearmament dramatically.

By 1935, the army had increased from 7 to 21 divisions. Conscription was introduced in the same year; the army increased to 36 divisions and over half a million men. In March 1935, Hermann Göring, one of Hitler's ministers, revealed the existence of the Luftwaffe, which by this time had around 2,500 planes. Hitler justified this level of rearmament on the grounds that Britain and France had failed to disarm and that Germany needed to be able to protect itself against the growing Soviet Army.

Joachim von Ribbentrop

Ribbentrop started off as Hitler's adviser on foreign policy. In 1935 he negotiated the Anglo–German Naval Agreement, and in August 1936 he was appointed ambassador to Britain. He hoped to arrange an alliance with Britain but ultimately failed in this goal; he was not helped by his arrogant behaviour. After this, he became negative towards Britain, seeing it as weak. In 1938 he became foreign minister, a post he kept until 1945.

Challenging the Treaty of Versailles: The remilitarization of the Rhineland

▲ Disputed territories around Germany, 1935–38

Early in 1936, Hitler turned his attention to the Rhineland. This area had been demilitarized under the terms of the Treaty of Versailles. In order to provide security for France, no military installations or garrisons were permitted on the left bank or within 50 kilometres of the right bank of the River Rhine.

For Hitler, the remilitarization of the Rhineland would be an important step in his plans for strengthening Germany; he would be able to build fortifications there to prevent an attack from France.

The timing of Hitler's actions in 1936 was led both by domestic and international considerations. In Germany, rising prices and food shortages were causing unrest among the population and Hitler needed to distract attention from economic problems. Internationally, the Abyssinian crisis provided an ideal opportunity to take action. Mussolini's break with the British and French over this crisis meant that he was now seeking closer ties with Hitler, and so he agreed not to oppose Hitler's takeover of the Rhineland. Hitler also knew that he could take advantage of the fact that Britain and France were distracted by both this crisis and the fallout from the Hoare–Laval Pact (see page 204).

Hitler's excuse for moving troops back into the Rhineland was the Franco–Soviet Mutual Assistance Treaty (see page 214), which was ratified on 4 March 1936. He argued that this violated the spirit of the Locarno Pact and threatened Germany with encirclement.

Source skills

A speech by Hitler, March 7 1936.

To this [the Locarno] Pact Germany made a contribution which represented a great sacrifice because while France fortified her frontier with steel and concrete and armaments, and garrisoned it heavily, a condition of complete defencelessness was imposed upon us on our Western Frontier.

France had not concluded this Treaty with a European power of no significance … Soviet Russia is the exponent of a revolutionary political and philosophical system … Its political creed is … world revolution.
It cannot be foreseen whether this philosophy will not be victorious … in France as well.

But should this happen … then … this new Bolshevik state would be a section of the Bolshevik International, which means that a decision as to aggression or non-aggression would not be taken in two different states … , but orders would be issued from one headquarters, … not in Paris but in Moscow.

This gigantic mobilisation of the East against Central Europe is opposed not only to the letter but to the spirit of the Locarno Pact.

Cited in Norman H. Baynes. 1969.

First question, part a – 3 marks

According to Hitler, how has France gone against the spirit of the Locarno Pact?

Both Hitler's generals and the German Foreign Office were hesitant about marching into the Rhineland, viewing it as a dangerous action likely to provoke a response from Britain and France. However, Hitler decided to take a gamble, hoping that the diplomatic disarray caused by the Abyssinian crisis would prevent Britain and France from taking any effective action. However, he later said,

> *the 48 hours after the march into the Rhineland were the most nerve-wracking of my life. If the French had marched into the Rhineland, we would have had to withdraw with our tails between our legs.*

German troops moved into the Rhineland on 7 March 1936. In fact, this was not a surprise to the British and the French, who had received intelligence warnings that this was about to happen. However, no action was taken by either the British or the French to stop the remilitarization, despite the fact that the Germans invaded with a relatively weak military force.

The successful invasion was accompanied by a peace offer, which was again intended to make Hitler look as though he was a man of peace and to divert the attention of Britain and France away from his challenge to the post-war settlement. The offer included demilitarizing the Rhineland, providing Britain and France created similar zones on their sides of the frontier as well. He also suggested that he was interested in negotiating new security pacts with his neighbours and returning to the League of Nations.

Source skills

First question, part b – 2 marks
What is the message of this photograph?

Examiner's hint: *How many marks would you give the following answer?*

The overall message here is that both the German troops and the occupants of the Rhineland were happy about the German action. This can be seen by the expressions on the faces of both the soldiers and the citizens who are also giving flowers to the troops. The Nazi flags that are flying from every building would also indicate support for the remilitarization.

ATL Thinking and communication skills

Read the views of historians Kershaw and Craig on the impact of the remilitarization of the Rhineland. Identify and make notes on:

- why this success was important to Hitler's position in Germany
- why it changed the international situation.

Source A

Ian Kershaw, *Hitler* (1991), page 124.

The remilitarisation of the Rhineland was important in the context of rearmament; it matched the revisionist expectations of the traditional conservative-nationalist elites; and it was hugely popular among the masses of the population – even in circles otherwise distinctly cool about the Nazi regime. As the re-establishment of German sovereignty over territory which no one disputed was Germany, it would have been on the agenda of any nationalist German government. And given the well-known divisions between Britain and France in their stance towards Germany, it was an issue which more than most stood a likely chance of success. But precisely the manner in which Hitler achieved his notable triumph was guaranteed to give a massive boost to his leadership position. He had been proved right again, in the teeth of Foreign Office hesitancy and military anxiety. And his popularity among the masses … had never been higher.

Source B

Gordon A. Craig. *Germany 1866–1945* (1978), page 691.

With the [invasion of the Rhineland] … Hitler had effectively destroyed the post-First World War security system. The German remilitarisation of the Rhineland was a victory not merely in the sense that it enhanced German prestige. Its psychological effect was to reveal the exclusively defensive nature of French strategical thinking, and this had devastating consequences among France's allies. Before the year was out, the King of the Belgians was seeking release from the obligations incurred by the treaties of 1920 and 1925, and his government had abandoned the intention of extending the Maginot Line into Belgium and had set a course back towards strict neutrality. There were tremors in the Little Entente as well, where politicians with an eye to the main chance began to weigh the advantages of getting on to Hitler's bandwagon. All in all, the Führer had good reason to exult, as he viewed the disarray of French fortunes, "The world belongs to the man with guts! God helps him".

ATL Communication skills

Go to http://www.britishpathe.com/video/scraps-of-paper.

Watch the Pathé News clip showing Hitler's invasion of the Rhineland. What impression does the footage and the commentary give about Germany at this time?

TOK

Review the historian's accounts in Source A and Source B above. Discuss the use of *reason* in the accounts given by each historian. To what extent are their views influenced by *expectation* and hindsight?

Increasing the influence of Nazism: The Spanish Civil War

Spain became the battlefield for a European-wide struggle between the forces of communism and socialism on the one hand and the forces of Fascism on the other. — Henig, 1985

Mussolini and Hitler were pushed closer together when they both intervened in the Spanish Civil War on the side of Franco.

As you will have read in the previous chapter, the Spanish Civil War began in 1936 with a nationalist revolt led by the army against the republican Spanish government.

Both sides appealed to the international community for help in this conflict. General Franco led the Nationalists and he asked for help from Germany and Italy, while the Republican government hoped to get support from Britain, France and the Soviet Union.

Germany did not send ground troops but played a key role in transporting Franco's troops from Morocco to Spain at the start of the conflict, and German bombers of the Condor Legion caused havoc by attacking civilian centres, most notoriously Guernica in April 1937. German submarines also attacked government ships in the Mediterranean. Nevertheless, in contrast to Mussolini (see page 141), Hitler placed limits on the extent of German involvement.

Hitler had several reasons for intervening in this civil war:

- He wanted a friendly government in Spain that would supply Spanish mineral resources and also provide military bases for German submarines.

- He would be able to test out his air force and see the effects of air attacks on civilian populations.

- He was able to pose as the defender of European civilization against the Communist threat.

- A pro-Fascist government in Spain would further undermine French security.

What were the results of this conflict for Hitler's position in Europe?

- The war dragged on for three years, polarizing opinion in Europe.

- It reinforced suspicions between Britain and France on the one hand and the Soviet Union on the other, thereby preventing a strong anti-Fascist alliance.

- It distracted the West, and Britain's failure to take any strong action (see page 217) led Hitler to believe that he would not face further opposition to expansion in Eastern Europe.

Changing diplomatic alignments: The Rome–Berlin Axis and the Anti-Comintern Pact

The most important result of the Spanish Civil War on diplomatic alignments was the improved relations between Hitler and Mussolini. Hitler recognized King Victor Emmanuel III of Italy as the "Emperor of Abyssinia" and worked with Italy to prevent a British initiative to update the Locarno Treaties. On the Italian side, opposition to German influence in Austria was now removed. In July 1936, with Mussolini's approval, Hitler signed an agreement with Chancellor Schuschnigg of Austria, whereby Schuschnigg promised to pursue a policy *based on the principle that Austria acknowledges herself to be a German state* in return for a German commitment to non-intervention.

The new atmosphere of cooperation between Germany and Italy culminated in the signing of the Rome–Berlin Axis between Hitler and Mussolini in October 1936. It consisted of a series of secret protocols setting out their mutual interests (see page 143). This was followed up in November of the same year by an agreement with Japan; the Anti-Comintern Pact was directed against the Communist International and stated that, in the case of an attack by the Soviet Union, the signatories would consult on measures to "safeguard their common interests". The militant nature of this agreement indicated the beginning of the openly aggressive phase of Hitler's foreign policy.

Hitler was delighted, as these agreements demonstrated that Germany was no longer isolated but an important player on the world stage.

ATL **Self-management**

Refer back to Chapter 2.3. Compare and contrast the importance of involvement in the Spanish Civil War for the foreign policies of Mussolini and Hitler.

Class discussion

To what extent had Hitler succeeded in removing the most important restrictions of the Treaty of Versailles by the end of 1936?

Ruth Henig. *The Origins of the Second World War*, page 30 (1985).

In the process [of the Four Year Plan], Germany was to make every effort to become more self-supporting by developing a wide range of synthetic materials, by stockpiling essential raw materials, and by concluding bilateral trade agreements with states in eastern and south-eastern Europe whereby food and raw materials were supplied to Germany in exchange for manufactures and armaments. Romania was a particular target for German advances because she could supply vitally needed supplies of oil.

First question, part a – 3 marks

According to Henig, in what ways did Hitler plan to make Germany prepared for war?

Read the full text of the Hossbach Memorandum at:

avalon.law.yale.edu/imt/hossbach.asp.

Make bullet point notes on the key points made.

In pairs or small groups, discuss the significance of this meeting.

The impact of the economy on Hitler's foreign policy: The Four Year Plan

By 1936, rearmament was not progressing fast enough for Hitler. Indeed, the consumer economy was starting to struggle: there were shortages of butter and meat, as well as shortages of vital imports of raw materials and of foreign exchange. The economics minister, Dr. Hjalmar Schacht, favoured spending less on armaments in order to enable more exports to be produced, thus encouraging foreign trade.

However, Hitler believed that Germany's economic problems could only be solved by the acquisition of more land and living space. He decided to go all out for autarky, bringing the economy more closely under party control, in order to prepare for war. This was to be done via a Four Year Plan, which Hitler introduced in September 1936 under the leadership of Göring.

Believing that this would make the pace of rearmament too fast and that it would cause an economic crisis, Schacht resigned. However, there is no doubt that Hitler was now in a strong position. As the historian Ian Kershaw writes:

> By the end of the year [1936], with the German-Italian axis secured … the creation of the anti-Comintern pact with Japan, the Spanish Civil War all providing renewed evidence of the passivity and uncertainty of the western democracies, and the German economy committed full tilt to preparation for war, the contours of growing international tension and an escalating arms race in the latter 1930s were all set. And out of the various interwoven crises of 1936, Hitler's own power position had emerged buttressed and reinforced. — Kershaw, 1991

The impact of Nazism on Germany's foreign policy: The Hossbach Memorandum

> The conference marks the point at which the expansion of the Third Reich ceased to be latent and became explicit. — Wiliamson, 1995

On 5 November, Hitler called a special meeting that was attended by his top generals and his war ministers: Hermann Göring (air), Werner von Fritsch (army), Erich Raeder (navy), Werner von Blomberg (defence) and Foreign Minister Konstantin von Neurath. Hitler told the meeting that what he was to say was to be regarded as "his last will and testament".

We know about this meeting because the main points were compiled and written down five days later by Hitler's military assistant, Colonel Hossbach, from notes that he made at the time. The document was filed without having been seen by Hitler.

At the conference, Hitler gave an overview of Germany's international situation and proposed several actions that now needed to be taken. The following extracts are taken from Hossbach's memorandum:

> The aim of German foreign policy was to make secure and to preserve the racial community and to enlarge it. It was therefore a question of space. The question for Germany was: where could she achieve the greatest gain at the lowest cost? German policy had to reckon with two hate inspired antagonists, Britain and France, to whom a German colossus in the centre of Europe was a thorn in the flesh … Germany's problem could only be solved by the use of force. If the resort to force with its attendant risks is accepted … there then

remains still to be answered the questions "When"? and "How"? In this matter there were three contingencies to be dealt with.

Case 1: Period 1943–5

After that date only a change for the worse for our point of view could be expected … Our relative strength would decrease in relation to the rearmament which would then have been carried out by the rest of the world. … If the Führer was still living it was his unalterable determination to solve Germany's problem of space by 1943–5 at the latest …

Case 2

If internal strife in France should develop into such a domestic crisis as to absorb the French army completely and render it incapable of use for war against Germany, then the time for acting against the Czechs would have come.

Case 3

If France should be so embroiled in war with another state that she could not "proceed" against Germany. For the improvement of our political-military position our first objective, in the event of our being embroiled in war, must be to overthrow Czechoslovakia and Austria simultaneously in order to remove the threat to our plan in any possible operation against the West.

If Germany made use of this war to settle the Czech and Austrian question, it was to be assumed that Britain – herself at war with Italy – would decide not to act against Germany.

While none of the military leaders objected to the planned destruction of Czechoslovakia, Blomberg and Fritsch were unhappy about a policy that could lead to war with Britain and France before Germany was sufficiently prepared. However, all those who were hesitant about Hitler's aims – (Blömberg, Fritsch and Neurath) were ruthlessly removed from power in February 1938 when Hitler appointed himself Supreme Commander of the German army. These changes were accompanied by the retirement of 16 high-ranking generals and the transfer of 44 others, thus removing anyone who might be less than committed to Hitler's goals. As Kershaw writes, *"Following the Reichstag Fire and the Rohm crisis [Night of the Long Knives], the Blömberg-Fritsch affair was the third great milestone on the way to Führer absolutist power"* (quoted in Darby, 2007).

How significant is the Hossbach Memorandum as evidence of Hitler's foreign policy objectives?

A copy of Hossbach's minutes of this meeting were used at the **Nuremberg Trials** as evidence of Hitler's planning for war. However, AJP Taylor points out that the memorandum is only a copy and indeed only a fragment of a copy of the original, which has disappeared. Taylor also argues that the purpose of the meeting was not actually to discuss foreign policy aims but to convince conservative military and financial experts of the need to continue with the rearmament programme, and to isolate Schacht, who opposed it. Taylor states that *"Hitler's exposition was in large part day-dreaming and unrelated to what followed in real life"* (Taylor, 1969).

However, other historians would still argue that, while it cannot be used as a road-map for war, the Hossbach Memorandum did clearly set out Hitler's central goal: *"to make secure and to preserve the racial community and enlarge it"*. It also made clear Hitler's war-like and expansionist intentions and Hitler's sense of urgency; this was all taken seriously by those present.

Source skills

Second question – 4 marks

With reference to its origin, purpose and content, assess the values and limitations of the Hossbach Memorandum as evidence of Hitler's foreign policy plans after 1937.

Class discussion

Refer back to Hitler's foreign policy ideas in *Mein Kampf* (see pages 117–118). What continuities are there in his aims as set out in 1923 in *Mein Kampf* and those as they appear in the Hossbach Memorandum? What change in attitude do you see concerning Britain?

In pairs, review Italy's position on a potential naval war with Britain. What would be the Italian view of the "cases" discussed in this meeting?

The Nuremberg Trials

A series of military tribunals, held by the Allied forces after World War II. Key members of the political, military, and economic leadership of Nazi Germany were put on trial charged with crimes against peace and crimes against humanity.

Full document question: Hitler's remilitarization of the Rhineland

Source A

A British report by the heads of the three armed services on their ability to fight a war against Germany in 1936.

> We would at once emphasise ... that any question of war with Germany while we were as at present heavily committed to the possibility of hostilities in the Mediterranean would be thoroughly dangerous. As regards naval operation against Germany, our minimum requirements could only be carried out by weakening naval forces in the Mediterranean to an extent which would jeopardise our position there vis-à-vis Italy ... As regards the Army and the Air Force, the purely defensive provisions already made in the Mediterranean have drawn upon the resources of these two Services to such an extent that until those reinforcements have returned to this country we should be quite incapable of dispatching a Field Force or providing any proper defence in the air. To bring home these forces with their equipment ... would take in the case of the army two months ... and even longer in the case of the Air Force.
>
> At the moment our coast defence artillery requires modernisation to a large extent, we have no anti-submarine defences for a number of our most important ports, and the number of our anti-aircraft guns and searchlights is quite inadequate to deal with the air threat from Germany.

Source B

A cartoon published in *Punch* magazine on 18 March 1936.

THE GOOSE-STEP

"GOOSEY GOOSEY GANDER,
WHITHER DOST THOU WANDER?"
"ONLY THROUGH THE RHINELAND—
PRAY EXCUSE MY BLUNDER!"

Source C

Ruth Henig, a British academic historian, in an academic book, *The Origins of the Second World War* (1985).

> On 7 March 1936, token German forces marched into the Rhineland and Hitler announced that the German government was remilitarizing it because of the threat to Germany posed by the Franco-Russian alliance which had just been ratified by the French Senate ... The remilitarization was a further challenge to the Versailles settlement and to the

British government's wish to secure peaceful and orderly revision. For the British government had already gone out of its way to indicate to Hitler that ministers were willing to agree to German remilitarization of the Rhineland as part of a more general package of measures which might include an air-pact, German return to the League of Nations, some peaceful revision of Germany's eastern frontiers and the return of former German colonies. Now Hitler had shown once again, in his rearmament policies that he preferred to achieve his objectives by unilateral military action rather than by participating in multilateral diplomatic discussions. … In retrospect, many politicians and commentators claimed that this was the point at which Hitler should have been challenged, and that after March 1936 he could not be stopped from plunging Europe into war.

Source D

A speech by Hitler to the Reichstag following the remilitarization of the Rhineland, Saturday 7 March 1936.

The German government has continuously emphasised during the negotiations of the last years its readiness to observe and fulfil all the obligations arising from the Rhine Pact so long as the other contracting parties were ready on their side to maintain the pact. This obvious and essential condition can no longer be regarded as being fulfilled by France. France has replied to Germany's repeated friendly offers and assurances of peace by infringing the Rhine Pact through a military alliance with the Soviet Union directed exclusively against Germany. In this manner, however, the Locarno Rhine Pact has lost its inner meaning and ceased to exist …

In order, however, to avoid any misinterpretation of its intentions and to establish beyond doubt the purely defensive character of these measures, as well as to express its unalterable longing for a real pacification of Europe between states in equal rights and equally respected, the German government declares itself ready to conclude new agreements for the creation of a system of peaceful security for Europe … After three years, I believe that today the struggle for German equality of rights can be deemed concluded …

We have no territorial claims to make in Europe. Above all, we are aware that all the tensions resulting either from erroneous territorial provisions or from the disproportion between the size of its population and Lebensraum can never be solved by wars.

First question, part a – 3 marks

According to Source A, why would it be difficult for Britain to resist German aggression in 1936?

First question, part b – 2 marks

What is the message of Source B?

Second question – 4 marks

Compare and contrast the views expressed in Source C and Source D regarding Hitler's motives for his actions in 1936.

Third question – 6 marks

With reference to its origin, purpose and content, assess the value and limitations of Source C for a historian studying the reasons for the remilitarization of the Rhineland.

Fourth question – 9 marks

Using these sources and your own knowledge, examine the reasons for Hitler's remilitarization of the Rhineland in 1936.

References

Baynes, N. 1969. *The Speeches of Adolf Hitler: April 1922–August 1939*. H. Fertig. New York, USA

Craig, G. 1978. *Germany 1866–1945*. Oxford University Press. New York, USA

Darby, G. 2007. *Hitler, Appeasement and the Road to War*. Hodder, UK

Henig, R. 1985. *The Origins of the Second World War*. Routledge. London, UK

Kershaw, I. 1991. *Hitler*. Longman. London, UK.

Steiner, Z. 2011. *The Triumph of the Dark: European International History 1933–1999*. Oxford University Press. New York, USA

Wiliamson, DG. 1995. *The Third Reich*. Longman. London, UK

2.5 German expansion, 1938–1940

▲ German troops march into Poland following the start of hostilities on 1 September 1939

Conceptual understanding

Key concepts

→ Causation

→ Change

→ Perspective

Key questions

→ Examine the ways in which Hitler went further than challenging the post-war settlement after 1937.

→ To what extent was Hitler successful in carrying out his foreign policy aims?

→ Discuss the consequences of Hitler's actions for the international situation.

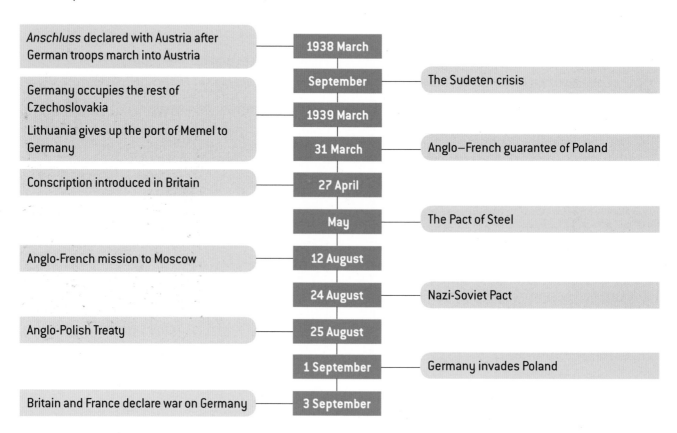

Anschluss declared with Austria after German troops march into Austria	1938 March	
	September	The Sudeten crisis
Germany occupies the rest of Czechoslovakia	1939 March	
Lithuania gives up the port of Memel to Germany	31 March	Anglo–French guarantee of Poland
Conscription introduced in Britain	27 April	
	May	The Pact of Steel
Anglo-French mission to Moscow	12 August	
	24 August	Nazi-Soviet Pact
Anglo-Polish Treaty	25 August	
	1 September	Germany invades Poland
Britain and France declare war on Germany	3 September	

Following the shake-up of his military command in 1937 after the Hossbach Conference, Hitler was in a position to start taking more risks in his foreign policy. The first of these was the takeover of Austria; the next was the takeover of Sudetenland. These actions completed the revision of the post-war settlement and also put Hitler in a position to pursue his goal of *Lebensraum* in the East.

Challenging the post-war settlement after 1937

Anschluss, 1938

Between 1938 and 1939, Hitler was able to achieve the aims that he had set out at the Hossbach Conference in 1937: the annexation of Austria and the dismemberment of Czechoslovakia. However, this was not achieved in the way that Hitler had anticipated; indeed, historian Alan Bullock sees *Anschluss* as "a striking example" of Hitler's ability to combine "*consistency in aim, calculation and patience in preparation with opportunism, impulse and improvisation in execution*" (Bullock, 1967: 204).

Despite his failure to take Austria in 1934, Hitler had already made much progress in establishing Nazi influence in the country. In July 1936, an Austro–German agreement had been signed, which agreed the following:

- Germany reaffirmed its recognition of Austria's independence.

- Both powers agreed not to interfere in each other's internal affairs.

- Austria would conduct a foreign policy consistent with it being a "German state".

In addition, secret clauses gave prominent Austrian Nazis, such as Arthur Seyss-Inquart, a role in the government.

However, in 1938 the opportunity to take over Austria directly arose due to the actions of Austrian Chancellor Kurt Schuschnigg. Schuschnigg was alarmed by the activities of the Austrian Nazis and he requested an interview with Hitler. However, when Schuschnigg arrived at the meeting in Berchtesgaden on 12 February 1938, Hitler launched into an attack on Austria:

> *Hitler: "The whole history of Austria is just one interrupted act of high treason. That was so in the past, and is no better today. The historical paradox must now reach its long-overdue end. And I can tell you here and now, Herr Schuschnigg, that I am absolutely determined to make an end of all this. The German Reich is one of the Great Powers, and nobody will raise his voice if it settles its border problems … Who is not with me will be crushed … I have chosen the most difficult road that any German ever took …"*

> *Schuschnigg: "Herr Reichkanzler, I am quite willing to believe it … We will do everything to remove obstacles to a better understanding, as far as possible …"*

> *Hitler: "That is what you say, Herr Schuschnigg. But I am telling you that I am going to solve the so-called Austrian problem one way or the other … I have only to give the order and your ridiculous defence mechanism will be blown to bits …"*

Chancellor Schuschnigg's recollection of the conversations at Berchtesgaden, 12 February 1938, written shortly afterwards from memory

Class discussion

Discuss the events that were happening in Asia at this time. What expansionist moves had Japan made by early 1938? Do you think events in Asia had any influence on the international response to German expansion?

▲ Schuschnigg, Chancellor of Austria

Source skills

Second question – 4 marks

With reference to its origin, purpose and content, assess the value and limitations of Schuschnigg's account of his meeting with Hitler for historians studying the Austrian crisis of 1938.

Examiner's hint:

Here are some points that you could consider in your answer:

Values

- A value of the origin is that Schuschnigg was present at the meeting and so would have first-hand knowledge of what was said.

- Schuschnigg wrote the conversation down soon after the meeting so it would have been fresh in his mind.

- The purpose is of value as Schuschnigg made a record of the meeting which he saw as important.

Limitations

- Schuschnigg's account was written afterwards from memory, so he is unlikely to have been able to remember the conversation so precisely as it is here.

- His purpose would be to gain sympathy for his treatment, so it is possible that he might want to exaggerate Hitler's attack on Austria.

- Certainly, the language used by Hitler here is very aggressive in contrast to Schuschnigg's very reasonable tone which could support the idea that he is exaggerating.

After being submitted to two hours of abuse, Schuschnigg was forced to agree to a list of demands that included releasing all imprisoned pro-Nazi agitators, lifting the ban against the Nazi Party and appointing Seyss-Inquart as interior minister. Pro-Nazis were also to be made the ministers of war and of finance, and the economic systems of the two countries were to be assimilated. These demands would effectively end Austrian independence; Schuschnigg was told that if he did not agree, Hitler would march into Austria.

Schuschnigg attempted a desperate last action: he announced a plebiscite for 13 March 1938, in which Austrians were to vote on whether or not they wanted a *"free and German, independent and social, Christian and united Austria"*. Austrians could only answer "yes" or "no"; given the wording, along with the fact that Schuschnigg's own political party was in charge of the plebiscite, there was a good chance that a Yes vote could be secured. This would then give him a chance to break free of his agreement with Hitler.

Hitler, therefore, decided to act before this could happen. Mussolini gave his assurances that he would not object to *Anschluss* and Hitler mobilized his army. When Schuschnigg found that no help was coming from Italy, Britain or France, he resigned. Hitler marched into Austria on 12 March 1938.

ATL **Communication skills**

In pairs review Chapter 2.3 and then discuss the reasons for the change in Mussolini's position on Anschluss by 1938.

On 13 March, apparently in a spur of the moment decision following an emotional visit to his home town of Linz, Hitler announced the incorporation of Austria into the Reich. This was subsequently confirmed by 99% of the population in a plebiscite on 10 April.

Historian Klaus Fischer sums up the impact of *Anschluss*:

> *The Anschluss and the methods that brought it about had far-reaching consequences. Hitler had gambled successfully again. He became convinced that his strategy of ruthless power politics had been vindicated and that it was the only effective policy against his war-weary and vacillating opponents. Aside from reinforcing Hitler's belief in the effectiveness of international blackmail and intimidation, the Anschluss also had far-reaching consequences in the field of diplomacy. It promoted the friendship of the two Fascist tyrants – Hitler and Mussolini, and this further polarised European powers. Another consequence of the Anschluss was that Germany's strategic position was greatly enhanced. With Vienna at his disposal Hitler had acquired direct access to the whole of south-eastern Europe. From Vienna it was only a footstep to Czechoslovakia, Hungary and Yugoslavia.* — Fischer, 1995

▲ Austrian crowds greeting Hitler after *Anschluss*

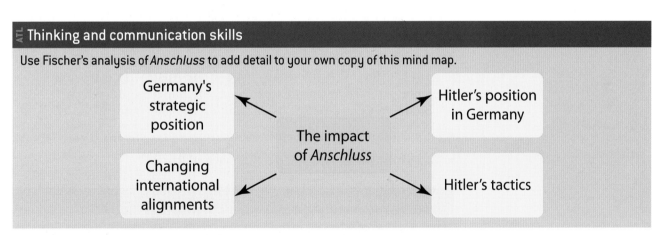

ATL | Thinking and communication skills

Use Fischer's analysis of *Anschluss* to add detail to your own copy of this mind map.

Germany's strategic position

Changing international alignments

The impact of *Anschluss*

Hitler's position in Germany

Hitler's tactics

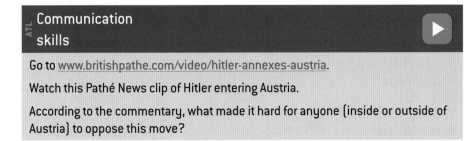

ATL | Communication skills

Go to www.britishpathe.com/video/hitler-annexes-austria.

Watch this Pathé News clip of Hitler entering Austria.

According to the commentary, what made it hard for anyone (inside or outside of Austria) to oppose this move?

The Sudeten crisis

Hitler's action against Czechoslovakia was a virtuoso performance, diminished only by the fact that his antagonists made things easier for him than he deserved. — Craig, 1978

After the success of annexing Austria, Hitler turned his attention to Czechoslovakia. There were several reasons for this:

▲ Partition of Czechoslovakia, 1938–39

- Hitler considered Slavs to be *untermenschen* (racially and socially inferior).

- Many Czechs had resisted Austrian rule in the old Austro–Hungarian Empire and had fought for Russia during the First World War, rather than for Austria.

- Czechoslovakia was the only successful independent state created by the Versailles Settlement; it consisted of many different peoples and had therefore proved that ethnically diverse people could live together.

- One of the ethnic groups in the new Czechoslovakia was German. These Germans had formally lived in the Austro–Hungarian Empire and now lived in the area known as the Sudetenland, which bordered Germany (see its location on the map above).

- Czechoslovakia was an enthusiastic supporter of the League of Nations.

- Czechoslovakia was allied to France and Russia.

ATL | Thinking and social skills

In pairs, consider how each of the bullet points above would contribute to Hitler's hostile attitude towards Czechoslovakia.

The Sudeten Germans

The Sudetenland – a mountainous area, rich in mineral resources – had been given to Czechoslovakia in order to give the new state a strong frontier and to ensure its prosperity. The Czechs had then further strengthened this frontier by building defences. In addition, Czechoslovakia had a strong arms industry and a well-organized army.

However, the Sudeten Germans themselves, some 3.5 million people, had not accepted their position in Czechoslovakia. As part of the former Austrian Imperial ruling nation, they resented their loss of status and regarded themselves as victims of Czech discrimination. With the impact of the Great Depression and high unemployment, their sense of grievance grew.

The leader of the Sudeten Germans, Konrad Heinlein, became the mouthpiece for Sudeten discontent and for demands to the Czech government for self-government. He led the Sudeten German Party, which, from 1935, was funded by Nazi Germany. Hitler encouraged Heinlein to make continual demands on the Czech government and to keep up a relentless programme of agitation and subversion. On 24 April 1938, Heinlein presented the Czech government with his Eight Demands in the form of the Karlsbad Programme; these demands included autonomy and various special rights.

Initially, however, Hitler was reluctant to use force against Czechoslovakia. He told Heinlein that he would solve the Sudeten issue "in the not too distant future", but did not commit himself to any clear plan on how this was to be achieved. In addition, many of Hitler's generals warned him that Germany was not ready for a war at this stage.

▲ Konrad Heinlein, leader of the Sudeten German Party

The May Crisis, 1938

Hitler changed his mind with regard to taking action against Czechoslovakia as a result of the so-called May Crisis. On 20 May, rumours started circulating that the Germans were making military preparations near to the Czech border. As a result, the Czech government ordered partial mobilization, and Britain and France sent warnings to Germany.

In fact, the rumours were unfounded and Hitler had to tell the powers involved that no such preparations to attack Czechoslovakia were underway. He found this action humiliating, as it looked as though he had responded to British and French threats. On 28 May, in what was known as Operation Green, Hitler told his generals: "*It is my unalterable decision to smash Czechoslovakia by military action in the near future*".

Throughout the summer of 1938, tensions increased in the Sudetenland as the Sudeten Germans, on instructions from Hitler, increased their violence against the Czech government. On 5 September, the Czech President Edvard Beneš agreed to all demands of the Sudeten Germans for self-government. However, Heinlein was told by Hitler to reject this offer, thus proving that Hitler was interested only in conquest and not in justice for the Sudeten Germans. Meanwhile, the German press whipped up a frenzy of anti-Czech feeling by showing pictures and film footage of the apparent ill-treatment of Sudeten Germans.

Speech made by Hitler on 12 September 1938 at the annual Nuremberg Rally.

I am speaking of Czechoslovakia. This is a democratic State founded on democratic lines by forcing other nationalities without asking them into a structure manufactured by Versailles. As good democrats they began to oppress and mishandle the majority of the inhabitants …

If this were a matter foreign to us … we would regard the case as so many others, merely as an interesting illustration of the democratic conception of self-determination, and simply take note of it. But it is something most natural which compels us Germans to take an interest in this problem. Among the nationalities being suppressed in this State there are 3,500,000 Germans. That is about as many persons of our race as Denmark has inhabitants … That conditions in this nation are unbearable is generally known. 3,500,000 people were robbed in the name of a certain Mr Wilson of their right to self-determination. Economically these people were deliberately ruined and afterwards handed over to a slow process of extermination. The misery of the Sudeten Germans is without end. They are being oppressed in an inhuman and intolerable manner and treated in an undignified way …

This may be a matter of indifference to the democracies … but I can only say to the representatives of the democracies that it is not a matter of indifference to us, and I say that if these tortured creatures cannot obtain rights and assistance by themselves they can obtain both from us …

We can quite understand that the French and British defend their interests in the world. I can assure the statesmen in Paris and London that there are also German interests which we are determined to defend in all circumstances … You will understand that a Great Power cannot suddenly submit … to such a base attack … What the Germans demand is the right of self-determination which other nations possess … if the Democracies, however, should be convinced that they must in this case protect with all their means the oppressors of the Germans, then this will have grave consequences.

In pairs, read Hitler's speech and consider what evidence this document provides of:

- Hitler's political views
- Hitler's tactics with regard to taking over the Sudetenland
- the nature of Nazi propaganda.

Hitler's speech at the Nuremberg Rally caused more unrest in the Sudetenland, but this was brought under control by the Czech government, which declared martial law.

Go to www.youtube.com/watch?v=hprV2nQRvbc, or search for "The German people persecuted at Sudetenland".

Watch this German propaganda film. According to the film, how are the Sudeten Germans being persecuted?

Chamberlain's intervention

It was at this point that Britain decided to act. The full reasons and nature of this involvement are discussed in more detail in the next chapter. However, Chamberlain desperately wanted to avoid a war, and so now flew three times to meet Hitler to try to make a deal over the Sudetenland.

Berchtesgaden, 15 September 1938

▲ Chamberlain arriving at Berchtesgarden

At this meeting, it was agreed that the Sudeten German areas of Czechoslovakia should be transferred to Germany. Chamberlain persuaded his Cabinet and the French to agree to this deal. The Czechs finally agreed after two days of persuasion.

Godesberg, 22–23 September 1938

Chamberlain flew to Godesberg to tell Hitler the good news, but Hitler was furious. He wanted an excuse for a war with Czechoslovakia, not a peaceful handover of the Sudetenland. He insisted that the demands of the Hungarians and the Poles for territory in Czechoslovakia should also be met, and that German troops should be allowed to occupy the Sudetenland on 28 September.

▲ Chamberlain leaving Godesberg

It now seemed as though war was inevitable. The Czechs rejected Hitler's terms and the French said they would support Czechoslovakia. As mentioned previously, the Czechs had good defences and a strong army. They hoped that with the help of their allies, France and the Soviet Union, they could resist a German attack.

Munich, 29 September 1938

▲ Chamberlain, Daladier, Hitler and Mussolini at the Munich Conference

With Britain and France now showing that they were prepared to fight, and with his own generals pointing out that Germany was not yet ready for war, Hitler agreed to a further conference. Mussolini stepped in as a mediator to prevent war, and a Four Power Conference was held in Munich. Here, a plan presented by Mussolini (though written by Hitler!) was agreed on.

The plan included the following points.

- The German occupation of the Sudetenland would take place by 1 October and an international commission would determine a provisional new frontier by 10 October. The international commission would also supervise plebiscites in areas of dispute.
- Czechs would be allowed to leave and Germans allowed to join the Sudeten territories (neither the plebiscites nor the transfer of populations actually happened).
- Poland was to be given Teschen.
- Hungary was to get South Slovakia.
- Germany, along with the other powers, guaranteed the independence of the rest of Czechoslovakia.

Neither the Czech President, Beneš nor the Soviet leader, Stalin were invited to the Munich Conference. The Czechs were told that if they resisted this agreement they would receive no help from Britain or France, even though France had guaranteed the Czech borders at Locarno. The Czechs therefore had no option but to agree. Beneš resigned a few days later.

Following the conference, Chamberlain got Hitler to sign a statement in which he agreed to settle all matters of international interest through consultation. Hitler, however, was determined not to be deprived of his war against Czechoslovakia. On 21 October, he gave orders for the *"liquidation of the remainder of the Czech state"*.

Source skills

Gordon A. Craig. *Germany 1866–1945* **(1990).**

Munich seemed to convince Hitler that he could do no wrong, and his policy now betrayed an impatience that had not characterised it earlier. In his search for new triumphs, economic factors no longer had the power to restrain him, for it was clear that the country's readiness for war was as good as it could be without measures of domestic discipline that he was disinclined to take; and it seemed possible, in any case, that conquests might repair deficiencies. Moreover, the acceleration of Hitler's campaign against the Jews at the end of 1938 contributed to the mounting pace of his external policy. One

of the complaints that he made against the government of Czechoslovakia was that "the Jews in Czechoslovakia were still poisoning the nation" against Germany and would have to be dealt with. As he turned to new objectives, it is clear that the conquest of space and the destruction of Jewry were inextricably connected in his thoughts.

First question, part a – 3 marks

According to Craig, what was the impact of the Munich Conference on Hitler?

Beyond the Treaty of Versailles: The liquidation of Czechoslovakia

ATL Communication skills

▲ German troops enter Prague in March 1939

What does this photo suggest about the attitude of the citizens of Prague towards the takeover of the rest of Czechoslovakia?

ATL Thinking and social skills

1 According to Craig in the source above, what factor linked Hitler's domestic and foreign policies?

2 With a partner, discuss what conclusions Hitler might now draw as to the attitude of the West regarding any future action he might take.

As a result of the Munich Conference, Czechoslovakia lost 70% of its heavy industry, a third of its population and both the natural mountainous defences and the man-made fortifications of the Sudetenland. Slovakia and Ruthenia were given self-government for internal affairs, though were still ultimately controlled from Prague.

Clearly, Hitler saw the Munich Agreement as *"a stepping stone to the liquidation of the Czech state"* (Stackelberg, 1999: 173). From early 1939, Hitler encouraged the Slovaks to cause disruption and to ask for complete independence. He was willingly helped in this by Father Jozef Tiso, who was head of the fascist Slovak People's Party.

As with Austria, Hitler was given the excuse to directly get involved when the new Czech President, Emil Hacha, moved troops into Slovakia to crush this agitation. Prompted by Hitler, Tiso proclaimed full independence for Slovakia and asked for German protection.

In the hope of saving Czechoslovakia, Hachá now asked to see Hitler. This, of course, was a mistake; Hachá was forced to sign over Bohemia and Moravia to Hitler.

On 15 March 1939, German troops occupied the rest of Czechoslovakia. On 16 March, Bohemia and Moravia were declared a protectorate of Germany; Slovakia was to be an independent state under the protection of Germany and Ruthenia was occupied by Hungarian troops.

This action led to a change in British policy towards Germany. On 18 March, Chamberlain told the British Cabinet that *"no reliance could be placed on any of the assurances given by the Nazi leaders"* (see page 223).

German expansion: Poland

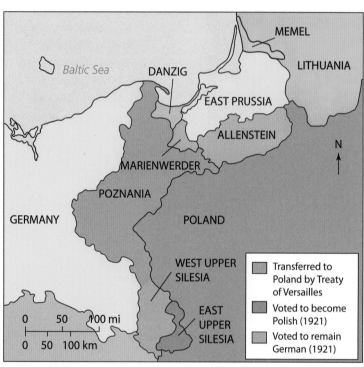

▲ The Polish Corridor after the First World War

It was now clear that Hitler's next target would be Poland. Poland had been dismantled as a country in the 18th century and partitioned between Prussia, Russia and the Austrian Empire. However, following Wilson's aims of self-determination at Versailles, it had been recreated as a nation. It was this part of the Treaty of Versailles that was probably most resented by the Germans, as West Prussia had been given to Poland to allow it access to the sea, thereby splitting East Prussia off from the rest of Germany. This piece of land, known as the Polish Corridor, also included the city of Danzig, which became a "free city" run by the League of Nations, allowing both Poland and Germany to use it as a sea port.

Less than a week after the occupation of Prague, the Germans proposed to Poland that Danzig should be returned to Germany, and that Germany should have direct access to East Prussia via a German-controlled road and rail link. This was actually a more legitimate demand than the German claim to the Sudetenland, which had not been part of Germany before the First World War. However, Poland's foreign minister Colonel Beck refused, seeing this as the start of an attack on Polish territory.

Britain's guarantee to Poland

In March 1939, Hitler asked the Lithuanian government to hand over Memel. Lithuania was a Baltic state that had been made independent from Russia in 1919; Memel was a city and strip of land bordering East Prussia that had a substantial German population. Lithuania was in no position to stand up to Hitler and the land was handed over four days later.

Britain now decided to act and, on 30 March, a guarantee was offered to Poland to give help in the event of a German attack:

> *In the event of any action which clearly threatened Polish independence, and which the Polish Government accordingly considered it vital to resist with their national forces, His Majesty's Government would feel themselves bound at once to lend the Polish Government all support in their power. They have given the Polish Government an assurance to this effect.*
>
> *I may add that the French Government have authorised me to make it plain that they stand in the same position in this matter as do His Majesty's Government.*

The Anglo–Polish Treaty failed to make Hitler more cautious in his actions. Indeed, he was furious about this opposition to his plans, commenting, *"I'll cook them a stew that they'll choke on"*. Two days after the British guarantee to Poland, Hitler responded by declaring the Anglo–German Naval Agreement invalid and ending the 1934 Non-Aggression Pact with Poland. He then ordered his Chief of Staff, Keitel, to prepare for the attack on Poland. This was known as Operation White, and the plan was for a limited war on Poland rather than for a wider war involving Britain and France.

Changing international alignments: The Pact of Steel, May 1939

Pact of Steel

International tensions continued to rise with Mussolini's invasion of Albania (see page 147). Although this action was caused by Mussolini's attempt to show his independence of Hitler and to increase his own international importance, to Britain and France this looked like a coordinated action between the dictatorships. Thus, Britain and France immediately issued guarantees to both Greece and Romania.

The Germans supported Mussolini's action in Albania, and Mussolini found that he needed Hitler's support given the hostile reaction of Britain and France. He thus agreed to sign the Pact of Steel with Germany, whereby each power agreed to come to the aid of the other if it became involved in hostilities "contrary to its wishes and desires". However, Mussolini was wary of getting involved in a full-scale conflict, and privately he made it clear to Hitler that Italy would not be ready for war for another three or four years.

Nevertheless, Hitler was intent on an immediate war with Poland. The day after the signing of the Pact of Steel, he told his generals: *"we are left with the decision: to attack Poland at the first suitable opportunity"*. As Kershaw writes, *"War for [Hitler] was no conventional military conflict. It represented the decisive step towards the fulfilment of his 'idea', the accomplishment of his 'mission'"* (Kershaw, 1991: 134).

TOK

You have already reflected on the role of the individual in history when considering Italy's foreign policies under Mussolini. In pairs consider the role of Hitler in shaping and directing events. Intentionalist historians view the role of individuals and personalities as key forces of historical change. To what extent do you agree with this idea. Refer to your study of German expansion in the 1930s. Other historians, and particularly Marxist historians argue that economic forces are the key factor. Investigate historians' views on German expansion in the 1930s. How far can you identify political or cultural perspectives of the historians from their accounts?

Source skills

Source A

The Italo–German Alliance, 22 May 1939 (the Pact of Steel).

The German Reich Chancellor and His Majesty the King of Italy and Albania, Emperor of Ethiopia, consider that the time has come to confirm through a solemn pact the close relation of friendship and affinity which exists between National Socialist Germany and Fascist Italy.

… Firmly bound together through the inner unity of their ideologies and the comprehensive solidarity of their interests, the German and the Italian people are determined also in future to stand side by side and to strive with united effort for the securing of their Lebensraum [living space] and the maintenance of peace. In this way, prescribed for them by history, Germany and Italy wish, in a world of unrest and disintegration, to carry out the assignment of making safe the foundations of European culture … have agreed upon the following terms:

ARTICLE I.

The Contracting Parties will remain in permanent contact with each other, in order to come to an understanding of all common interests or the European situation as a whole.

ARTICLE II.

In the event that the common interests of the Contracting Parties be jeopardized through international happenings of any kind, they will immediately enter into consultation regarding the necessary measures to preserve these interests. Should the security or other vital interests of one of the Contracting Parties be threatened from outside, the other Contracting Party will afford the threatened Party its full political and diplomatic support in order to remove this threat.

ARTICLE III.

If it should happen, against the wishes and hopes of the Contracting Parties, that one of them becomes involved in military complications with another power or other Powers, the other Contracting Party will immediately step to its side as an ally and will support it with all its military might on land, at sea, and in the air.

Berlin 22 May 1939 in the XVII year of the Fascist Era.

Source B

A photograph taken in Berlin, May 1939, following the signing of the Pact of Steel.

First question, part a – 3 marks

According to Source A, what common factors unite Italy and Germany?

First question, part b – 2 marks

What is the message of Source B?

ATL Thinking skills

Look at the articles of the agreement. Who do you consider would benefit the most from this alliance?

The Nazi–Soviet Pact

In the summer of 1939, both the Western democracies and Hitler approached the Soviet Union for an alliance. Despite Hitler's loathing of communist Russia and his plans for *Lebensraum* in the East, an alliance with the Soviet Union at this stage was highly desirable. It would prevent the Soviets forming an alliance with Britain and France, and would secure Soviet neutrality in a war with Poland, thus preventing a two-front conflict.

In fact, the Soviet Union had initially favoured an alliance with Britain and France. In 1934, the Soviet Union had joined the League of Nations and, alarmed by the growing power of Hitler, had hoped that collective security would work to prevent Hitler's aggression. However, the Western democracies were still suspicious of a communist government and had worked to appease Hitler. The French alone had signed a defensive pact with the Soviet Union in response to German rearmament in 1935, but this collapsed after the Munich Agreement.

Despite the Munich Agreement and what seemed to Stalin a capitulation to the Nazis, he renewed a proposal of a military alliance with the West following Hitler's occupation of Prague. However, negotiations with the democracies dragged on, both sides ultimately distrusting each other (see Chapter 2.7). Meanwhile, Stalin had also made it clear to the Germans that he would welcome an agreement and as a result, on 24 August 1939, Germany pulled off one of the most controversial and cynical alliances in modern history: the Nazi–Soviet Pact.

Under this Non-Aggression Pact, the Soviet Union and Nazi Germany each pledged to remain neutral in the event of either nation being attacked by a third party. In addition, the pact included a secret protocol dividing Northern and Eastern Europe into German and Soviet spheres of influence: the Baltic states and Bessarabia in Romania were to be in the Russian sphere, and Poland was to be divided between the two powers.

A cartoon by Herblock, 1939, called "Little Goldilocks Riding Hood".

Communication and social skills

In pairs or small groups, discuss the meaning of the cartoon above.

Why was an agreement between the Soviet Union and Nazi Germany so surprising and shocking to Poland, and also to the rest of the world?

Source skills

Source A

The Nazi–Soviet Pact, 23 August 1939

The Government of the German Reich and The Government of the Union of Soviet Socialist Republics desirous of strengthening the cause of peace between Germany and the U.S.S.R., and proceeding from the fundamental provisions of the Neutrality Agreement concluded in April, 1926 between Germany and the U.S.S.R., have reached the following Agreement:

Article I. Both High Contracting Parties obligate themselves to desist from any act of violence, any aggressive action, and any attack on each other, either individually or jointly with other Powers.

Article II. Should one of the High Contracting Parties become the object of belligerent action by a third Power, the other High Contracting Party shall in no manner lend its support to this third Power.

Article III. The Governments of the two High Contracting Parties shall in the future maintain continual contact with one another for the purpose of consultation in order to exchange information on problems affecting their common interests.

Article IV. Neither of the two High contracting parties shall participate in any grouping of powers whatsoever that is directly or indirectly aimed at the other party.

Article V. Should disputes or conflicts arise between the High Contracting Parties over problems of one kind or another, both parties shall settle these disputes or conflicts exclusively through friendly exchange of opinion or, if necessary, through the establishment of arbitration commissions.

Article VI. The present Treaty is concluded for a period of ten years, with the proviso that, in so far as one of the High Contracting Parties does not advance it one year prior to the expiration of this period, the validity of this Treaty shall automatically be extended for another five years.

Article VII. The present treaty shall be ratified within the shortest possible time. The ratifications shall be exchanged in Berlin. The Agreement shall enter into force as soon as it is signed.

The section below was not published at the time the above was announced.

Secret additional protocol

Article I. In the event of a territorial and political rearrangement in the areas belonging to the Baltic States (Finland, Estonia, Latvia, Lithuania), the northern boundary of Lithuania shall represent the boundary of the spheres of influence of Germany and U.S.S.R. In this connection the interest of Lithuania in the Vilna area is recognized by each party.

Article II. In the event of a territorial and political rearrangement of the areas belonging to the Polish state, the spheres of influence of Germany and the U.S.S.R. shall be bounded approximately by the line of the rivers Narev, Vistula and San.

The question of whether the interests of both parties make desirable the maintenance of an independent Polish State and how such a state should be bounded can only be definitely determined in the course of further political developments.

In any event both Governments will resolve this question by means of a friendly agreement.

Article III. With regard to Southeastern Europe, attention is called by the Soviet side to its interest in Bessarabia. The German side declares its complete political disinterest in these areas.

Article IV. This protocol shall be treated by both parties as strictly secret.

Moscow, August 23, 1939.

Source B

▲ The signing of the Nazi–Soviet Pact

First question, part a – 3 marks

According to Source A, what measures were to be followed to maintain peace between the two countries?

First question, part b – 2 marks

What is the message of Source B?

For Hitler, this alliance meant that he could have a free hand in Poland and that he could avoid fighting a war on two fronts. He could also get valuable raw materials from the Soviet Union. He clearly regarded it as a short-term expedient due to his long-term plans for attaining *Lebensraum* in the East.

For Stalin, there were also considerable advantages, as follows.

- It would keep the Soviet Union out of a war. This was important as it faced a threat in the East from Japan, and the army was weakened after **Stalin's purges** (see glossary box).

- There was always the hope that Germany and the West would weaken each other in the war and that the Soviet Union would emerge as the strongest nation.

- He got considerable territorial gains from the pact: half of Poland and the opportunity to take over Finland and the Baltic States.

- The Soviet Union could keep trading with Germany: Germany was to send mechanical goods to the Soviet Union in return for raw materials and foodstuffs (see Source B below for the importance of this to Germany).

> **Stalin's purges**
> During the 1930s, Stalin killed or "purged" anyone considered to be a threat. This included peasants, workers, political opponents and even senior military officers. In fact, approx 35,000 officers were either shot or imprisoned.

Two contrasting views of the Nazi–Soviet Pact

ATL Thinking and communication skills

Source A
Molotov's comments to the Supreme Soviet on the ratification of the Non-Aggression Pact, 31 August 1939.

The chief importance of the Soviet-German non-aggression pact lies in the fact that the two largest States of Europe have agreed to put an end to enmity between them, to eliminate the menace of war and to live at peace one with the other …

Only the instigators of a general European war … can be dissatisfied with this position of affairs …

It is really difficult for these gentlemen to understand the purpose of the Soviet-German non-aggression pact, on the strength of which the USSR is not obliged to involve itself in war either on the side of Great Britain against Germany, or on the side of Germany against Great Britain.

Is it really difficult to comprehend that the USSR is pursuing and will continue to pursue its own independent policy based on the interests of the peoples of the USSR and only these interests?

Source B
Comment by Dr Julius Schnurre, Head of the Economic Policy Division of the German foreign ministry, 24 October 1939.

The Agreement means a wide open door to the East for us. The raw material purchases from the Soviet Union and from the countries bordering the Soviet Union can still be considerably increased. But it is essential to meet the German commitments to the extent required. In view of the great volume this will require a special effort. If we succeed in expanding exports to the East in the required volume, the effects of the English blockade will be decisively weakened by the incoming raw materials.

Questions
1. What do Sources A and B indicate about the different ways in which the Soviet Union and Germany viewed this pact?

2. Does this pact support the idea that Hitler did *not*, in fact, have a clearly planned foreign policy, but was taking advantage of situations as they arose?

3. Which country do you consider gained most from this pact?

Source skills

A cartoon by David Low, "Rendezvous", published in the *Evening Standard* newspaper on 20 September 1939.

RENDEZVOUS

▲ The text reads: (Hitler to Stalin) *"The scum of the Earth, I believe?"*; (Stalin to Hitler) *"The bloody assassin of the workers, I presume?"*.

First question, part b – 2 marks

What is the message of this source?

The outbreak of war

Despite Britain's and France's assurances to Poland, Hitler did not believe that they would take any action at all, let alone declare war. As historian Roderick Stackelberg writes:

> *Hitler could not conceive that Britain and France, having failed to fight for a militarily strong and democratic Czechoslovakia a year before despite the assurance of Soviet aid, would now fight to save a militarily weak and undemocratic Poland without the prospect of Soviet aid".* — Stackelberg, 1999

Hitler was therefore taken back when he heard that Britain and Poland had signed a full military alliance on 25 August. At the same time, Mussolini informed him that he was not ready for war. Hitler thus delayed his attack on Poland planned for 26 August until 1 September. Hoping to cause a division between Britain and Poland, he also gave a last-minute proposal to Britain. This involved guaranteeing the British Empire and trying to reach an agreement on disarmament on the condition that Britain give Germany a free hand in Danzig and the Polish Corridor. However, this was not taken up by Britain. The Poles also refused further negotiation.

On 31 August, Mussolini proposed that a conference should be held to resolve the crisis. However, Hitler wanted war and was not prepared to wait for any peace initiatives. That same evening, Germany claimed that one of its wireless stations near the Polish border had been attacked by Poles. In reality, SS soldiers dressed in Polish uniforms had staged the attack. To make it appear authentic, they left behind the bodies of convicted criminals who had been dressed in Polish uniforms, killed by lethal injection and shot. This so-called Polish attack was used as the excuse for war. At 4.45am on 1 September 1939, German troops invaded Poland and German planes bombed Warsaw.

On 3 September, the British government presented an ultimatum to Germany to call off the attack by 11.00am. When no response had been received by this time, Britain and France declared war. Hitler hoped that the war on Poland would remain a localized affair; in fact, he had unleashed the most destructive war of all time. As historian Donald Watt concludes:

> *What is extraordinary in the events which led up to the outbreak of the Second World War is that Hitler's will for war was able to overcome the reluctance with which everybody else approached it. Hitler willed, desired, lusted after war, though not the war with France and Britain, at least not in 1939. No one else wanted it, though Mussolini came perilously close to talking himself into it.* — Watt, 2001

Hitler's actions after the declaration of war

Following the British declaration of war, Hitler launched an attack on Poland. Subjected to a "blitzkrieg" style of war, the Poles were quickly defeated, and Germany and the USSR divided up Poland along the so-called Ribbentrop–Molotov line as had been agreed in the Nazi-Soviet Pact of 1939. The Germans were now able to transfer most of their forces to the west.

The phoney war

In October 1939, Hitler offered peace proposals but very few people in Britain now trusted Hitler, and these were not taken up. However, there was no direct action from Hitler against the West for the next few months. This was the period known as "the phoney war".

Hitler takes over Europe

The calm of the phoney war was broken in April 1940. These are the key events, 1939–40:

- Hitler's troops occupied Denmark and landed at the Norwegian ports in April 1940.

- 10 May, Germany attacked Holland, Belgium and France simultaneously. Again, Hitler achieved swift victories. The Dutch surrendered after four days; Belgium at the end of May. British troops had to evacuate from Dunkirk in June 1940 as the invading German troops swept through France.

- After the British had left, the Germans moved southwards; Paris was captured 14th June and France surrendered 22nd June. The Germans occupied northern France and the Atlantic coast; unoccupied France was allowed its own government under Marshal Petain; however it had no real independence

- To secure the defeat of Britain in the planned invasion called "Operation Sea lion", the Germans needed control of the air over the English Channel. This led to the Battle for Britain during the summer and autumn of 1940 as the British Royal Air Force fought Luftwaffe planes in the skies above the coast of Britain.

- Although on the verge of defeating the RAF, Hitler switched to the bombing of London and other British cities. This marked the start of the Blitz. Hitler hoped that this would break the morale of the British, however by the middle of 1941, this was still not the case. It was at this point that Hitler decided to turn back to one of his main foreign policy aims: achieving lebensraum in the East. Thus, Hitler launched Operation Barbarossa against the Soviet Union in June 1941 with Britain still undefeated. Hitler anticipated that the attack against the Soviet Union would end in a speedy Soviet defeat, after which he would be able to return to finish off Britain. However, far from ensuring a victorious finale, the invasion of the Soviet Union would ensure that the war would go on for much longer and that Hitler would eventually be defeated.

ATL Self-management and thinking skills

Task one

Return to the question on page 161.

What new examples to explain Hitler's success in achieving his aims can you add to these headings?

- Hitler's tactical skill
- Luck
- The role the distractions and differences of the other powers played

What other factors played a role?

Task two

Review Hitler's actions between 1933 and 1939. Decide how far you agree with Bullock's claim that Hitler was able to combine "consistency in aim" with "opportunism and improvisation" in how he conducted his foreign policy.

Task three

How far had Hitler fulfilled his foreign policy aims?

In Chapter 2.2, we identified Hitler's aims were to:

- destroy the Treaty of Versailles
- unite all Germans
- gain more *Lebensraum* (living space) for the Germans
- gain Britain and Italy as allies.

For each of these aims, identify the extent to which it was achieved and give evidence for your conclusions.

Task four

You have read about the pacts and treaties signed by Japan, Italy and Germany between 1933 and 1939. Copy and complete the following table to consolidate your understanding of these agreements.

Agreement	Countries involved	Effect/impact of this treaty	Reasons for the outcome
Non-Aggression Pact, 1934			
Stresa Front, 1935			
Anglo-German Naval Treaty, 1935			
Rome–Berlin Axis, 1936			
Anti-Comintern Pact, 1936			
Pact of Steel, 1939			
Nazi–Soviet Pact, 1939			
Anglo–Polish Treaty, 1939			

Task five

Comparing and contrasting case studies.

a In pairs, compare and contrast the aims and methods of Mussolini's and Hitler's foreign policies in the 1930s.

b In pairs, compare and contrast the successes and failures of Mussolini's and Hitler's foreign policies in the 1930s.

c In small groups compare and contrast the aims, methods and results of the foreign policies of the expansionist states in Europe and Asia.

Full document question: The outbreak of war, September 1939

Source A

Germany's reply to Britain's ultimatum, received at 11.20am, 3 September 1939.

The German Government and the German people refuse to receive, accept, let alone fulfil, demands in the ultimatum made by the British Government.

1. On our eastern frontier there has for many months already reigned a condition of war. Since the time when the Versailles Treaty first tore Germany to pieces, all and every peaceful settlement was refused to all German Governments. The National Socialist Government also has since the year 1933 tried again and again to remove by peaceful negotiations the worst ... breaches of justice of this treaty. The British Government have been among those who, by their intransigent attitude, took the chief part in frustrating every practical revision. Without the intervention of the British Government ... a reasonable solution doing justice to both sides would certainly have been found between Germany and Poland. For Germany did not have the intention nor had she raised the demands of annihilating Poland. The Reich demanded only the revision of those articles of the Versailles Treaty which already at the time of the formulation of that Dictate had been described by understanding statesmen of all nations as being in the long run unbearable, and therefore impossible for a great nation and also for the entire political and economic interests of Eastern Europe. ... The blame for having prevented this peaceful revision lies with the British Cabinet policy ...

2. The German people and their Government do not, like Britain, intend to dominate the world, but they are determined to defend their own liberty, their independence, and above all their life ... we shall therefore answer any aggressive action on the part of England with the same weapons and in the same form.

Source B

A cartoon by David Low published in the UK newspaper, the *Evening Standard*, on 21 October 1939.

SOMEONE IS TAKING SOMEONE FOR A WALK

Source C

Hitler's speech to his commanders-in-chief, 22 August 1939.

I have called you together to give you a picture of the political situation, in order that you may have some insight into the individual factors on which I have based my decision to act and in order to strengthen your confidence …

It is easy for us to make decisions. We have nothing to lose, we have everything to gain … [O]ur economic situation is such that we cannot hold out more than a few more years … We have no other choice, we must act. Our opponents will be risking a great deal and can gain only a little. Britain's stake in a war is inconceivably great. Our enemies have leaders who are below average. No personalities. No masters, no men of action …

The relationship with Poland has become unbearable … My proposals to Poland were frustrated by England's intervention. Poland has changed her tone toward us. A permanent state of initiative cannot be allowed to pass to others … The probability is still great that the West will not intervene. We must take the risk with ruthless determination … [S]pecial reasons fortify me in my view. England and France have undertaken obligations which neither is in a position to fulfil … The West has only two possibilities for fighting against us: 1. Blockade: it will not be effective because of our autarky and because we have sources of supply in Eastern Europe. 2. Attack in the West from the Maginot Line: I consider this impossible.

Source D

Hitler's speech to party leaders at Obersalzberg, 22 August 1939.

Our strength lies in our quickness and in our brutality; Genghis Khan sent millions of women and children to death knowingly and with a light heart. History sees in him only the great founder of States. I have given the command and I shall shoot everyone who utters one word of criticism. And so for the present only in the East I have put my death-head formations in place with the command relentlessly and without compassion to send into death many women and children of Polish origin and language. Only thus we can gain the living space that we need …

To be sure a new situation has arisen. I experienced those poor worms Daladier and Chamberlain in Munich. They will be too cowardly to attack. They won't go beyond a blockade. Against that we have our autarchy and Russian raw materials.

Poland will be depopulated and settled with Germans. My pact with the Poles was merely conceived of as a gaining of time. As for the rest, gentlemen, the fate of Russia will be exactly the same as I am now going through with in the case of Poland. After Stalin's death – he is a very sick man – we will break the Soviet Union. Then there will begin the dawn of the German rule of the earth.

First question, part a – 3 marks

According to Source A, how had Britain caused the outbreak of hostilities in September 1939?

First question, part b – 2 marks

What is the message of Source B?

Second question – 4 marks

With reference to its origin, purpose and content, assess the values and limitations of using Source A as evidence of Hitler's aims in 1939.

Third question – 6 marks

Compare and contrast Sources A and C regarding Hitler's motivations for the attack on Poland.

Fourth question – 9 marks

Using the sources and your own knowledge, examine the reasons for Hitler's attack on Poland in September 1939.

References

Bullock, A. 1967. *Hitler and the Origins of the Second World War*. Oxford University Press. Oxford, UK

Craig, G. 1978. *Germany 1866–1945*. Oxford University Press. Oxford, UK

Fischer, K. 1995. *Nazi Germany: A New History*. Constable. London, UK

Stackelberg, R. 1999. *Hitler's Germany*. Routledge, UK

Watt, D. 2001. *How War Came*. Pimlico. London, UK

2.6 The international response to Italian aggression (1935–1940)

▲ Stanley Baldwin, Prime Minister of Britain 1935–37

Conceptual understanding

Key concepts
→ Consequence
→ Change
→ Significance

Key questions
→ Discuss the reasons for the British and French policy of appeasement.
→ Examine the response of the international community to Italian aggression.

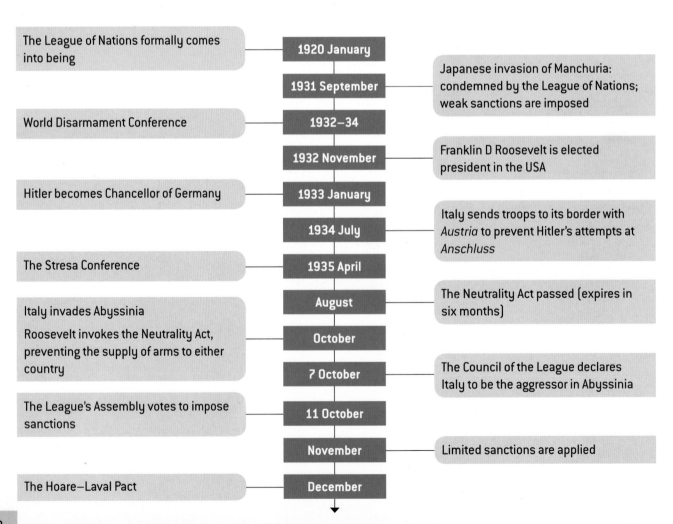

The League of Nations formally comes into being	**1920 January**	
	1931 September	Japanese invasion of Manchuria: condemned by the League of Nations; weak sanctions are imposed
World Disarmament Conference	**1932–34**	
	1932 November	Franklin D Roosevelt is elected president in the USA
Hitler becomes Chancellor of Germany	**1933 January**	
	1934 July	Italy sends troops to its border with *Austria* to prevent Hitler's attempts at *Anschluss*
The Stresa Conference	**1935 April**	
	August	The Neutrality Act passed (expires in six months)
Italy invades Abyssinia Roosevelt invokes the Neutrality Act, preventing the supply of arms to either country	**October**	
	7 October	The Council of the League declares Italy to be the aggressor in Abyssinia
The League's Assembly votes to impose sanctions	**11 October**	
	November	Limited sanctions are applied
The Hoare–Laval Pact	**December**	

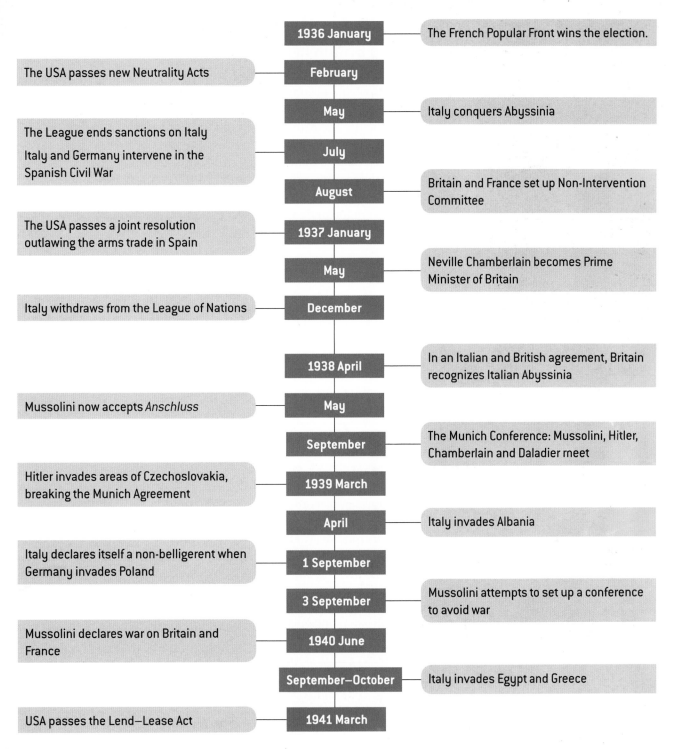

	1936 January — The French Popular Front wins the election.
The USA passes new Neutrality Acts	**February**
	May — Italy conquers Abyssinia
The League ends sanctions on Italy Italy and Germany intervene in the Spanish Civil War	**July**
	August — Britain and France set up Non-Intervention Committee
The USA passes a joint resolution outlawing the arms trade in Spain	**1937 January**
	May — Neville Chamberlain becomes Prime Minister of Britain
Italy withdraws from the League of Nations	**December**
	1938 April — In an Italian and British agreement, Britain recognizes Italian Abyssinia
Mussolini now accepts *Anschluss*	**May**
	September — The Munich Conference: Mussolini, Hitler, Chamberlain and Daladier meet
Hitler invades areas of Czechoslovakia, breaking the Munich Agreement	**1939 March**
	April — Italy invades Albania
Italy declares itself a non-belligerent when Germany invades Poland	**1 September**
	3 September — Mussolini attempts to set up a conference to avoid war
Mussolini declares war on Britain and France	**1940 June**
	September–October — Italy invades Egypt and Greece
USA passes the Lend–Lease Act	**1941 March**

Neville Chamberlain, prime minister of Britain, 1937–40

What was the policy of appeasement and why was it pursued by Britain in the 1930s?

Appeasement, in this political and historical context, was a diplomatic policy of making concessions to nations in order to avoid conflict. The policy is most closely associated with Britain's foreign policy in the late 1930s, in particular the Munich crisis of 1938. Appeasement failed to prevent the outbreak of war and came to be seen as a weak and dishonourable policy. It allowed both Mussolini and Hitler to get away with territorial demands, which encouraged Hitler to ask continuously for more, resulting in the outbreak of war in 1939. However, for most of the inter-war years, appeasement was seen as a positive idea, and as part of a long-standing tradition of trying to settle disputes peacefully.

In Britain, there were many reasons to follow a policy of appeasement in the 1930s:

1 Public opinion

The Franchise Act of 1918 had increased the number of voters in Britain from 8 million to 21 million; for the first time, women over the age of 30 were given the vote, and from 1928, this was lowered to the age of 21. This huge increase in the electorate meant that politicians were more likely to take notice of public opinion, which was against war and in favour of collective security.

The horror of the First World War had created a widespread feeling that this should be "the war to end all wars". This anti-war feeling was seen clearly in February 1933, when the Oxford Union debating society voted that "This House would not fight for King and Country". The destruction by German bomber aircraft of Guernica in Spain in 1937 showed the vulnerability of London to attack from the air and highlighted the need to prevent another war that would clearly have a devastating effect on civilians on the British mainland. As Stanley Baldwin told the House of Commons in 1932, "*I think it is as well … for the man in the street to realise that no power on earth can protect him from being bombed. Whatever people may tell him, the bomber will always get through*". It was widely believed that there would be 150,000 casualties in London in the first week of war.

The British public put faith in the League of Nations to maintain peace through collective security. There was even a League of Nations Union in Britain, which had more than 400,000 supporters in 1935. The Union carried out a "peace ballot" in 1935, which appeared to show that the British public fully supported the League and its principles.

2 The demands of the dictators seen as justified

Many British politicians felt that the Treaty of Versailles was too harsh and that Hitler had genuine grievances relating to the First World War. Increasingly, there was a belief that the First World War had been caused by all the powers, not just by Germany and her allies, and thus there was support for the idea of revising the more punitive clauses of the treaty. In particular, Chamberlain believed, mistakenly, that it was possible to do business with Mussolini and Hitler, and to sort out the grievances of these countries rationally and without recourse to war.

In addition, many conservative politicians saw the threat of communism as more dangerous than the threat of fascism.

3 The lack of an alternative policy

Support for appeasement was found in all political parties and there was no clear anti-appeasement party to provide a coherent political alternative. The Labour Party, which was the political party in opposition, supported collective security but did not support rearmament.

4 Economic pressures

There were also economic reasons for following a policy of appeasement. Already weakened severely by the First World War, the Great Depression worsened Britain's economic situation further still. By the 1930s, Britain was facing competition from other countries that were overtaking its industrial production. It also faced high unemployment: 3 million people were unemployed in the early 1930s. These economic difficulties made it hard to spend money on armaments; no government would be able to maintain support if it cut welfare benefits in order to finance rearmament. It was also feared that rearming too quickly would cause a balance of payments crisis, with too many imports of machinery and raw materials. For these reasons, although rearmament started again in 1932, it was not until 1937 that defence spending increased dramatically.

The Anti-Appeasers

Some individuals did speak out against appeasement:

Foreign Secretary Anthony Eden resigned in February 1938 because he disagreed with Chamberlain's policy of appeasement of Italy.

Winston Churchill called for rearmament to be stepped up and vehemently opposed concessions to Germany (though he did not oppose the appeasement of Mussolini over Abyssinia). He supported the idea of a Grand Alliance of the Anti-Fascist powers.

Duff Cooper was Secretary of State for War (1935–1937) and then First Lord of the Admiralty in Chamberlain's government until he resigned in protest at the Munich Agreement in September 1938.

You will have seen plenty of David Low's cartoons in this book. These appeared in the *Evening Standard* newspaper and were consistently critical of appeasement throughout the 1930s. Low was attacked in the right-wing press as a "war-monger" and his cartoons were banned in Germany.

TOK

There have been many critics of the policy of appeasement as pursued by Britain and France in the 1930s. As you have read here, those involved at the time seem to have had a different view and this perspective was supported by public opinion. In pairs discuss the extent to which history looked different in the past. Create a poster: "History itself looked different in the past" outlining your ideas. Include references to the material you have covered in this book.

Thinking skills

What does the foreign office report on defence expenditure show about Britain's expectations for a future war? How might France react to this report?

Britain was in a weak military position and, by 1937, with threats from Japan, Italy and Germany, this position was becoming increasingly dangerous. As a result, the British Chiefs of Staff concluded that, until rearmament was further advanced, it should be the main aim of foreign policy to reduce the number of Britain's enemies. This was reiterated in January 1938 in this statement: *"We cannot foresee the time when our defence forces will be strong enough to safeguard our territory, trade and vital interests against Germany, Italy and Japan simultaneously"*.

5 Global commitments

Britain had to consider its worldwide commitments alongside its obligations to European countries and the League of Nations. Indeed, most politicians considered British interests to be more global than European. Preservation and defence of the Empire was held to be essential if Britain was to remain a great world power, which was its priority. However, Britain's imperial commitments were now so vast that they were becoming increasingly difficult to administer and defend.

In addition, the Dominions (the self-governing parts of the British Empire, such as Canada, Australia and New Zealand) made it clear at the 1937 Imperial Conference that they were not prepared to help Britain in another European war.

6 Defence priorities

Worried about the cost of its expenditure, the Treasury was also putting pressure on the Foreign Office. In 1937, the Treasury put forward a report on defence expenditure in which the priorities for defence were to be, in order of importance:

- military preparation sufficient to repulse air attacks
- the preservation of trade routes for the supply of food and raw materials
- the defence of the Empire
- the defence of Britain's allies.

7 The impact of Neville Chamberlain

Clearly, the financial pressures, the commitments of Empire and the comments from the Chiefs of Staff meant that Chamberlain, when he became Prime Minister in 1937, would have little choice but to follow a policy that looked for conciliation rather than confrontation with Germany and Italy. However, Chamberlain's own personal views also had an impact. He detested war and was determined to resolve international tension and to use negotiation and diplomacy to bring about a peaceful settlement of Europe. Chamberlain ran foreign policy very much alone, with the aid of his chief adviser, Sir Horace Wilson, but without consulting his Cabinet. He had little faith in the League or in Britain's allies, France and the USA; he distrusted the Soviet Union, and he believed that Britain should take the lead in negotiating with Hitler. Right up to the moment that war broke out, Chamberlain continued to hope that he could achieve a "general settlement" of Europe to maintain peace.

ATL Communication skills

Go to www.youtube.com/watch?v=gR8ISozEbcs, or search for "Why Appeasement?"

Watch a summary of the reasons for Britain's policy of appeasement. Make notes on the first 10 minutes of this video clip.

Add notes to the points above on the reasons behind Britain's policy of appeasement.

Class discussion

How might the policy of appeasement encourage expansionist states?

Why did France align its foreign policy to Britain's policy of appeasement in the 1930s?

France certainly did not agree with many of Britain's views regarding Germany and the Treaty of Versailles, and there was no indication in the 1920s that it would follow a policy of appeasement. It faced huge debts after the First World War and, unlike Britain, had suffered economically from the impact of the fighting on its land; about 10% had been laid to waste, which had an impact on industrial and agricultural resources. The huge loss of life, and the resultant trauma to French society, meant that the French population wanted Germany punished and permanently weakened to prevent any future German attack. France had been invaded twice by Germany between 1870 and 1914 and the French wanted to prevent a resurgent Germany at all costs.

When the USA failed first to ratify the Treaty of Versailles and then to join the League of Nations, the French felt abandoned. When Britain also showed some sympathy with the view that Germany had been treated too harshly at Versailles, the French were appalled at this apparent collapse of the Anglo–American guarantee of the post-war settlement. The French subsequently attempted to uphold the terms of the treaty by force when they occupied the Ruhr in 1923. However, the occupation ended in defeat for France and was followed by a period of appeasement under Foreign Minister Aristide Briand; this can be seen in the Dawes Plan of 1924, the Locarno Agreements of 1925 and the evacuation of French troops from the Rhineland in 1930.

In an attempt to strengthen its position, France also tried to find other allies and signed a series of bilateral agreements through the 1920s with Belgium (1920), Poland (1920 and 1925), Czechoslovakia (1924), Romania (1926) and Yugoslavia (1927). Czechoslovakia, Romania and Yugoslavia had signed a mutual defence agreement in what became known as the "Little Entente". France supported this alliance.

However, the frequent changes of government and ideological conflicts in France in the 1930s meant that it was unable to take any action against Germany. German reparations ended and, coupled with the impact of the Great Depression, the French economy stagnated. The franc had been overvalued, exports fell and unemployment increased. In 1932, a coalition of socialists and radicals won the general election. Edouard Herriot was initially elected Prime Minister, but due to his failure to redress the economic issues he was forced to resign and was replaced by Edouard Daladier. Daladier did not bring stability, however,

▲ Edouard Daladier, the French Prime Minister in 1938

Thinking and social skills

In pairs compare and contrast the British and French reasons for pursuing a policy of appeasement towards the aggressor states in the 1930s. Are there more similarities or more differences?

Self-management skills

Review Chapter 2.3 on Mussolini's expansion in the 1930s. Consider the extent to which a policy of appeasement would have encouraged Mussolini's aggression.

and there were six different Cabinets in less than two years. Economic problems fostered the growth of right-wing leagues, some of whom emulated Mussolini's Fascists. Right-wing activity galvanized left-wing unity and led to the formation of the Popular Front, an alliance of left-wing parties. In January 1936, the Popular Front won a resounding victory in the general elections under the leadership of Prime Minister Leon Blum. However, Blum's government was criticized by the right for expensive domestic reforms when they believed France should have been rearming. Blum was also criticized for his attempts to take a firm stance against internal Fascist threats. Daladier returned as Prime Minister in May 1938 and managed to establish some political stability as he moved to the right and supported a huge in arms spending. These continual changes in government meant that there was little continuity in how to deal with Hitler.

In addition, there was a conflict between France's foreign policy and its military planning. Despite a series of guarantees to the states of Eastern Europe, which would have required France to demonstrate some offensive capability, its military planning in the 1930s was entirely defensive. This was in contrast to its offensive action in the 1920s, and most clearly seen in the building of the Maginot Line, a chain of fortresses along the Franco–German border. Furthermore, France's air force was ineffectual and its army limited. As a result, the French became increasingly dependent on Britain. When Britain decided on a policy of appeasement in the 1930s France had to follow its strongest ally's line.

How was the international response to aggression in the 1930s affected by the weaknesses of the League of Nations?

Refer back to Chapter 1.3, page 62, to review the aims of the League.

The international response to acts of expansion and aggression in the 1930s should have been dealt with through the mechanism to facilitate collective security: the League of Nations. However, the League had many limitations:

- It lacked the credibility and economic power of its founding nation, the USA.

- Its key organ of power was the Council, which was led by Britain, France, Italy and Japan, with Germany joining in 1926. The latter three countries were "revisionist" powers who wanted to revise the Treaty of Versailles.

- The Soviet Union was not a member until September 1934.

- The League's structure and organization was inefficient.

- It was impotent in the face of the aggressive military fascist states, and each time it failed to act effectively it lost more authority.

Without the economic and diplomatic power of the USA, it was up to Britain and France to uphold the League's resolutions and enforce its decisions. However, Britain was inclined to look after its own interests first, while France had little faith in the League's ability to contain Mussolini's Italy or Hitler's Germany.

What was the impact of US foreign policy on the international response to the expansionist powers?

As has been discussed in Chapter 1.3, the USA did not join the League of Nations in 1919 and it pursued a policy of isolationism in the inter-war period. The USA wanted to be free to engage in trade and investment globally and wished to avoid being drawn into conflicts that were not in its own interests. This policy continued during the 1930s and was strengthened by the impact of the Great Depression and by public opinion, which was staunchly anti-war. Memories of the First World War also remained fresh in the minds of Americans. US isolationists advocated a policy of non-involvement in the affairs of both Europe and Asia. In 1935, the USA passed the Neutrality Act designed to keep the USA out of a possible European war by banning the sale of armaments to belligerents.

▲ Franklin D Roosevelt, US president from 1933

Source skills

A.J.P. Taylor. *The Origins of the Second World War* **(1961).**

American isolationism completed the isolation of Europe. Academic commentators observed, rightly, that the problem of the two dictators would be "solved", if the two World Powers, Soviet Russia and the United States, were drawn into European affairs. This observation was a desire, not a policy. Western statesmen would have grasped eagerly at material backing from across the Atlantic. This was not on offer. The United States were unarmed except in the Pacific; and neutrality legislation made it impossible for them to act even as a base of

supply. President Roosevelt could provide only moral exhortation; and this was the very thing which Western statesmen feared. It would tie their hands in dealing with Hitler and Mussolini; it would work against the concessions which they were ready to make. Great Britain and France had already too much moral capital; what they lacked was material strength. None was forthcoming from the United States.

First question, part a – 3 marks

What, according to AJP Taylor, was the impact of the USA's policy of isolationism?

What was the impact of Soviet foreign policy on the international response to the expansionist powers?

Western hostility towards the Soviet Union also affected its response to Italian and German aggression. The Western democracies had cut off all diplomatic and economic ties with the Bolshevik government in 1917 and had invaded Russia in an attempt to overthrow the new regime. This failed, but the USSR was not included in the Paris Peace talks and the Russian Bolshevik leader, Vladimir Lenin, had called the League of Nations, on its foundation, "a band of robbers". Relations remained hostile until the end of the 1920s when some diplomatic links and economic agreements were made. Britain remained particularly concerned with the potential threat from communism and, following a "red scare" in 1927, did not restore diplomatic links until 1930.

Source skills

A Soviet poster by D. Melnikova, produced in Moscow, in the Soviet Union, June 1930. The text reads "Proletarians of all countries, Unite!".

First question, part b – 2 marks

What is the message of the artist in this poster?

ATL **Thinking and social skills**

Look at the details of this Soviet poster. In pairs or groups, discuss how the Western democracies of the 1930s might have reacted to this Soviet propaganda.

ATL **Communication and social skills**

Work in pairs. Create a diagram to show the factors influencing the policy of appeasement that France and Britain took towards Mussolini and Hitler in the 1930s.

Class discussion

Should the Western democracies have worked with the USSR to form a "Popular Front against Fascism"? What advantages would this have had? Why were the Western democracies reluctant to ally with the USSR?

The Soviet Union under Stalin (from 1929) wanted to build "socialism in one country", which meant that it would not commit to exporting the revolution until the process was complete in the USSR. Nevertheless, the activities of the Communist International in Europe and Asia alarmed the democracies. Stalin's foreign policy began to shift away from hostility towards the West when the Soviet Union became threatened by the expansionist policies of Japan in Asia, and by Hitler's stated aim of acquiring *Lebensraum* in the East of Europe at the expense of the Soviet Union. Between 1931 and 1932, Stalin signed non-aggression pacts with Afghanistan, Finland, Lithuania, Latvia, Estonia, Poland and France. There was a tangible shift in Soviet foreign policy towards the pursuit of a "Popular Front" against fascism. To this end, the Soviet Union joined the League of Nations in 1934 and signed mutual assistance pacts with France and Czechoslovakia in 1935.

However, the aim of forming a Popular Front against fascism failed because Britain and France were following a policy of appeasement. It was clear to the Soviet Union during the Spanish Civil War that Britain in particular feared communism more than fascism. The final catalyst for the Soviet Union to abandon its attempts to work with the British and French in order to contain the fascist aggressors came at the Munich Conference in September 1938. Despite its assistance pact with Czechoslovakia and the territorially strategic importance of that country to the Soviet Union, Stalin was not invited to the Munich Conference.

What was the international response to the Italian invasion of Abyssinia in 1935–36?

Both the French and the British had attempted to keep Mussolini on side as a key guarantor of the post-war settlement, specifically to contain German ambitions to unite with Austria. As previous chapters have described, the three countries had come together to form the Stresa Front in March 1935. At this meeting, the French gave Mussolini the impression that they would tolerate an Italian expansion in East Africa. French Foreign Minister Pierre Laval had suggested that Italy could go ahead and acquire political influence in Abyssinia, as the French interests there were only economic. Although the French had not condoned a military takeover of the country, Mussolini believed at this point that they would not resist.

Britain had been silent on the matter of Abyssinia when Mussolini mentioned his plans during the Stresa Conference. Mussolini hoped this meant Britain would have the same attitude as the French. The Italians were concerned about the potential British response to military action, particularly as the British could threaten to attack the Italian navy.

The British demonstrated that they wanted to appease Italian expansionist plans when Foreign Secretary Anthony Eden went to Rome in June 1935, with a plan that would give Italy the Ogaden region of Abyssinia and compensate Emperor Haile Selassie's Abyssinia with access to the sea via British Somaliland. The Italians now saw that Britain wanted to accommodate them, and so they rejected the plan. This perception was further reinforced by a report Italy had "acquired" from the British foreign office, stating that Britain would not resist an Italian invasion of Abyssinia.

When Mussolini invaded Abyssinia in October 1935, there was widespread international public outrage and condemnation from the League of Nations. British public opinion was against the invasion and in favour of action by the League. As there was a general election in Britain in November 1935, public opinion at the time was all the more important; a pro-League stance had helped the National government to secure power in November 1935. However, as you will see from the sequence of events below, the League proved ineffective in dealing with the crisis.

Source skills

Source A

Laura Fermi, Jewish-Italian writer and political activist, who emigrated to the USA in 1938 to escape from Mussolini's Italy, in *Mussolini* (1966).

In England, in view of the coming elections, the "peace ballot", and public opinion, the government embraced an all-out policy in favor of the League of Nations and the imposition of economic sanctions on aggressor nations. At the end of September Winston Churchill spoke in London and "tried to convey a warning to Mussolini", as he recalls in The Gathering Storm: "To cast an army of nearly a quarter-million men, embodying the flower of Italian manhood, upon a barren shore two thousand miles from home, against the goodwill of the whole world and without command of the sea, and then in this position embark upon what may well be a series of campaigns against a people and in regions which no conqueror in four thousand years ever thought it worthwhile to subdue, is to give hostages to fortune unparalleled in all history."

It is tempting to speculate what effect these words may have had on Mussolini, if he read them, as Churchill believed he did. The chance seems negligible that at this late date, committed as he was to the Ethiopian war by both the fatalistic drive of his own determination and the amount of money he had spent in the undertaking, Mussolini would have allowed this warning to dissuade him. (To an interviewer from the Morning Post, he said that the cost of preparation was already 2 billion lire – 100 million pre-war dollars – and asked "Can you believe that we have spent this sum for nothing?") …

While taking up a position against the Ethiopian war and for the League's policies, Great Britain was unofficially assuring France that she would try to water down the sanctions on Italy, if imposed, and connived with France in an embargo on arms to Ethiopia through the control of the port of Djibouti, the only access to Abyssinia from the sea. It is said that Haile Selassie, placing pathetic confidence in traditional British justice, could not understand why it was so difficult to procure the modern arms and equipment he needed and was trying so desperately to buy. But then, during the war, the unofficial embargo was lifted, in part at least.

Source B

A cartoon by David Low, published in the UK newspaper, the *Evening Standard*, on 24 July 1935.

▲ The text reads "On the throne of justice. See no Abyssinia; Hear no Abyssinia; Speak no Abyssinia".

First question, part b – 2 marks

What is the message of the cartoonist in Source B?

Second question – 4 marks

With reference to its origin, purpose and content assess the values and limitations of Source A for historians studying the international response to the Abyssinian crisis in 1935–36.

The response of the League, Britain and France

- On 6 December 1935, following the Wal Wal incident (see page 137), Abyssinian Emperor Haile Selassie asked the League of Nations to arbitrate; however the League's arbitration committee found neither side responsible.

- On 7 January 1935, a Franco–Italian agreement was made. In return for Italian support to contain Hitler, France gave Italy parts of French Somaliland, improved the official status of Italians living in Tunisia and tacitly allowed Mussolini to do as he pleased in Abyssinia.

- On 17 March 1935, following a large build-up of Italian forces in East Africa, Emperor Haile Selassie appealed directly to the League, as a member state, for its support. The Italian mobilization continued and on 11 May Selassie appealed to the League again.

- On 20 May, the League held a special session to discuss the crisis and on 19 June Selassie requested League observers be sent to the region. Talks between officials from Italy and Abyssinia broke down at The Hague.

Despite Anglo–French efforts to appease Mussolini and British attempts via Anthony Eden to find a peaceful resolution, it was clear from the beginning of July that Italy wanted a war of conquest. The British declared an arms embargo on both sides on 25 July, perhaps in response to Mussolini's assertion that sales of arms to Abyssinia would be seen as "unfriendliness" towards Italy. It also removed its warships from the Mediterranean, an act which enabled Mussolini to have free movement of supplies to East Africa.

At the end of September, Selassie again asked for neutral observers, but on 28 September he also began to mobilize his poorly equipped and outdated army. Without a declaration of war, Italian forces invaded Abyssinia on 3 October.

On 7 October, the League duly found Italy the aggressor and began the process of imposing sanctions; however, this process was slow and the sanctions were limited. They did not embargo key war materials, such as coal, steel and oil, and the sanctions were not carried out by all members of the League. The British government had not wanted to implement harsh sanctions as Britain wanted to revive the Stresa Front and to maintain good relations with Mussolini. However, the British government was also under pressure to uphold the authority of the League.

Nevertheless, Britain decided not to close the Suez Canal, a significant route for Mussolini's troops and for supplies to East Africa, to Italian shipping. Austria, Hungary and Nazi Germany ignored the sanctions completely. The USA actually increased exports to Italy. The sanctions, therefore, did little to impede the Italian war effort and, as discussed in the previous chapter, they in fact rallied Italian domestic support behind Mussolini.

Even when the Italians used chemical weapons in Abyssinia, the League failed to take further action.

The Hoare–Laval Pact

In their attempt to maintain the Stresa Front against a resurgent Germany, the French and British came up with an appeasing plan to end the conflict and the tension it had caused. In December 1935, French foreign secretary, Pierre Laval and British counterpart, Samuel Hoare drew up the Hoare–Laval Pact, which sought to pacify Mussolini by giving him most of Abyssinia. Selassie would receive access to the sea. However, the plan was leaked in the French press. Public opinion in both Britain and France was outraged by this apparent duplicity and demanded support for the League's policy. The British and French governments were forced to denounce the pact and sanctions continued. Laval and Hoare resigned.

Abyssinia (1935) and bordering countries

The Hoare–Laval proposal

BRITISH ▢ FRENCH ▩ ITALIAN ▢

Assigned to Italy ▩   Italian sphere of economic influence ▓

Thinking and communication skills

Read this source. Discuss the key impact of the Hoare–Laval Pact on domestic politics in Britain and France.

Using this source, identify political opposition to appeasing Mussolini that existed in Britain and France.

A.J.P. Taylor. 1961. *The Origins of the Second World War* **(1961) pages 126–127.**

Early in December Hoare took the plan to Paris. Laval welcomed it. Mussolini, warned by his equally erring experts that the war was going badly, was ready to accept it. The next step was to present it at Geneva; then, with the League's concurrence, to impose it on the Emperor of Abyssinia – a beautiful example, repeated at Munich, of using the machinery of peace against the victim of aggression. But something went wrong. Hardly had Hoare left Paris on his way to Geneva than the so-called Hoare-Laval plan appeared in the French press. No one knows how this happened. Perhaps Laval doubted whether the National government were solidly behind Hoare and therefore leaked the plan in order to commit Baldwin and the rest beyond redemption. Perhaps Herriot, or some other enemy of Laval's, revealed the plan in order to ruin it, believing that, if the League were effective against Mussolini, it could then be turned against Hitler. Maybe there was no design at all, merely the incorrigible zest of French journalists …

At any rate the revelation produced an explosion in British public opinion. The high-minded supporters of the league who had helped to return the National government felt cheated and indignant … Baldwin first admitted that the plan had been endorsed by the government; then repudiated both the plan and Sir Samuel Hoare. Eden took Hoare's place as Foreign Secretary. The Hoare-Laval plan disappeared. Otherwise nothing was changed. The British government were still resolved not to risk war.

The results of the international response to the Abyssinian crisis

The Hoare–Laval pact sealed the fate of the League of Nations in 1935. It had been exposed as a sham. The attention of Britain and France was drawn away from East Africa and closer to home when Hitler remilitarized the Rhineland in March 1936. France was prepared to let Mussolini complete his conquest in return for his support against Hitler, and the French would not support any further action regarding sanctions.

Source skills

Telegram from Haile Selassie to the League of Nations, 6 May 1936.

We have decided to bring to an end the most unequal, most unjust, most barbarous war of our age, and have chosen the road to exile in order that our people will not be exterminated and in order to consecrate ourselves wholly and in peace to the preservation of our empire's independence … we now demand that the League of Nations should continue its efforts to secure respect for the covenant, and that it should decide not to recognize territorial extensions, or the exercise of an assumed sovereignty, resulting from the illegal recourse to armed force and to numerous other violations of international agreements.

First question, part a – 3 marks

What, according to Haile Selassie, should the League of Nation's do in response to Italian aggression in Abyssinia?

Selassie fled on 2 May, and the Abyssinian capital, Addis Ababa, fell to Italian forces. However, there was no official surrender by Abyssinia and a guerrilla war continued against the Italians. Selassie made pleas for support from the League and on 30 June, despite the jeering of Italian journalists, he made a powerful speech criticizing the international community for its inaction. He moved for a resolution to deny recognition of the Italian conquest. He concluded with the ominous and prophetic statement, "It is us today. It will be you *tomorrow*".

Despite Selassie's impassioned speech, his resolution failed; on 4 July, the League voted to end its sanctions, which were lifted on the 15 July. The new "Italian Empire" was recognized by Japan on 18 November 1936 in return for recognition of its own occupation of Manchuria. In 1938, Britain and France recognized Italian control of Abyssinia, although the USA and USSR refused to recognise the Italian Empire.

Thinking and social skills

Go to www.youtube.com/watch?v=oyX2kXeFUlo, or search for "Emperor Haile Selassie of Ethiopia addresses League of Nations".

Watch Haile Selassie's speech at the League of Nations, June 1936.

Source skills

Source A

Article from the UK newspaper, *The Guardian*, 3 October 1935.

Mussolini's long-expected invasion of Abyssinia began at dawn yesterday, with thousands of young Italian infantrymen cheering as they crossed the border from Eritrea and began the heavy slog up the valleys.

Italian bombing planes roared overhead, striking first at the border town of Adowa, scene of Italy's humiliating defeat at the hands of the Abyssinians in 1896. Two of the bombers were reported to be piloted by Mussolini's sons, Vittorio, aged 19, and Bruno, aged 18, while a third had his son-in-law, Count Galeazzo Ciano, as pilot.

Tonight the Italian force, under General Emilio de Bono and numbering 100,000 men, including Eritrean soldiers, is reported to be advancing on a 40-mile front and to be within 12 miles of Adowa. Another army, commanded by General Graziani, is mounting a drive north from Italian Somaliland, but is reported to be held up by rain-soaked tracks …

The Abyssinian Ministry of Foreign Affairs has telegraphed the League of Nations in Geneva, denouncing the Italian aggression as a breach of the League Covenant. The Abyssinians claim that the first bombs on Adowa struck a hospital bearing the Red Cross. Mussolini raised the curtain on his African adventure with a speech on Wednesday afternoon from the balcony of his office in the Palazzo Venezia, in Rome. "A solemn hour is about to break in the history of our fatherland," he said. The wheel of fate had begun to turn and could not be stopped.

In London, the British cabinet held a two-hour meeting on the crisis in the morning, and in the afternoon key ministers and service chiefs were called to Downing Street. It is being stressed that any action by Britain must be coordinated with France. But the French are saying they will not do anything to upset the accord they recently reached with Italy.

Source B

Speech by Sir Samuel Hoare, British Foreign Secretary, to the League at Geneva, 11 September 1935.

I do not suppose that in the history of the Assembly there was ever a more difficult moment for a speech … On behalf of the government of the United Kingdom, I can say that they will be second to none in their intention to fulfill within the measure of their capacity, the obligations which the Covenant lays upon them. The League stands, and my country stands with it, for the collective maintenance of the Covenant, especially to all acts of unprovoked aggression.

Source C

Extract from speech by Haile Selassie to the League of Nations, June 1936.

I, Haile Selassie, Emperor of Abyssinia, am here today to claim that justice which is due to my people and the assistance promised to it eight months ago when fifty nations asserted that aggression had been committed in violation of international treaties … What real assistance was given to Ethiopia by the fifty-two nations who had declared the Rome Government guilty of breach of the Covenant and had undertaken to prevent the triumph of the aggressor? … I noted with grief, but without surprise that three powers considered their undertakings under the Covenant as absolutely of no value … What, then, in practice, is the meaning of Article 16 of the Covenant and of collective security? … It is collective security: it is the very existence of the League of Nations. It is the value of promises made to small states that their integrity and independence be respected and ensured … it is the principle of the equality of states … In a word, it is international morality that is at stake.

First question, part a – 3 marks

What key criticisms of the League's response to the Abyssinian Crisis are made in Source C?

Second question – 4 marks

With reference to its origin, purpose and content, assess the values and limitations of Source B for historians studying the international reaction to the Abyssinian crisis.

Without doubt, the international response to the Abyssinian crisis had a profound effect on European diplomacy. It had fatally undermined the League of Nations as a credible body for dealing with aggressor states. It also ended the Stresa Front. Both France and Britain believed after this conflict that appeasement was the only route they could take to avoid a conflict with Hitler's Germany. Thus the crisis had shifted the balance of power to Germany's advantage. Mussolini would now move towards a full alliance with Hitler.

Source skills

A cartoon by David Low, published on 4 October 1935, "The man who took the lid off".

THE MAN WHO TOOK THE LID OFF.

First question, part b – 2 marks

What is the message of the cartoon?

ATL Thinking and social skills

In pairs or small groups, read Source A and discuss the key points it makes. Discuss the reasons it gives for British hesitation. To what extent do you agree that France's position held Britain back?

ATL Research and communication skills

In pairs, research headlines and press reports on the invasion of Abyssinia from around the world in October 1935. Make sure you reference your sources appropriately and include a correctly formatted works cited list.

Present your headlines and press reports to the class and assess whether there was international consensus against the Italian action.

How did the USA respond to the invasion of Abyssinia?

President Roosevelt sent Mussolini a personal message on 18 August 1935. He stated that the US government and people believed that the failure to arrive at a peaceful settlement in East Africa would be a calamity and would lead to adverse effects for all nations.

However, the United States would not take any direct action, as was made clear in a radio address by Secretary of State Hull on 6 November 1935. In this broadcast, he said it was the USA's duty to remain aloof from disputes and conflicts with which it had no direct concern.

Source skills

The Secretary of State to the United States Delegation at Geneva, by telegram, Washington, October 17 1935, 6.00pm.

October 15, 8 p.m. It is important that, if possible, daily newspaper rumors and reports from Europe about the attitude or policy of this Government toward some phase of the Italo-Ethiopian controversy, and especially reports that foreign governments or agencies are just about to inquire of this Government whether it can or will cooperate with foreign Governments or peace agencies in one way or another, shall be minimized to the greatest possible extent ... Every leading official abroad knows that prior to the outbreak of the war our chief purpose was to aid in preserving peace, whereas after hostilities began our chief object is and will be to avoid being drawn into the war ...

First question b – 3 marks

What key points are made in this source with regards to the US response to the Italian invasion of Abyssinia?

Second question – 4 marks

With reference to its origin, purpose and content, assess the values and limitations of this source for historians studying the international response to the Italian invasion of Abyssinia.

The end of the appeasement of Mussolini's Italy

How did Britain and France respond to the Italian invasion of Albania, 7 April 1939?

Britain, along with France, condemned the Italian invasion of Albania and, as Italy had previously guaranteed the sovereignty of the Balkans, this was a turning point for Chamberlain. He no longer trusted the dictators and now went as far as to guarantee Greek borders with British military support. Churchill had urged a more direct response by sending in the Royal Navy, but Chamberlain did not agree. Mussolini was, however, surprised at the appeasers' commitment to Greece.

ATL Thinking skills

G. Bruce Strang. *On the Fiery March: Mussolini Prepares For War*, page 247 (2003).

Italian leaders were ignorant of the real British reaction. Despite the comparatively muted protests, the aggressive nature of Italian policy did provoke a response. The foreign policy committee decided on 10 and 11 April to issue a guarantee to Greece, and, under intense French pressure, agreed to extend one to Romania, while making a concerted effort to bring Turkey into an eastern Mediterranean security arrangement. Greece accepted its guarantee, although it refused in the first instance to join in guaranteeing other countries independence. In Turkey, the Inonii government cited constitutional difficulties, and, more seriously, concerns about its own security in the absence of a British guarantee. Nevertheless, on 13 April both Chamberlain and Daladier issued public statements in their respective parliamentary chambers guaranteeing Greece and Romania against aggression. Although the issuing of guarantees would in the end be significantly less than an ironclad, interlocking security system against Axis aggression, it did signal that the patience of the Western democracies with Axis aggression was eroding. Chamberlain wrote to his sister, "Mussolini has behaved like a snake and a cad." Chamberlain thought the invasion showed Mussolini's "complete cynicism". The Prime Minister had reached the conclusion that "any chance of future rapprochement with Italy has been blocked by Mussolini just as Hitler has blocked any German rapprochement". Mussolini's decision to invade Albania may have brought potential gains in Italy's strategic situation but at the cost of further alienating the Chamberlain cabinet and furthering the division of Europe into two competing blocks. By the middle of April, British strategic intelligence listed Italy amongst Britain's likely enemies. British planners also shifted the emphasis in war planning to concentrate the British fleet in the eastern Mediterranean at the expense of the commitment to the Far East, a clear signal that resistance to Axis aggression had assumed a higher priority after Mussolini's attack.

Question

In pairs, and with reference to the source above, discuss the extent to which the invasion of Albania in 1939 marked a turning point in British policy towards Italy.

What was the reaction of Britain to Italian expansion in 1940?

As you have read in Chapter 2.3, when Italy joined the war in June 1940 Mussolini's forces invaded Egypt and invaded Greece from Albania. The British then counter-attacked Italian forces in North Africa in Operation Compass and pushed them out of Egypt, defeating them at Beda Fomm in Libya in February 1941. The British Navy, which had been feared by the Italian navy (as you have read earlier), had sunk half the Italian fleet in harbour at Taranto on the 11th November, 1940. The British then occupied Crete.

ATL Communication and thinking skills

From Andrew Roberts. The Storm of War: A new History of the Second World War, (2009) page 120–121.

In mid-September Mussolini, fancying himself a second Caesar, sent [his] Tenth Army to invade Egypt with five divisions along the coast, taking Sidi Barraini. He stopped 75 miles short of the British in Mersa Matruh, while both sides were reinforced. It was a nerve-wracking time for the British in Egypt… On 8th December 1940, Lieutenant-General Richard O'Connor, commander of the Western Desert Force [numbering only 31,000 men, 120 guns and 275 tanks], counter-attacked fiercely against a force four times his size, concentrating on each fortified area in turn. Operation Compass had close support from the Navy and RAF, and, aided by a collapse in Italian morale, by mid-December O'Connor had cleared Egypt of Italians and 38,000 prisoners were taken.

Question

In pairs discuss what this source suggests about how the Italians were pushed back in North Africa in 1940.

Therefore, the initial military response by the British led to reversals for the Italians. However, the British were in turn pushed back when German forces arrived. The British evacuated Greece in May 1941 and had been pushed back by German forces to El Alamein in Egypt by June 1942.

Full document question: The international response to Italian aggression, 1935–36

Source A

Extract from the Covenant of the League of Nations, 1919.

Article 16 – Should any member of the League resort to war in disregard of its covenants under Articles 12, 13 or 15, it shall be deemed to have committed an act of war against all other members of the League, which hereby undertake immediately to subject it to the severance of all trade or financial relations, the prohibition of all exchange between their nationals and the nationals of the covenant-breaking state, and the prevention of all financial, commercial or personal business between the nationals of covenant-breaking state and the nationals of any other state, whether a member of the League or not.

It shall be the duty of the Council in such cases to recommend to the several governments concerned what effective military, naval or air force the members of the League shall contribute to the armed forces to be used to protect the covenants of the League.

Source B

A photograph of US protesters, 1936.

Source C

Sir Samuel Hoare's resignation speech, delivered in the House of Commons in London, 19 December 1935.

It was clear … that Italy would regard the oil embargo as a military sanction or an act involving war against her. Let me make our position quite clear. We had no fear whatever, as a nation, of any Italian threats. If the Italians attacked us … we should retaliate with full success. What was in our mind was something very different, that an isolated attack of this kind launched upon one Power … would almost inevitably lead to the dissolution of the League.

… It was in an atmosphere of threatened war that the conversations began, and … the totality of the member States appeared to be opposed to military action.

… [It] seemed to me that Anglo-French co-operation was essential if there was to be no breach at Geneva. For two days M. Laval and I discussed the basis of a possible negotiation …

… These proposals are immensely less favourable to Italy than the demand that Mussolini made last summer.

… I believe that unless these facts are faced… either the League will break up, or a most unsatisfactory peace will result from the conflict that is now taking place. It is a choice between the full co-operation of all the member States and the kind of unsatisfactory compromise that was contemplated in the suggestions which M. Laval and I put up.

Source D

Ruth Henig, a British academic historian, in an academic book *The Origins of the Second World War* (1985).

The bargain they tentatively struck was immediately leaked in the French press, and reports of the "Hoare-Laval pact" caused an uproar in Britain. The government was forced to repudiate Hoare's negotiations in Paris, and Hoare himself resigned, to be replaced by Anthony Eden, who was perceived as a strong League supporter. The British government now led the way at Geneva in calling for economic sanctions against Mussolini, and dragged a reluctant French government behind it. But the French would not support oil sanctions, whilst the British were reluctant to agree to the closure of the Suez Canal, both measures which would have caused major problems for the Italian war effort. The French had not abandoned hopes of restoring the Stresa front, and the British did not want to run a serious risk of unleashing a naval war in the Mediterranean – even though British naval commanders there were confident that the outcome would be a British victory. For such a war would threaten vital imperial communications, and Japan would not be slow to exploit the situation to further its own expansionist ambitions in China. So League action was muted, with the result that Italian troops were able to overrun Abyssinia, crush resistance by the use of poison gas amongst other weapons, and proclaim the Italian conquest of a League member state. The League of Nations had suffered its second serious setback in five years, and this time had failed to prevent aggression much nearer to Europe.

Once again, the great powers had shown their inability to work together to resolve serious threats to peace or to protect the interests of weaker League members. These lessons were not lost on Hitler.

First question, part a – 3 marks

In Source A, what key points are made about the League regarding its response to a member state resorting to war?

First question, part b – 2 marks

What is the message of the photograph in Source B?

Second question – 4 marks

With reference to its origin, purpose and content, assess the values and limitations of Source C for historians studying the international response to the Abyssinian crisis.

Third question – 6 marks

Compare and contrast the views expressed in Source C and D regarding the Hoare–Laval Pact.

Fourth question – 9 marks

Using the sources and your own knowledge, examine the impact of the Anglo–French response to the Abyssinian crisis.

References

Fermi, L. 1966. *Mussolini*. University of Chicago Press. Chicago, USA

Henig R. 1985. *The Origins of the Second World War.* Routledge. London, UK

Roberts, A. 2009. *The Storm of War*: *A New History of the Second World War.* Allen Lane, UK.

Strang, GB. 2003. *On the Fiery March: Mussolini Prepares for War.* Praeger. Westport CT, USA

Taylor, AJP. 1961. *The Origins of the Second World War.* Penguin. Harmondsworth, UK

US Department of State. 1943. *Peace and War: United States Foreign Policy, 1931–1941.* Government Printing Office. Washington DC, USA

Warner, G. 1968. *Pierre Laval and the Eclipse of France.* Eyre and Spottiswoode. London, UK

2.7 The international response to German aggression, 1933–1940

The international reaction to the actions of Germany, 1935–39, has been the subject of much criticism and debate amongst historians. As you read this next section, consider the options available to Britain and France at each

▲ A cartoon by David Low, "What's Czechoslovakia to me, anyway?" 18 July 1938

stage of German expansion, and the extent to which the decisions that Britain and France took encouraged German aggression.

What was the international reaction to German rearmament?

As we have seen, there was sympathy in Britain towards Germany's desire to reverse certain aspects of the Treaty of Versailles. Following Germany's withdrawal from the Disarmament Conference and the League of Nations in 1933 (see page 157), Britain worked hard to get Germany back into the conference. It proposed that Germany should be allowed to have an army of 200,000 (rather than the 100,000 stipulated in the Treaty of Versailles), that France should also reduce its army to 200,000, and that Germany should be allowed an air force half the size of the French air force.

However, the realization in 1935 that Germany was introducing conscription and already had an air force ended attempts by the British and French to bring Germany back into the League of Nations and to establish new conditions for rearmament. Germany's actions blatantly contravened the terms of the Treaty of Versailles. This was obviously a concern to the other powers, who could see that Germany was now catching up militarily. German military expenditure increased from 2.7 billion marks in 1933 to 8 billion marks in 1935; while this was still a relatively low proportion of the gross national product (GNP), it was nonetheless a worry to Britain and France. It was clear that such rearmament would strengthen German demands for further treaty modifications and that, indeed, Germany would be able to achieve these by force if it could not get them by peaceful means.

In response to German rearmament, and following Hitler's threatening moves over Austria in 1934, a conference was held at Stresa in Italy, and was attended by the prime ministers and foreign ministers of France, Britain and Italy. The ministers drew up a formal protest at Hitler's disregard of the Versailles provisions regarding disarmament, and they reaffirmed their commitment to Locarno and to Austrian independence.

This collective action, as you have read in Chapter 2.3, was known as the Stresa Front, and it could have acted as a deterrent to Hitler's plans. However, three developments now took place that undermined this united front.

- First, France concluded the Franco–Soviet Mutual Assistance Treaty with Russia, in 1935. This coincided with Russia's entry into the League of Nations; with Poland in a pact with Germany (see page 159), it was important to keep Russia on side. However, Italy was unwilling to conclude any pact with a communist government. Britain was also worried about using a communist country to contain Germany and opposed France's idea of surrounding Germany with alliances, believing that this would lead to Germany feeling encircled.

- The second development was initiated by Britain and it offended both the French and Italian governments. Britain was unwilling to enter a naval race with Germany at a time when its naval strength was already stretched to capacity; there was also a concern that Japan might want to renegotiate the terms of the naval treaties of Washington and London (see page 22). This made it tempting to respond to Hitler's offers to limit the German fleet to 35% of the British fleet, which in fact gave the opportunity for the German navy to triple its size. On 18 June, this percentage was agreed in the Anglo–German Naval Agreement. The agreement also allowed a German submarine fleet equal to Britain's. The Versailles restrictions on the German navy had thus been completely set aside.

Ruth Henig summarises the effect of this treaty in Source A below.

Source skills

Source A

Ruth Henig. *The Origins of the Second World War* (1985).

While such an agreement may have been militarily desirable from a British point of view, it was politically inept. It drove a wedge between Britain on the one hand and the French and Italians on the other, at a time when it was vitally important for the three powers to work together. The British government could claim that it was possible to do business with Nazi Germany in the field of arms limitation. But they had, in the process, condoned German violation of the Treaty of Versailles by agreeing to a German navy considerably in excess of that stipulated by the treaty, and they had not attempted to secure the prior agreement of the other major signatories, France and Italy. What was now to stop Hitler repudiating other provisions of the treaty, fortified by the knowledge that the British government was, if not tacitly supporting him, most unlikely to offer strenuous opposition?

Source B

A cartoon by David Low, 24 June 1935 (with added annotations), depicting French prime minister Pierre Laval, Italian prime minister Benito Mussolini and British prime minister Ramsay MacDonald in a boat labelled *"Collective isolation"*. The text reads *"3 wise men of Stresa went to sea in a Barrel. If the Barrel had been stronger, my story would have been longer."*

The Anglo-German Naval Agreement—Mussolini furious

Germany watching: also a reference to the terms of the Anglo-naval Treaty?

Rough seas indicating tricky international situation

"Collective isolation" opposite of collective security

The Stresa "boat" totally inadequate for the rough seas

First question, part a – 3 marks

According to Source A what were the key limitations of the Anglo–German Naval agreement?

First question, part b – 2 marks

What is the message of the cartoon in Source B?

- The third development which undermined the Stresa Front was Mussolini's invasion of Abyssinia in October 1935. In fact, this left the Stresa Front in ruins. After this, Hitler was able to pursue his aims with greater confidence.

What was the international reaction to the remilitarization of the Rhineland?

When Hitler marched into the Rhineland in 1936, violating both the Treaty of Versailles and the Locarno Treaties, he faced no opposition from either Britain or France.

> **Examiner's hint:** *Use the annotations on the cartoon to help you write your answer. Here is a starting sentence:*
>
> *The overall message of this cartoon is that the Stresa Front is weak and unlikely to last long. This is shown by the fact that … (use the details of the cartoon to back up your points)*

The French government at the time was only a "caretaker" government and thus was not in a position to consider war. The divisions in French society made a clear response impossible and neither left nor right wanted to propose a war against Germany with forthcoming elections.

In addition, the general staff of the French army had exaggerated the number of German forces marching into the Rhineland, putting them at 265,000 when in fact there were only 30,000. To deal with an invasion of such supposed size, the French would have to mobilize its army and General Gamelin, the Chief of Staff, told French ministers that this would lead to a long, drawn-out war for which there was little support in France.

The French thus looked to Britain for a response, but Prime Minister Stanley Baldwin's government made it clear that they, too, were unwilling to contemplate war over the Rhineland. One reason for this was Britain's overstretched military commitments, and in 1936 the Chief of the Imperial General Staff made it clear that the armed forces were not in any position to fight a successful war against Germany (see page 168).

Significantly, the British also did not see Hitler's action as particularly threatening. As the British politician Lord Lothian put it, *"The Germans … are only going into their own back garden"*. Hitler of course, had also offered negotiations at the same time as invading (see page 163), a move that historian William Craig calls "a diplomatic smokescreen"; this made it easier to aim for a settlement rather than to confront Hitler directly. Foreign Minister Anthony Eden wrote:

> *It seems undesirable to adopt an attitude where we would either have to fight for the [demilitarized] zone or abandon it in the face of a German reoccupation. It would be preferable for Great Britain and France to enter … into negotiations … for the surrender on conditions of our rights in the zone, while such a surrender still has got a bargaining value.* — Eden, 1936

The failure to stop Hitler at this point, especially given that his troops had instructions to turn back if confronted, is often seen as a turning point: the last chance to stop Hitler without war. Harold Macmillan, a Conservative politician, wrote in the Star newspaper, *"There will be no war now. But unless a settlement is made now – a settlement that can only be made by a vigorous lead from this country – there will be war in 1940 or 1941"*. However, at the time, this was the view only of a minority. The reality is that it would have been hard for the British government to act given that political and public opinion were firmly in favour of peace and of negotiating with Germany.

Source skills

A.J.P. Taylor. *The Origins of the Second World War* (1964).

It was said at the time, and has often been said since, that 7 March 1936 was "the last chance" … when Germany could have been stopped without all the sacrifice and suffering of a great war. Technically, on paper, this was true: the French had a great army, and the Germans had none. Psychologically it was the reverse of the truth … The French army could march into Germany; it could extract promises of good behaviour from the Germans, and then it would go away. The situation would remain the same as before, or, if anything, worse –

the Germans more resentful and restless than ever. There was in fact no sense in opposing Germany until there was something solid to oppose, until the settlement of Versailles was undone and Germany rearmed. Only a country which aims at victory can be threatened with defeat. 7 March was thus a double turning point. It opened the door for Germany's success. It also opened the door for her ultimate failure.

First question, part a – 3 marks

According to Taylor, why was opposing Germany in the Rhineland **not** a good idea.

The international reaction to the Spanish Civil War: The Non-Intervention Committee

In France, a Popular Party government with similar views to the republican government in Spain was elected in June 1936. The new prime minister, Leon Blum, wanted to support the Spanish government; it was not in French interests to have on its border a right-wing regime that could join with Italy and Germany to encircle France. However, Blum feared opposition if he directly intervened and knew that Britain was unlikely to support such a move. He therefore came up with the idea of non-intervention, whereby all of the European countries would commit to keeping out of the conflict.

Baldwin's government in Britain wanted to prevent the Spanish Civil War becoming a wider conflict and so agreed with the French plan. However, British motives were different from those of the French. Baldwin's largely Conservative government believed that the nationalists would probably win the war and so did not want to make an enemy of the Spanish nationalist leader, General Franco. In addition, the British government did not want to upset Mussolini. It also viewed the Republican government as communist (an impression reinforced by the fact that it received aid from the Soviet Union). There were many British business interests in Spain, and investors believed that they faced financial risks if Franco lost resulting in a socialist or communist government in Spain. They also supported Franco's tough anti-union position.

A total of 16 countries signed the Non-Intervention Pact. However, three of the key members of the Non-Intervention Committee (NIC) – Germany, Italy and the Soviet Union – ignored the NIC commitment completely and, as we have seen, sent substantial aid into Spain.

In addition, Britain's policy of non-intervention favoured the nationalists:

- It focused on preventing aid to the Republic and allowed the Nationalists, rather than the Republicans, to use Gibraltar as a communications base.

- In December 1936, Britain signed a trading agreement with the Nationalists that allowed British companies to trade with the rebels.

- Franco, not the Spanish republicans, was able to get credit from British banks.

TOK

In small groups investigate a current civil war or conflict and find out how the international community has responded. How does your understanding of the international response to the Spanish Civil war in the 1930s help you to make sense of the complexity of responding to civil conflicts today?

The policy of non-intervention thus played a key role in allowing Franco to win the civil war in Spain. Non-intervention worked against the Republicans, while Hitler and Mussolini continued to give effective aid to the Nationalists.

The failure of non-intervention further discredited the appeasement policies of Britain and France. Hitler had ignored non-intervention, which was also the policy of the League of Nations, and had successfully helped a right-wing government to power. The Western democracies thus appeared weak to Hitler, and this encouraged him further in his actions.

What was the international response to *Anschluss*?

With *Anchluss* in May 1938, Hitler had again violated the Treaty of Versailles which specifically forbade the union of Germany and Austria. He invaded an independent state and was in a stronger position to attack Czechoslovakia. Yet, apart from British and French protests to Berlin, there was limited international response. Why was this?

- France was paralysed by an internal political crisis and did not even have a government at the time of *Anschluss*. Ministers threatened to call up reservists to strengthen France's army but needed Britain's support, which was not forthcoming.

- Italy was now increasingly dependent on German friendship and refused to respond to Chancellor Schuschnigg's appeals for help.

- The League of Nations was discredited after the Abyssinian affair and *Anschluss* was not even referred to the League for discussion.

- In Britain, there was a feeling that Germany's union with Austria was inevitable. Chamberlain made a statement in the House of Commons in which he condemned Germany's actions and the way in which *Anschluss* had taken place, but also stated, "*the hard fact is … that nothing could have arrested this action by Germany unless we and others with us had been prepared to use force to prevent it*".

Source skills

Source A

David Faber. *Munich, 1938* (2008).

On 14 March *The Times* newspaper told its readers that "our correspondent leaves no room for doubt about the public jubilation with which [Hitler] and his army were greeted everywhere". The Labour Party, recalling the brutality of Dollfuss a few years earlier against Austrian socialists, had little inclination to speak up now for Schuschnigg. Even the Archbishop of Canterbury appealed to the House of Lords for "calmness and balance of judgement". The union of Germany and Austria "sooner or later was inevitable" he told his fellow peers, and "finally, may bring some stability to Europe". At the Foreign Office too, the general feeling was one of relief.

Source B

A cartoon by David Low, "Not only the Austrians voted", published in the UK newspaper, the *Evening Standard*, on 12 April 1938.

First question, part a – 3 marks

According to Source A, what factors influenced Britain's attitude towards *Anschluss*?

First question, part b – 2 marks

What is the message of Source B concerning *Anschluss*?

What was the international reaction to German aggression in Czechoslovakia?

France's reaction

Following *Anschluss*, it was clear to Britain and France that Czechoslovakia would be the focus of Hitler's next foreign policy moves. France had two treaties with Czechoslovakia, signed in 1924 and 1925, which committed France to assisting Czechoslovakia in the event of a threat to their common interests. However, the French also saw that they were in no position to keep to these treaty obligations. They argued that Czechoslovakia could not be defended, and French Prime Minister Daladier and Foreign Minister Bonnet were only too happy to follow Britain's lead in finding a way out of a military showdown with Germany.

> **Examiner's hint:** *Don't forget to use the details of the cartoon to support your two points. Start by annotating it in the same way as we annotated the cartoon on page 215. Make sure you look at the title to give you a hint as to the meaning of the cartoon.*

Britain's reaction

Many British politicians had sympathy with Czechoslovakia, as it had survived as a democracy for a longer period than the other new states in central and eastern Europe. However, Chamberlain did not believe that Czechoslovakia was worth fighting for. He saw Czechoslovakia as a "highly artificial" creation and one that was ultimately unsustainable. He had some sympathy with the Sudeten Germans and believed that he could organize a peaceful and negotiated handover of the Sudetenland to Germany.

In any case, Britain was not in a position to offer military help to Czechoslovakia. Chamberlain wrote in his diary that,

> We could not help Czechoslovakia – she would simply be a pretext for going to war with Germany … I have therefore abandoned the idea of giving guarantees to Czechoslovakia, or the French in connection with her obligations to that country.

Given their determination to avoid a conflict over Czechoslovakia, Britain and France worked hard to find a diplomatic solution. Following Hitler's speech of 12 September 1938 at the Nuremberg Rally (see page 176), Chamberlain decided to seize the initiative and to fly to meet Hitler in Germany. This was a radical move in the world of diplomacy, as at this time prime ministers did not fly abroad to meet other leaders one to one. This was the first time that Chamberlain had flown; as historian David Reynolds has pointed out, it also marked the first of the 20th century summits between world leaders.

At the meeting, Hitler demanded that all areas of Czechoslovakia in which Germans comprised over 50% of the population should join Germany. This would be supervised by an international commission. Chamberlain agreed, but said that he would have to get the agreement of the Czechs and the French first. Chamberlain privately remarked that,

> In spite of the hardness and ruthlessness I thought I saw in his face, I got the impression that here was a man who could be relied upon when he had given his word.

Over the following week, Chamberlain was able to get agreement for this deal from the British Cabinet and the French government, despite the fact that this would mean ignoring their alliance with Czechoslovakia. The Czechoslovakian government, led by President Edvard Beneš, was told that, if these proposals were rejected, the Czechs would have to face Germany on their own. Czechoslovakia accepted the plan on 21 September 1938.

On 22 September, Chamberlain flew back to Germany, expecting to have a discussion at Bad Godesberg about the proposals that had previously been discussed and were now agreed upon. However, Hitler now said that the previous proposals did not go far enough. He wanted the claims of Hungary and Poland to Czech territory met and he wanted to occupy the Sudetenland no later than 1 October.

Back in Britain, many of Chamberlain's colleagues rejected the Godesberg proposals. France now said it would honour its commitments to Czechoslovakia; the Czechs said that the new proposals were unacceptable. All countries started preparing for war. In Britain, trenches were dug in London's parks and 38 million gas masks were distributed. On 27 September, Chamberlain made the following radio broadcast:

> *How horrible, fantastic and incredible it is that we should be digging trenches and trying on gas-masks because of a quarrel in a far-away country between people of whom we know nothing. I would not hesitate to pay even a third visit to Germany if I thought it would do any good.*
>
> *Armed conflict between nations is a nightmare to me; but if I were convinced that any nation had made up its mind to dominate the world by fear of its force, I should feel it must be resisted. Under such a domination, life for people who believe in liberty would not be worth living, but war is a terrible thing, and we must be very clear, before we embark on it, that it is really the great issues that are at stake.*

Thinking and Communication skills

Task one

In what way does the cartoonist Low in the cartoon at the start of this chapter disagree with Chamberlain?

Task two

Go to www.britishpathe.com/video/the-crisis-latest/query/Sudeten.

Watch Chamberlain's broadcast on this Pathé News clip. What is the British attitude towards Chamberlain as shown in the clip?

Go to www.youtube.com/watch?v=cPoOTNPYKnQ, or search for "Peace in our time? (1938 Munich Crisis) Part 2 of 11".

Watch part of the video *Peace in our Time?* What point is the narrator making about Czechoslovakia and the British attitude towards Czechoslovakia?

How useful is this documentary for a historian investigating the Munich Crisis?

Task three

Go to www.youtube.com/watch?v=BFIsYffrTFO, or search for "Hitler and Chamberlain: The Munich Crisis 1938".

Watch this documentary by historian David Reynolds on the Munich Conference. How does this compare to the documentary *Peace in our Time?* in terms of presentation and content? (You will need to watch the rest of *Peace in our Time?* to answer this question.)

Hitler agreed to a third conference, which was to be chaired by Mussolini. As you can see in the Pathé News clip below, this last hope for peace was greeted with much enthusiasm in Britain. Neither the Czech president, Edvard Beneš, nor the Soviet leader, Stalin, was invited to the conference, which agreed to give the Sudetenland to Germany (see page 178 for full details of the Munich Agreement). For Chamberlain, however, the highlight of the conference, was securing from Hitler a joint declaration that Britain and Germany would only deal with problems through negotiation and would not attempt to use force. For Chamberlain, this meant "peace in our time" (though this was a phrase that he later said he regretted using).

Communication skills

Go to www.youtube.com/watch?v=SetNFqcayeA, or search "Neville Chamberlain returns from Germany with the Munich Agreement".

Watch the Pathé News clip showing Chamberlain returning to Britain.

What exactly has Hitler agreed to according to the signed declaration?

What information concerning the agreement is **not** given in this clip?

There was much relief in Britain that war had been averted. The British press mostly supported Chamberlain's policy and Chamberlain had support from the majority of his party. However, even at the time, there was criticism of the agreement. Winston Churchill called British policy "*a total and unmitigated disaster*", and Duff Cooper, First Lord of the Admiralty, resigned from the government. The Labour and Liberal Parties both opposed the agreement. Clement Attlee, leader of the Labour Party, said:

> *We have been unable to go in for carefree rejoicing. We have felt that we are in the midst of a tragedy. We have felt humiliation. This has not been a victory for reason and humanity. It has been a victory for brute force … We have today seen a gallant, civilised and democratic people betrayed and handed over to a ruthless despotism.*

Class discussion

In pairs, discuss the extent to which you agree with the historian Richard Overy's appraisal of the Munich Agreement that it "*represented a realistic assessment of the balance between Western interests and Western capabilities*" (Overy, 2008).

The invasion of Czechoslovakia: The end of appeasement

Hitler's takeover of the rest of Czechoslovakia in March 1939, caused great shock and outrage in Britain. It was now clear that Hitler's aims were not limited; he had broken a signed agreement and his invasion of Czechoslovakia could not be justified by any claim to be uniting Germans. There was a shift of opinion in Britain, and Chamberlain was put under pressure to take a firmer stand against Hitler.

He made his new stance clear in a speech on 17 March 1939:

Is this the last attack upon a small state or is it to be followed by others? Is this, in effect, a step in the direction of an attempt to dominate the world by force? ... While I am not prepared to engage this country in new and unspecified commitments operating under conditions which cannot now be foreseen, yet no greater mistake could be made than to suppose that because it believes war to be a senseless and cruel thing, this nation has so lost its fibre that it will not take part to the utmost of its power in resisting such a challenge if it were ever made.

ATL Communication skills

What does Chamberlain's speech reveal about his change in policy towards Hitler?

What was the international reaction to Hitler's demands regarding Poland?

Given Hitler's actions over Memel, and German demands over Danzig, on 31 March 1939, Britain offered a guarantee to Poland which said that, if it was the victim of an unprovoked attack, Britain would come to its aid. France gave a similar assurances.

These guarantees were controversial. Poland was a right-wing military dictatorship and anti-Semitic; it had also accepted Japanese and Italian expansion, and had taken territory from Czechoslovakia as part of the Munich Agreement. Moreover, actually sending military aid to Poland would be even more difficult than acting to support Czechoslovakia.

Nevertheless, Britain's guarantee to Poland did act as a warning to Hitler, and it did allow Britain to feel that it was taking more direct action against Hitler to deter further aggression. In fact, Chamberlain still believed that he could use diplomacy to get Hitler to negotiate.

When Mussolini invaded Albania on 7 April, Britain and France also gave guarantees to Greece and Romania. In May, Britain further strengthened its position in the Eastern Mediterranean by negotiating an agreement with Turkey for mutual assistance in case of war in the Mediterranean area.

Meanwhile, both Britain and France stepped up military preparations. The Pact of Steel confirmed that Italy could not now be detached from Germany and this strengthened military collaboration between the two countries. In March, the British government announced that it was doubling the territorial army, and in April conscription was introduced. In fact, by 1939, it was clear that Britain and France were in a much stronger military position than they had been in 1938, and this fact, too, allowed them to take a firmer stand against Hitler. In Britain, air defence and the introduction of radar was near completion. The rearmament programme was also set to reach a peak in 1939–40, by which time it was estimated that Britain would, militarily, be on roughly equal terms with Germany.

Negotiations with the Soviet Union

If Britain and France were to be able to assist Poland in the event of a German attack, then help from the Soviet Union would be key. The French were more enthusiastic about this than the British as they had a long tradition of Franco–Soviet/Russian cooperation. Many British politicians on the left also felt that such an alliance had to be established quickly; however, there was still a reluctance on the part of the British government to follow this line of action. It had ignored the Soviet Union's approaches during the Austrian and Sudeten crises, and Stalin had not even been invited to the Munich Conference.

Even in 1939, Chamberlain was unenthusiastic about an alliance with the Soviets, confessing to *"the most profound distrust of Russia"*. There were also other, more practical, reasons to be concerned about such an alliance:

- The Soviet army was militarily weak after Stalin's purges.

- An alliance could alienate other Eastern European countries that Britain hoped to win over to form a diplomatic front against Germany.

- If Germany felt hemmed-in this could actually push it towards war.

- An alliance might push Poland, where Stalin was also distrusted, and Spain into an alliance with Hitler.

In April 1939, despite these misgivings, Chamberlain finally bowed to pressure and agreed to start negotiations. However, the expectations of what should be included in such an agreement were different for the Soviets on the one hand, and the French and British on the other. Britain and France just wanted the Soviets to join in the guarantees to Poland, but the Soviets proposed instead a mutual assistance treaty by which Britain, France and Russia would all come to one another's aid in the event of an attack. This was to prevent the Soviet Union being left to deal with Germany in the East alone.

In addition, Stalin demanded that the Soviet Union should have the right to intervene militarily in neighbouring states if they were threatened internally by local fascist forces. This was rejected outright by the British and French, who saw this as an excuse to interfere with, or even take over, other countries. There were other reasons for the failure of the negotiations as explained by historian Richard Overy in Source A, below.

Source skills

Source A

Richard Overy. *Origins of the Second World War* (2008).

Talks continued throughout the summer, though both sides complained endlessly about the obduracy and deviousness of the other. In August the Soviet side insisted on full military discussions before any more progress could be made. Again the west showed what Molotov later condemned as a "dilatory" attitude. The British delegation was sent on a long trip by sea instead of by air. When it arrived the Soviet negotiators, all top military and political figures, found that the British had sent a junior representative, who had no powers to negotiate and sign an agreement. This slight deeply offended Soviet leaders. It was soon discovered that the western delegations had no real plans for the military alliance, and had not even secured agreement for the passage of Soviet forces across Poland to fight the German army. The discussions, which had begun on 12 August 1939, broke up after three days and were not revived.

Source B

A cartoon by David Low, published in the UK newspaper the *Daily Mail*, 5 April 1939.

First question, part a – 3 marks

What, according to Source A, were the reasons for the failure of the Anglo-Soviet talks?

First question, part b – 2 marks

What is the message of Source B?

ATL Self-management and communication skills

Review the relationships between the Soviet Union and the Western democracies and Germany between 1933 and 1939. Refer back to the discussion of the reasons for the Nazi–Soviet Pact (see page 224; also pages 183–184).

Make notes under the following headings:

- the view of the British and French concerning an agreement with the Soviet Union
- the view of the Soviets on an agreement with the Western democracies
- the view of Germany on an agreement with the Soviet Union
- the view of the Soviets on an agreement with Germany.

Imagine that you are advising Stalin on whether to make an agreement with either Britain and France or with Germany.

Prepare a presentation to Stalin on the advantages and disadvantages of each course of action. Make sure you give evidence to support your points.

What is your final advice on the course of action that Stalin should take?

TOK

You have used your imagination in the task here as an "adviser" to Stalin. How do historians use their imagination when writing their accounts?

The international reaction to the invasion of Poland: The outbreak of war

Chamberlain continued to hope for a negotiated settlement but, as you have read in Chapter 2.6, last-minute attempts at diplomacy failed. Hitler invaded Poland on 1 September 1939. On 3 September, at 9.00am, Chamberlain issued an ultimatum to Germany. Germany did not reply and so war was declared at 11.00am that same day.

ATL Communication skills

Go to www.youtube.com/watch?v=rtJ_zbz1NyY, or search "Neville Chamberlain - Britain's declaration of war 1939".

Watch Chamberlain's broadcast to the British that war has been declared. What emotions is Chamberlain attempting to rouse in his speech?

Source skills

Richard Overy. *Origins of the Second World War* (2008).

[Hitler failed] to see that the western powers had reached their limit in 1939. Hitler was right to judge that Poland was not in itself of much intrinsic interest in British and French calculations, but he failed to see that both powers assessed the Polish crisis not on its own merits, but in terms of their global interests and great-power status. To fight for Poland was a means to assert British and French power in the Balkans, the Mediterranean and the Far East as well. Given favourable Allied intelligence on the military balance, and the threat of severe economic crisis if war preparations were continued at such a high level into the future, the Polish crisis was viewed as an unrepeatable opportunity to challenge German expansionism. If war had to come – and the Allies fervently hoped that Hitler would see reason before it did – the late summer of 1939 was a good time to declare it. This was particularly so given the nature of the Allied strategy of blockade and economic warfare, which could be made to bite across the winter months when Hitler would be unable to mount a major land offensive. The only incalculable element was the possibility of German bomb attacks in an effort to achieve the "knock-out" blow dreamed of by air theorists. Great efforts were made over the summer to complete the necessary civil defence preparations, to arrange the evacuation of women and children, and to prepare for gas attack.

First question, part a – 3 marks

According to this source, why was September 1939 an opportune time for Britain and France to make a stand against Germany?

ATL Research skills

Research the response of the international press to Hitler's invasion of Poland. Can you find headlines and articles about this act of aggression that are:

- negative
- positive
- neutral.

If possible, try to find newspapers from different regions and countries, and from different political backgrounds. You should spend no more than two hours on this task. Make sure your sources are appropriately referenced and that you make a list of works cited.

ATL Communication skills

Present your findings to the class in a 5–10-minute presentation.

What were the reactions of Britain and France to Hitler's actions, 1939–1940?

Despite the British and French promises of aid to Poland, they could offer no help to Poland against the Nazi onslaught which began in September. During the "phoney war", Britain prepared for the inevitable air attack. It also debated whether it should send aid to Finland which had been invaded by the Soviet Union. However, just as an Allied force was about to move, Finland capitulated. The Allies then decided to lay mines in Norwegian territorial waters in order to block Swedish iron ore getting to Germany. However the day after the Allies began mining, the Nazis occupied Denmark and invaded Norway. Allied troops were sent to help Norway, but the campaign was poorly planned and the Allied forces driven out.

The failure of the Norway campaign contributed to Chamberlain's decision to resign. The result was that Churchill took over as head of a coalition government in Britain.

With the defeat of France in 1940 and the evacuation of the British from Dunkirk, Britain stood alone against the German army. At this point, Hitler put forward another "peace offensive". It is possible that Chamberlain or other members of the British government would have been prepared to consider these proposals. However, Churchill was determined to continue fighting. His leadership was to prove key in the ensuing Battle of Britain and the Blitz where the Luftwaffe attacked London and other cities over the next few months.

During 1940, Britain attempted to find allies. However, the USA continued with its isolationist stance. Roosevelt persuaded Congress to amend the Neutrality Acts so that Britain could buy arms on "a cash and carry" basis. However, even when Britain stood alone against Nazi Germany at the end of 1940, most Americans were not in favour of getting involved in the war.

By the end of 1940, Britain was also suffering from Germany's U-boat campaign. Nevertheless, as explained at the end of chapter 2.5, Hitler's invasion of the Soviet Union was to ensure Germany's ultimate defeat. As Zara Steiner writes,

> *Each of the Axis powers were encouraged to embark on aggressive policies which were to bring the Soviet Union and the United States into what became in 1941 a global conflict. While the survival of Britain prevented a total German victory, only the entry of the Soviet Union and the United States ensured the destruction of Nazi Germany and, for the most part, dictated the outcome of the world war and the shape of the post-war settlement.*

— Steiner, p. 1064

The Second World War: The historical debate

How important was appeasement as a cause of the Second World War?

In the years following the end of the Second World War, there was much debate among historians as to the role of appeasement in causing the war. Sir Winston Churchill called the Second World War "the unnecessary war" that would not have taken place had Hitler been stopped earlier, for example in 1936 over the Rhineland or in 1938 over Czechoslovakia. The "appeasers" were seen as weak, frightened men who had been afraid to stand up to Hitler and who had failed to realize that they were dealing with a calculating and ruthless dictator. By consistently giving in to Hitler's demands they had encouraged his aggression and alienated the Soviet Union. Appeasement also meant that Hitler had gambled on that policy continuing when he invaded Poland, which was the trigger for war. AJP Taylor argued that Hitler did not have a clear plan for how he would carry out his foreign policy aims, and that he in fact reacted to the actions of the European leaders:

the Fascist dictators would not have gone to war unless they had seen a chance of winning ... the cause of war was therefore as much the blunders of others as the wickedness of the dictators themselves — Taylor, 1961

Class discussion

Those who argue that appeasement was a weak policy suggest that other actions could have been taken by Britain and France. In pairs, consider the advantages and disadvantages of these alternative routes of action:

- using the League of Nations more effectively to stop the actions of the dictators
- being prepared to use force against Hitler when he marched into the Rhineland
- standing up to Hitler over the Sudetenland
- spending more on armaments in the early 1930s
- following Churchill's idea of establishing a Grand Alliance of the anti-Fascist countries against Hitler.

ATL Communication and social skills

Divide the class into two teams. The motion that you will be debating is:

"Appeasement was both the wrong policy for the 1930s and a flawed policy."

You will need three speakers on each side. The rest of the team should help research and write the speeches, and also prepare questions for the opposing team.

When British Cabinet minutes and government papers became available 30–40 years after the end of the Second World War, it became clear that Chamberlain had been dealing with a complex situation. Given the difficulties and constraints on Chamberlain – which included the realities of the British economy, British imperial commitments, as well as public opinion concerning the horror of another war and the injustices of the Treaty of Versailles on Germany – it becomes easier to see the forces that shaped appeasement as a policy. Richard Overy argues that Chamberlain's policy was, in fact, the right one for Britain at the time and paid off in the sense that Hitler was forced into a general European war earlier than he had planned, and at a date when Britain was in a stronger military position than it had been in 1938.

Indeed, most historians would now agree that it was the ambitions of Hitler that were the key cause of the Second World War. Ruth Henig sums up the debate:

We cannot be certain of the extent to which Hitler might have been encouraged in his expansion course by the lack of opposition he received. The view he already held that Britain and France were powers in serious decline, who would not put up any serious resistance to his eastern expansion was reinforced – and this may have speeded up his plans.

But historians are now in no doubt that Hitler was intent on expansion and was prepared to fight a war, or series of wars, to achieve his objectives.

The other powers ultimately had two choices: they could acquiesce in his plans or try to resist them. And whenever resistance came – whether over Nazi demands for the return of the Sudetenland, or Danzig and the Polish Corridor – it was likely to provoke war. — Henig, 1999

ATL Self-management skills

Go to www.youtube.com/watch?v=Eu78iaVsBEE, or search "World War II – Germany – Road To War".

Watch the documentary *Germany: Road To War* to review the key actions taken by Hitler and the responses of the Western powers. (Hitler's foreign policy starts 15 minutes into the clip.)

ATL Communication skills

Draw up your own timeline from 1933–40.

Above the timeline write the actions of Hitler and the actions of Mussolini (use a different colour for each dictator).

Below the timeline, write the actions of the Western democracies.

Make your timeline detailed and useful as a revision tool.

Full document question: The Munich Conference, 1938

Source A

Extract from *The Times*, a UK newspaper, 1 October 1938.

No conqueror returning from a victory on the battlefield has come home adorned with nobler laurels than Mr. Chamberlain from Munich yesterday; and the King and people alike have shown by the manner of their reception their sense of this achievement …

Had the Government of the United Kingdom been in less resolute hands, it is certain as it can be that war, incalculable in its range, would have broken out against the wishes of every people concerned. The horror of such a catastrophe was no less in Germany. So much is clear from the immense popular enthusiasm with which Mr. Chamberlain was greeted on each of his three visits … Indeed, these visits seem to have increased the Führer's understanding of his own people's sentiments, with a definite effect upon his policy.

Let us hope that he may go on to see the wisdom of allowing them at all times to know the sentiments of other peoples instead of imposing between them a smoke-screen of ignorance and propaganda. For our nation it remains to show our gratitude to Mr. Chamberlain, chiefly by learning the lessons taught by the great dangers through which we have been so finely led – that only a people prepared to face the worst can, through their leaders, cause peace to prevail in a crisis; but that the threat of ruin to civilisation will recur unless injustices are faced and removed in quiet times, instead of being left to fester until it is too late for remedy.

Source B

A cartoon, *"Still Hope"*, published in *Punch*, a UK magazine, 21 September 1938.

STILL HOPE

Source C

Speech by Winston Churchill in the House of Commons, 5 October 1938.

I will begin by saying what everybody would like to ignore or forget but which must nevertheless be stated, namely, that we have sustained a total and unmitigated defeat, and that France has suffered more than we have …

No one has been a more resolute and uncompromising struggler for peace than the Prime Minister. Everyone knows that. Never has there been such intense and undaunted determination to maintain and to secure peace. That is quite true. Nevertheless, I am not quite clear why there was so much danger of Great Britain or France being in a war with Germany at this juncture if, in fact, they were ready all along to sacrifice Czechoslovakia. The terms that the Prime Minster brought back with him … could easily have been agreed, I believe, through the ordinary diplomatic channels at any time during the summer …

All is over. Silent, mournful, abandoned, broken, Czechoslovakia recedes into darkness. She has suffered in every respect by her association with the Western democracies and with the League of Nations of which she has always been an obedient servant …

When I think of the fair hopes of a long peace which still lay before Europe at the beginning of 1933 when Herr Hitler first obtained power, and of all the opportunities of arresting the growth of the Nazi power which have been thrown away, when I think of the immense combinations and resources which have been neglected or squandered, I cannot believe that a parallel exists in the whole of history …

I do not grudge our loyal, brave people, who were ready to do their duty no matter what the cost … I do not grudge them the natural, spontaneous outburst of joy and relief when they learned that the hard ordeal would no longer be required of them at the moment; but they should know the truth … and do not suppose that this is the end. This is only the beginning of the reckoning.

Source D

Zara Steiner. *The Triumph of the Dark: European International History 1933–1999* (2011).

Chamberlain understood that his intervention was a high-risk strategy. Not only did he believe that Hitler might go to war, he also agreed with his civilian and military advisers that Britain was in no position to fight. There was virtual consensus in Whitehall that little could be done to protect Czechoslovakia against attack and that no peace treaty, even after a terrible war, could restore Prague to its 1919 position. The prime minster was convinced that "no state, certainly no democratic state ought to make a threat of war, unless it was both ready to carry it out and prepared to do so". Significantly, under crisis conditions, Britain's leaders assumed a worst-case scenario. The expectation of a future German bombing campaign, the number of aircraft and bombs, and the resulting casualty figures were all grossly exaggerated … it was assumed that Britain was at least two years behind the corresponding German air programme. Little was expected from the Czech army … there was no substantive planning with the French …

Chamberlain undoubtedly reflected the opinion of most British men and women, when on the evening of 27th September, he spoke of "a quarrel in a far-away country between people of whom we know nothing". While acknowledging the hardening of political and public mood, he still believed that the country wanted peace. There was no credible "war party" in Britain and no possible leader who could replace him.

First question, part a – 3 marks

According to Source A, why was Chamberlain greeted so enthusiastically on his return from Munich?

First question, part b – 2 marks

What is the message of Source B?

Second question – 4 marks

With reference to its origin, purpose and content, assess the values and limitations of Source C for historians studying the Munich Conference.

Third question – 6 marks

Compare and contrast the views expressed in Sources A and C regarding the outcome of the Munich Conference.

Fourth question – 9 marks

With reference to the sources and your own knowledge, examine the reasons for Chamberlain's decision to agree to Hitler's demands at Munich.

References

Eden, A. 1962. *Facing the Dictators: The Memoirs of Anthony Eden.* Houghton Mifflin. Boston, USA

Faber, D. 2008. *Munich, 1938.* Simon & Schuster. London, UK

Henig, R. 1999. *Modern History Review*, pages 29–31

Overy, R. 2008. *Origins of the Second World War*. Routledge. London, UK

Steiner, Z. 2011. *The Triumph of the Dark: European International History 1933–1939*. Oxford University Press. New York, USA

Taylor, AJP. 1964. *The Origins of the Second World War*. Penguin. Harmondsworth, UK

Writing the internal assessment for IB History

Key concepts

→ Causation   → Change

→ Consequence   → Perspective

→ Continuity   → Significance

Key questions

→ What is the purpose of the internal assessment in history?

→ How is the internal assessment structured and assessed?

→ What are some suggested strategies for choosing a topic and getting started?

→ What are some common mistakes students make?

→ What are good criteria for selecting sources?

→ What are the challenges facing the historian?

"Doing history": Thinking like a historian

The **internal assessment (IA)** is an engaging, inquiry-based **2200 word investigation** that provides teachers and students with the opportunity to personalize their learning. You will select, research and write on a historical topic of individual interest or curiosity.

The IA is an essential component of the IB History course. Students in both standard level (25%) and higher level (20%) will complete the same task as part of their course mark. Your teacher will evaluate your final draft, but only a small, random sample of your class' IAs will be submitted to the IB for moderation.

The purpose of the historical investigation is to engage students in the process of thinking like historians and "doing history" by creating their own questions, gathering and examining evidence, analyzing perspectives, and demonstrating rich historical knowledge in the conclusions they draw. Given its importance, your teacher should provide considerable time, guidance, practice of skills and feedback throughout the process of planning, drafting, revising and submitting a final

copy of the IA. In total, completing the IA should take **approximately 20 hours**. This chapter is designed to give both students and teachers some guidance for approaching these tasks.

Class discussion

How does the place and the time you live in affect the topics you might be interested in, or curious about? How might where and when you live affect the evidence and sources you have access to? Which topics could you investigate that students in other places could not? What does this tell us about the nature of history?

What does the IA look like?

The IA is **divided into three main sections**. Each of these sections will be explained and approached in more detail later in this chapter. Below is an overview of each section:

1. Identification and evaluation of sources (6 marks)

- Clearly state the topic in the form of an appropriate inquiry question.

- Explain the nature and relevance of two of the sources selected for more detailed analysis of values and limitations with reference to origins, purpose and content.

2. Investigation (15 marks)

- Using appropriate format and clear organization, provide critical analysis that is focused on the question under investigation.

- Include a range of evidence to support an argument and analysis, and a conclusion drawn from the analysis.

3. Reflection (4 marks)

- Reflect on the process of investigating your question and discuss the methods used by historians, and the limitations or challenges of investigating their topic.

Your history teachers can use the IA for whatever purposes best suit the school context, syllabus design or the individual learning of students. Nevertheless, you should be encouraged to select and develop your own question. The IA can be started at any point during the course, however the task is most effectively introduced after students have been exposed to some purposeful teaching and practice in historical methods, analysis and writing skills.

The IA is designed to assess each of the following History objectives:

Assessment objective 1: Knowledge and understanding

- Demonstrate understanding of historical sources.

Assessment objective 2: Application and analysis

- Analyse and interpret a variety of sources.

Assessment objective 3: Synthesis and evaluation

- Evaluate sources as historical evidence, recognizing their value and limitations.

- Synthesize information from a selection of relevant sources.

Assessment objective 4: Use and application of appropriate skills

- Reflect on the methods used by, and challenges facing, the historian.

- Formulate an appropriate, focused question to guide a historical inquiry.

- Demonstrate evidence of research skills, organization, referencing and selection of appropriate sources.

Beginning with the end in mind: what does success look like?

ATL Self-management skills

Throughout the process of planning, researching, drafting and revising your investigation, you should be continually checking the criteria. Ask your teacher and other students to provide specific feedback using the criteria. Continually ask yourself if your work meets the criteria.

Before getting started, you should look carefully at the assessment criteria to appreciate what each section of the IA demands. Teachers will **use the same criteria for both SL and HL**. It is important to have a clear understanding of what success will look like before you invest the time and hard work that this task will require. Teachers will use the criterion found in the IB History Guide to provide feedback to teachers and to assess the final draft. The assessment is based on "positive achievement", meaning that teachers will try to find the best fit according to the descriptors in each criterion. Students do not have to write a perfect paper to achieve the highest descriptors, and teachers should not think in terms of pass/fail based on whether scores are above or below 50% of the 25 marks in total.

To simplify the criterion and to provide some fixed targets for what success looks like, consider using the assessment tool provided on the next page.

Teacher, Peer and Self-Assessment Tool

Criterion A: Identification and evaluation of sources (6 marks)

Suggested word count: 500

Criteria for success	Strengths	Improvements needed
• Does the investigation have an **appropriate question clearly stated?**		
• Has the student selected, identified, and referenced (using a consistent format) **appropriate and relevant sources?**		
• Is there a **clear explanation of the relevance** of the sources to the investigation?		
• Is there detailed analysis and evaluation **of two sources** with explicit discussion of the **value and limitations**, with reference to their **origins, purpose and content?**		

Criterion B: Investigation (15 marks)

Suggested word count: 1,300

Criteria for success	Strengths	Improvements needed
• Is the investigation **clear, coherent and effectively organized?**		
• Does the investigation contain **well-developed critical analysis clearly focused on the stated question?**		
• Is there evidence from a **range of sources** used effectively to **support an argument?**		
• Is there **evaluation of different perspectives** (arguments, claims, experiences etc.) on the topic and/or question?		
• Does the investigation provide a **reasoned conclusion** that is **consistent with the evidence and arguments provided?**		

Criterion C: Reflection (4 marks)

Suggested word count: 400

Criteria for success	Strengths	Improvements needed
• Does the student **focus clearly** on what the investigation revealed about the **methods used by historians?**		
• Does the reflection demonstrate clear **awareness of the challenges** facing historians and/or the **limitations of the methods** used by historians?		
• Is there an **explicit connection** between the reflection and the rest of the investigation (question, sources used, evaluation and analysis)?		

Bibliography & formatting (no marks applicable)		
Suggested word count: Not included in total		
Criteria for success	**Strengths**	**Improvements needed**
• Is the **word count clearly stated** on the cover? *(2200 maximum)*		
• Is a single bibliographic style or format **consistently used**?		
• Is the bibliography **clearly organized** and **include all the sources** you have referenced or used as evidence in the investigation?		

Getting started: Approaches to learning history

To start generating ideas for a topic and to help you focus your question, use a research-based thinking routine such as **Think-Puzzle-Explore** (see Ritchhart, Church and Morrison, 2011. *Make Thinking Visible*, Jossey-Bass).

Think: What topics do you **think** might interest you?

Puzzle: What **puzzles** you about these topics?

Explore: How can you **explore** more about each of these topics?

Ideally, you will have opportunities throughout the IB History course to explore and develop understandings about the methods and the nature of history. This will prepare you to better develop the skills necessary for the IA and the other assessment papers in the IB History course. Additionally, these kinds of learning activities provide clear links to TOK.

• Debate controversial historical events and claims.

• Compare and corroborate conflicting sources of evidence.

• Take on, role play or defend different perspectives or experiences of an event.

• Discuss the value and limitations of historian's arguments and evidence.

• Develop criteria for selecting and comparing historical sources.

• Gather and analyze a variety of different kinds of sources (photos, artwork, journal entries, maps, etc.) focused on the same event or issue.

• Co-develop good questions and carry out an investigation of a historical event as a entire class.

• Read an excerpt from a historian's work and identify which parts are analysis, evidence and narrative.

If students better understand that history is more than simply memorizing and reporting on facts, dates and chronological narratives, then they are more likely to be curious, engaged and motivated learners of history. Accordingly, they will more likely develop appropriate questions for their investigation and have a better understanding of how to organize and write effective analysis.

Selecting a topic and appropriate questions

Before beginning, ask your teacher to find some examples of student IAs with examiner's feedback. These can be found on the **IB Online Curriculum Centre** or in the **Teachers' Support Materials** for History. Examine the formatting and layout of each component to visualize in advance what your IA might look like, and the steps that will be required to complete them.

Once you have some general understanding of the IA components and are familiar with the assessment criteria, it is time to select a topic focus. Students often do not know how to begin selecting a topic. Identify a historical topic of interest and get to know it well by conducting some background reading from a general history textbook or an online encyclopaedia. You may find some information that will help you narrow the topic focus quickly. These kinds of sources often outline the differing perspectives, interpretations and controversies that make for an engaging investigation. Well-written textbooks and articles will also include references, annotated bibliographies and footnotes of additional, more detailed sources that will help in the research stage.

After selecting a topic, formulating an appropriate research question can also be very challenging. It is essential that you take the time to carefully think about what kinds of topics help produce good questions for investigations. Before you begin any writing, **you should submit a proposal** to your teacher to ensure that the investigation will be successful.

Some teachers recommend that students write about a topic related to their course syllabus, but there are a countless number of possible topics and you are better off choosing topics that interest you and motivate you to learn. The topic must be historical however, so students **may not investigate any topic that happened within the last ten years.** All investigations will take one of three forms:

1　**An investigation of a historical theme, issue, person or event based on a variety of sources.**

2　**An investigation based on fieldwork of a historical building, place or site.**

3　**An investigation of a local history.**

When selecting a historical topic, students often fail to select a topic that is manageable. For example, examining all of the causes of the Second World War is too broad for the purposes of a 2200 word investigation. Many students also select topics that cannot be researched in depth because there are not enough readily available primary and/or secondary sources.

Investigating a historically-themed film or piece of literature can be very engaging; but many students write better papers when they focus the investigation on a particular claim, portrayal or perspective contained in the work, rather than the entire work itself. Students who choose to investigate a historical site, or to investigate local or community history, often have an opportunity to engage in experiences that are more authentic to the work of professional historians, but these can also produce a lot of challenges when looking for sources. Whatever the topic that you select, it is essential to formulate a good question.

One of the most common errors students make when planning and writing the IA is formulating a poor question about their topic. Formulating a good question is essential for success and helps ensure that the IA is a manageable and researchable investigation. Consider the following criteria when formulating a good question:

1 The question is researchable.	• *There is an adequate variety and availability of sources related to your topic.* • *The sources are readable, available and in a language that is accessible.*
2 The question is focused.	• *Questions that are vague or too broad make it difficult to write a focused investigation limited to 2200 words.* • *Questions that are too broad make it difficult to manage the number of sources needed to adequately address the topic.*
3 The question is engaging	• *Interesting, controversial or challenging historical problems make better questions.* • *Questions with obvious answers (i.e. Did economic factors play a role in Hitler's rise to power?) do not make good investigations.*

Using the concepts to formulate good questions

The IB History course is focused on **six key concepts: change, continuity, causation, consequence, significance and perspectives**. Each of these concepts shape historians' thinking about the kinds of questions they ask and investigate. Therefore, they are helpful to students as a framework for formulating good IA questions. Using the historical thinking concepts, you may be able to generate several good questions about any historical topic that can be eventually focused into successful investigations.

Concepts	Possible investigation prompts

change
- What changes resulted from this topic?
- To what extent did this event, person or issue cause change?

continuity
- To what extent did the topic remain the same?
- Did this event, person or issue cause progress or decline?

causation
- What were the long term, short term and immediate causes?
- What were the factors that caused the event related to the topic?

Student's topic

consequence
- How has this topic had immediate and long-lasting effects?
- How significant were the effects of this topic?

significance
- To what extent is this topic significant? Is the significance of this topic justified?
- What events, people or issues are important to know about this topic?

perspectives
- What different perspectives or interpretations are there about this topic?
- How did people experience this topic?

To illustrate, a student interested in the Russian Revolution might use the concepts to brainstorm the following possible investigations:

Change: *In what ways did the Russian Revolution change Russian society?*

Continuity: *To what extent did Stalin's regime resemble the Tsarist system?*

Causation: *How significant were long term factors in causing the February Revolution?*

Consequence: *To what extent did Stalin's purges affect military preparedness?*

Significance: *How important was Lenin's role in the October Revolution?*

Perspectives: *To what extent did Doctor Zhivago capture the experience of upper class Russians during the Revolution?*

After generating some possible questions, students can bring greater focus to their topic. For example, a student interested in how women experienced Stalinism may narrow the focus to a particular place or event. A student investigating long-term causes of an event may have more success if the

question is focused on the significance of a specific, singular cause. For good examples of historical questions, you should consult past Paper 2 or Paper 3 examination questions.

You should notice that many of the questions above include more than one concept. Most good historical investigations will require students to think about perspectives because there will likely be multiple accounts of the issue under investigation, or there will be some controversy between historians. Here are some question exemplars showing how they capture more than one key historical concepts:

- *How significant was Allied area bombing in reducing German industrial capacity during the Second World War? (significance; consequence)*

- *To what extent did Gandhi's leadership achieve Indian independence? (significance; perspectives; causation)*

All successful IAs begin with a well-developed, thoughtful and focused question that is based on one or more of the historical concepts.

Categorize the following questions (Good – Needs Improvement – Poor) according to their suitability as a historical investigation according to the criteria provided above. Suggest ways the questions might be improved.

1 Which Second World War film is the most accurate?

2 To what extent did nationalism play a role in causing the First World War?

3 How did women win the right to vote in the United States?

4 Did Hitler use film for propaganda?

5 In what ways did Stalin start the Cold War?

6 To what extent was the influenza epidemic a factor in the collapse of the Central Powers in 1918?

Common problems when selecting a topic and question:

- Poorly focused question – too broad and unmanageable.
- Obvious question.
- Question is not researchable.

Getting organized: making a plan of investigation

Self-management skills

Create your own plan for completion with target dates and goals. Submit this with your proposed topic and question. Include some initial sources of information you will use.

Completing the IA successfully requires that students **create a plan for completion** that includes several important steps of the inquiry process. Some of the steps may overlap, but it is important that you organize your tasks and stay on track for completion by setting goals and due dates. Your teacher should read at least one draft and give some feedback to ensure that the IA is not plagiarised. A plan of investigation should include the following steps:

1 Planning	• Select a topic and formulate a question.
	• Submit a proposal to your teacher.
	• Identify information sources.

2 Researching	• Gather information sources and evidence.
	• Carefully read and evaluate information.
3 Organizing and processing	• Create notes.
	• Record references using a standard citation format.
	• Create a bibliography.
	• Organize ideas into an outline.
	• Formulate an argument.
4 Drafting	• Write each section of the IA.
	• Revise and edit.
	• Check assessment criteria.
5 Sharing	• Submit a draft for feedback.
6 Revising	• Revise based on feedback from your teacher.
7 Publishing	• Submit final copy to your teacher.
	• Evaluate using criteria.

Getting organized: researching

Communication skills

When supporting historical claims, it is important to make your evidence visible to your reader. Make sure you use a standard bibliographic format to show the reader where your evidence was found. In the discipline of history, the University of Chicago style or MLA style is most commonly used because it provides significant information about the origins of the source, and the endnotes or footnotes format allows the historian to insert additional information about the source where necessary.

Take good notes during the research stage. Post-it notes are helpful to record thoughts and ideas next to key passages as you read and think about the information in relation to the question. Using different coloured highlighters to identify different perspectives on the question as you read can also be helpful. If using borrowed books, take a photo of important pages on a tablet device and use a note taking application to highlight and write notes on the page. Students who make their thinking visible as they read will have a easier time writing later in the process. Create a timeline of the event you are researching to ensure the chronology is clear in your mind.

It is strongly recommended that you record the bibliographic information and page numbers where you find important evidence and analysis. Many students wait until the very end of the writing process to compile their bibliography, but this is much more easily accomplished if the information is recorded throughout, instead of as an afterthought when the draft is finished. There are several easily accessible web sites that provide the most up-to-date versions of **MLA** (www.mla.org), and **Chicago Manual of Style** (www. chicagomanualofstyle.org), which are the two most common formats used for bibliographies in university history departments.

> **Common problems when planning and organizing an IA:**
> - Lack of general background knowledge of the topic.
> - No feedback on proposed topic and question.
> - No plan for completion.
> - Inaccurately recording page numbers and references.
> - Poorly organized notes; or no notes at all.

Internal Assessment skills

Create a proposal for the IA using the template shown.

Topic:	Student:
Research question:	
Proposed sources:	
Sources (2) proposed for evaluation in Section A:	

Section A: Identification and evaluation of sources

Section A is worth 6 of the 25 total marks. It is recommended that the word count does not exceed much more than 500 words. While this section does not count for a substantial portion of the marks, most students will not be successful without a strong Section A. There are three key aspects of this section.

1 **Clearly state the topic of the investigation. (This must be stated as a question).**

2 **Include a brief explanation of the two sources the student has selected for detailed analysis, and a brief explanation of their relevance to the investigation.**

3 **With reference to their origins, purpose and content, analyse the value and limitations of the two sources.**

> **Common problems with Section A:**
> - Question is not clearly stated.
> - Relevance or significance of selected sources not explained.
> - Student summarizes the content of selected sources.
> - Limited analysis.
> - Discussion of origins, purpose and content is in isolation to value and limitations.
> - Poorly chosen sources.
> - Speculates vaguely about the values and limitations of sources.
> - Reference to origins, purpose and content is not explicit.

Thinking about evidence: origins, purpose, value and limitations

Because it is built on a foundation of evidence, history is by nature interpretive and controversial.

This is not something many people understand – to them history is simply a long list of dates and dead people. While there are a great many things historians agree upon, there are countless historical questions that are enshrouded in debate and controversy. Since relatively few people personally witness the events they study, how one understands the past depends largely on which sources of evidence are used, and how they are interpreted. Even facts that historians generally agree upon can change over time. Philosopher Ambrose Bierce once said, *"God alone knows the future, but only a historian can alter the past."* Though the past cannot actually be changed, historical memory and understanding is always changing as each generation brings forward new questions, new evidence and new perspectives. This process of changing historical interpretations is referred to as **revisionism**. Revisionist historians are those who challenge **orthodox**, or generally accepted arguments and interpretations.

Besides revisionism, another reason why history is controversial is that accounts or evidence from the same events can differ drastically. People record events from different **origins and perspectives**, and for different **purposes**. Historical evidence might come from a limitless number of possible kinds of sources. Sources that all originate from the same time and place that we are investigating are typically referred to as **primary sources**. The interpretations and narratives that we find in documentaries, articles and books created by historians are called **secondary sources**.

Students often make the error of thinking that primary sources are more authentic and reliable, and therefore have more **value**, and fewer **limitations** than secondary sources. This isn't always the case. Being there does not necessarily give greater insight into events, and indeed, sometimes the opposite is true. Historians can look at events from multiple perspectives and use a wide range of evidence not available to the eyewitness. Students often speculate that a primary source is valuable and significant to their investigation, but

have poor reasons in support of this beyond the fact that it is a primary source.

It is important that you understand how to evaluate the value and limitations of sources with reference to the origins, purpose and content of the source. Discussing the origin, purpose and content outside the context of the value and limitations will result in a poor assessment.

Origins	• Where did the source come from? • Who wrote or created it? • Whose perspectives are represented? Whose are not?
Purpose	• Why was this created? • What purpose might this document have served?
Content	• What does the source mean? • What does it reveal or contain? • How useful is the information? Is it reasonable to believe it is accurate? Can it be corroborated?

Generally, the closer in proximity (place and time) the origin of a primary source is, the more **value** it has to historians. If students can find ways to **corroborate** (support, confirm) a source by other sources, then the source likely has greater value to the investigation. **Limitations** may include any factors that cause someone to question the truthfulness, validity or value of a source.

Keep in mind, that using the term **bias** is not always useful in history – it is important to be able to identify bias, but bias does not necessarily limit the value of a source. Students often make the error of assuming a source is unreliable because they detect bias. Remember that most people will have biased perspectives that are unique to their own experiences, time and place. This does not mean that you should blindly dismiss the evidence they offer us. You should ensure that you explain clearly how the bias affects the value of the content in the source used.

Internal Assessment skills

Use this template for taking notes from each of the sources used in the investigation.

Research Question:		
Source (bibliographic information):		
Primary or secondary source?	How is the source relevant/significant to the investigation?	Origins/Purpose? Value/Limitations?
Page#:	What evidence does the source provide? (quote, paraphrase, describe)	What is your interpretation? How does the content of the source relate to your question? What perspective does it add?

Selecting sources for the IA

One of the challenges to students writing a successful Section A is making sure that they choose two appropriate sources to evaluate. You should be able to clearly and effectively explain why the chosen sources are relevant and important to the investigation.

Often students make the mistake of relying too heavily on non-scholarly sources such as online encyclopaedia articles and general history textbooks. As stated, these are good starting points for finding a topic, but they are not good sources to build your investigation upon. They are especially poor choices to use for detailed analysis in this section. Before selecting sources consider the following:

- You will be expected to discuss as much detail about the origins and purpose of the source as possible. Be sure to choose sources where you can identify as much of the following as possible: when it was created; who created it; why it was created; where it was created. If much of this information is not readily identifiable, you will have difficulty evaluating value and limitations with explicit reference to the origins and purpose.

- Select sources or excerpts of sources that have clear significance to the question. You should be able to clearly, and explicitly explain why the content of the source is important to the investigation. Some students choose sources that are largely irrelevant or vaguely related to the question.

- The investigation should include an appropriate range of sources. As a general rule, you should include both primary and secondary sources, but this may not work with some types of investigations. While secondary sources on a topic are likely to be easily obtained, they often provide less to discuss in Section A. Interviews, personal correspondence, newspaper articles, journals, speeches, letters, and other primary sources often provide students with much more meaningful material to evaluate in Section A. Ideas about origins and purpose come more readily with primary sources than they might when using secondary sources which generally, but not always, strive to present balanced arguments and perspectives.

- Choose secondary sources that reference the evidence the historians used to support their arguments. You will find it less difficult to assess the validity of the evidence the historian uses, or how the evidence is interpreted in the arguments, if the historian has documented the evidence clearly.

- Consider using periodical articles. Many historians write excellent, concise articles on historical topics for peer-reviewed journals. These articles often have rich footnoting and bibliographies that you can use to find additional sources for the investigation.

- Be careful about relying too heavily on general web-based sources. Many online sources are not referenced or footnoted properly so it is difficult to validate information about the origins, purpose and authorship. On the other hand, a great number of rich primary sources can be found online, as well as articles written by respected historians.

- Consider using interviews. Some students have written exceptional IAs based on people's experiences, or by interviewing historians or other people with extensive knowledge and experience. When using interviews, record them as an audio file for reference and accuracy.

Analysing the selected sources

After stating the research question and explaining the two selected sources and their relevance to

the investigation, the largest portion of Section A should focus on analysing the two sources. Depending on the sources chosen, they can be discussed simultaneously and comparatively, or they can be discussed separately. Discussing them separately is often more advantageous because you can make the origins, purpose, value and limitations more explicit.

- It is important that any arguments about the value and limitations make specific references to the content, origins and purpose.

- Be careful that the value of a source is not dismissed on the basis of bias without a strong argument about why the bias limits the validity or reliability of the content.

- You should avoid summarizing the content too much. Summarize and describe content only to the extent necessary to construct a strong analysis about the source's value and limitations.

- You should be thorough in examining all aspects of the source's origins including date of origin, cultural context, author's background, publisher or other important details. If little information about the origins is identifiable, it is likely a poorly chosen source for analysis.

Internal Assessment skills

Use the Section A assessment criteria to discuss and evaluate this excerpt of a student's work. Identify where the student has explicitly discussed origins and purpose, and value and limitations.

This investigation will seek to answer the question **"What did the Tiananmen Square protest reveal about the democratic sentiments in China between 1980 and 1989?"** *Democratic sentiments are defined as people's attitudes toward democratic ideals. This investigation will analyze factors that influenced democratic sentiments from multiple perspectives, but will not assess the ethics and justification of the Chinese government's response to the protest.*

In order to take into account the opposing views on this event and keep the scope of the investigation manageable, I have made use of a variety of carefully selected sources. Two primary sources will be evaluated ...

Source 1: Prisoner of State: the secret journal of Zhao Ziyang[1]

The origin of the source is of great value because the author is Zhao Ziyang, the General Secretary of the Communist Party during the Tiananmen Square Protest (the Protest). Zhao attempted to use a non-violent approach to resolve the protest and spoke against the party's hardliners. After a power struggle, Zhao was dismissed and put under house arrest until his death in 2005. The content of the journal is translated from thirty audiotapes recorded secretly by Zhao while he was under house arrest between 1999 and 2000. The book is published in 2009 by Simon & Schuster, one of the largest and most reputable English-language publishers. The reputation of the author and publisher increases the reliability of this source.

Zhao's purpose for recording these tapes is to publicize his political opinions and express his regret for failing to prevent the massacre. This is valuable because Zhao was not allowed to publicize his opinions while under house arrest, so this source is the only surviving public record of Zhao's opinions and perspectives on the Protest. This source is also valuable because its author, Zhao, was directly involved in the government's decision-making process during the protest. It reveals the power struggle within the Communist Party through the lens of the progressive bloc.

However, its exclusivity may limit its value because there are no counterparts to compare with and to verify its claims. As a translated material, the source may not accurately present Zhao's intentions and may have lost some cultural expressions. In addition, this source may be biased in that Zhao speaks in favour of political reform and democracy, which does not represent the Party's position ...

[1] Zhao, Ziyang, Pu Bao, Renee Chiang, Adi Ignatius, and Roderick MacFarquhar. *Prisoner of the state: the secret journal of Zhao Ziyang.* New York: Simon & Schuster, 2009.

Section B: Investigation

Common problems with Section B:

- Too much narrative.
- Poor referencing of sources.
- Limited awareness of different positions or perspectives.
- Listing of evidence instead of integrating analysis and evidence.
- Overuse of quotations.
- Plagiarism.
- Poor organization and arguments that are difficult to follow.
- Few connections to the question and purpose of the investigation.
- Conclusions are not evidence-based.

It is essential that you keep Section B focused on the purpose of the investigation and construct an argument using all of the sources you have listed in the bibliography. No marks are awarded for the bibliography, but an incomplete treatment of your sources, or inaccurate referencing will cost you marks in this section. **Evidence must be integrated** with **very clear critical commentary** that leads the reader to an eventual **evidence-based conclusion** that addresses the question posed in Section A. Students often make the error of simply listing facts they researched, without explaining how they are relevant or relate to their question. The following points should be considered when writing this section.

- The investigation should be carefully organized. The synthesis of evidence and critical commentary should be carefully planned to ensure that there is logic and flow to the section, and that your argument is very clear.

- The type of question you pose for the investigation will determine how you organize your writing. For example, a question that invites comparisons (for example: whether a film portrays an event accurately) will require you to discuss both similarities and differences. "To what extent" questions will require you to discuss both perspectives of "ways no" and "ways yes".

- As you gather evidence and document your thinking in your notes, keep in mind you may need to adjust or change your question. You should give some consideration to planning and writing Section B before writing Section A.

- Where appropriate, discuss different perspectives of the topic. Historians may offer different interpretations, or there may be multiple experiences of an event.

- Quotes should be used sparingly. Most of your writing should summarize and paraphrase the evidence collected and explain explicitly how it relates to the investigation. Too many student papers read as long lists of quotes from sources. Quotes must be explained, or integrated as evidence in support of an argument, and add something specifically and convincingly to your argument.

- Any references to sources, or ideas that are not your own, should be referenced appropriately using endnotes or footnotes. If this is not completed carefully, you risk plagiarizing others' ideas as your own.

- You should avoid writing significant amounts of narrative. Retelling a historical narrative or sequence of events is not the purpose of the investigation. On the other hand, you should demonstrate a clear understanding of the chronology and historical context of the events you are analyzing.

- Your conclusion is essential. The conclusion must offer possible answers or solutions to the question identified in Section A. It should not read simply as a summary of points, but rather as a well-reasoned, convincing, evidence-based closure to the investigation.

- There is no suggested number of appropriate sources required for your investigation. The number of sources you should use depends entirely on your topic and the kind of investigation you are doing. Local or community history, for example, might offer a limited numbers of sources. Interviews or community archives that this kind of IA might require could yield fewer, but very rich primary sources. Wherever possible your sources should be varied and specific, rather than few and general.

Submitting your bibliography

The bibliography – an **alphabetically ordered list of sources** – should be inserted at the very end of your paper. It is mentioned here with Section B because it should be created as part of the writing process, not simply thrown together at the last minute before submitting the paper. This bibliography is not worth any marks but it is an essential component of the paper that is often overlooked or poorly completed. Any sources referenced as evidence in Section B must be included in your bibliography.

Internal Assessment skills

Use the Section B assessment criteria to evaluate an excerpt of this student's investigation. Has the student effectively integrated evidence and critical commentary?

…Sentimentality played a key role in the events leading up to the protest in 1989. Western democracy and parliamentary system were believed to be the panacea for China's social problems. As Zhao Ziyang stated in his memoir: "in fact, it is the Western parliamentary democratic system that has demonstrated the most vitality. It seems that this system is currently the best one available."[1] The death of Hu Yaobang, the former General Secretary of the Party who advocated strongly for democratic reform, created a unified sense of democratic sentiments that united both ideological and practical groups.[2] Hu's successor, Zhao Ziyang, an even more progressive leader, spoke publicly in favour of political reform. Zhao's rise in power gave people an optimistic belief in democracy, and encouraged other progressives to act more openly.

However, contrary to the revolutionary attitudes later in the protest, the democratic sentiment under Zhao's leadership was relatively constructive. Based on the Seven Demands[3] drafted by the protesters, it was clear that, in the beginning of the Protest, protesters did not intend to be anti-governmental or anti-communist; they merely demanded that the Party take actions to end corruption and grant citizens more political freedom.[4] As the leading figure behind the Party's progressive bloc, Zhao was generally in line with the protestors. Internally, he attempted to persuade hardliner party officials, particularly Deng, into making concession with the protestors.[5] He also allowed the media, such as the People's Daily and the China Central Television to bypass censorship and broadcast the protest…

[1] Zhao, Ziyang, Pu Bao, Renee Chiang, Adi Ignatius, and Roderick MacFarquhar. "Preface." In *Prisoner of the state: the secret journal of Zhao Ziyang*. New York: Simon & Schuster, 2009. xv.

[2] Meaning the intellectuals and the working class.

[3] Liang, Zhang. "The Tiananmen Papers." The New York Times. https://www.nytimes.com/books/first/l/liang-tiananmen.html (accessed May 26, 2014).

[4] Ziyang, op. cit.

[5] Zhao, Dingxin. *The power of Tiananmen state-society relations and the 1989 Beijing student movement*. Chicago: University of Chicago Press, 2001. 156.

Section C: Reflection

In Section C (approx. 400 words) you have the opportunity to reflect on what the investigation revealed to you about the methods used by historians and the challenges they face when investigating topics like your own. This section is worth the fewest marks (4), but it could make the difference between a good and an outstanding paper. You should no doubt already have an understanding that the study of history is beset with a number of challenges and limitations, some of which have been discussed earlier in this chapter. Section A is designed to give you an opportunity to reflect on this understanding, but it must be focused specifically on the nature of your topic and/or the kind of investigation you undertook, rather than a reflection on the nature of history in general.

Common problems with Section C:

- Limited understanding of the nature of history and the challenges facing historians.

- Limited understanding of the methods historians use to examine and study history.

- Poorly focused on the challenges specific to the student's topic.

Throughout your IB History course, your TOK and History teachers should provide opportunities for you to think about and discuss the challenges of determining historical truth and understanding.

History can often be determined largely by who writes it, his or her purpose, and the methods he or she decides to use. Consider also that where there is scant evidence, historians often make very authoritative sounding **speculations** – essentially educated guesses – where they fill in gaps in the historical record with judgments they think are reasonable to believe. But often we cannot with absolute certainty verify or prove beyond doubt that their accounts are correct.

Many of the inherent challenges of history stem from problems related to its evidence-based nature. History is also challenging because of how it is used for so many different purposes including political slogans, national narratives, personal and group identity, entertainment, advertising and countless other ways. The past the historian studies is not a dead past. History is living, changing and visible in the present. Therefore, there is no shortage of questions to consider in your reflection section.

- What is history? Is it more creative and interpretive as opposed to scientific and objective?

- How did the nature of your investigation present specific challenges to finding reliable evidence?

- What methods did historians use? How were they limited by time and place? How are they limited by ideology or world views?

- Is it possible to capture the entirety of an event?

- What are the challenges of causation? How far back in time should the historian search for causes? Can immediate causes ever be separated from long term causes?

- How might national identity, cultural norms, values or beliefs affect one's ability to reason and arrive at an understanding of history?

- How might mass culture, the entertainment industry or other powerful forces influence historical understanding?

- Who decides what topics and issues are important to record and study?

- How does bias and editorial selection impact what is recorded and reported on, and what is not?

- In what ways does the outcome of an event determine how it is recorded in history?

- How does technology affect understanding of history, or the methods the historian uses?

- How are value judgements in history determined? For example, how are terms like atrocity, terrorism or revolution treated now compared to the period under investigation? Should historians make moral judgements?

- In what ways does the idea of progress and decline affect our treatment of some historical events?

- What is the role of the historian? Can the historian ever be objective?

- Are all perspectives of history equally valid? If not, how do we determine which have greater value?

- How might knowledge of your investigation be used to solve complex problems in the present? How might it be abused?

In would be far too ambitious for you to consider all of these questions in Section C. It is essential however that you give considerable thought to what you learned about history from your investigation. You should demonstrate clear awareness of the challenges facing historians, and the limitations of specific methods used in investigating topics like your own. In other words, there should be a clear connection between the nature of history as a way of thinking, and your own investigation. For a greater understanding of the nature of history, the following books are very useful.

> E.E. Carr, 1961. *What is History?* Penguin Books. London, UK
>
> M. MacMillan, 2008. *The Uses and Abuses of History.* Viking. Toronto.
>
> J. L. Gaddis, 2004. *The Landscape of History.* New York, Oxford University Press.

Final touches: Wrapping up the IA

The Internal Assessment is arguably the best opportunity IB History students have to maximize their overall course mark. The final assessed mark is entirely in your hands because you control the process of topic selection, research, planning and writing. Before submitting to your teacher for final assessment, make sure you have completed the following:

- Select and thoroughly research a question of personal interest.
- Complete all sections fully, according to the criteria.
- Compare your IA to examples posted on the OCC or in the Teacher Support Materials.
- Include all relevant sources in your bibliography.
- Reference all sources using a consistent, standardized citation format.
- Edit and proofread your work carefully.
- Submit a draft for effective feedback from your teacher.
- Include a title page with your question, name, candidate number and total word count clearly listed.
- Include a table of contents.

Internal Assessment skills

Discuss and evaluate the student example below using the criteria for Section C:

Ever since Deng declared martial law on May 20th, 1989, the Tiananmen Square Protest had been a taboo topic in Mainland China. There are no public records of the Protest, and any discussion regarding the Protest is immediately censored. In the educational system, particularly, the Protest was considered "non-existent". The Party's illegitimate historical revisionism illustrates the extent to which history can be manipulated to influence public opinions. Therefore, historians have the morally imperative role to present a balanced account of the Protest.

However, historians hoping to investigate the Protest face a dilemma: most primary sources are not made public by the Chinese government, and most available sources are from the protestors' perspectives. Historians either have no primary sources to work with, or have a disproportionate number of pro-protest sources. This dilemma is a common problem caused by illegitimate historical revisionism, which made it difficult for historians to remain objective. Government records are not available. Media coverage during the Protest is censored. Government and military officers who gave orders during the Protest are not permitted to publicize their narratives. On the other hand, a large number of sources originate from political dissidents, protesters who sought asylum overseas, and families of protestors who were killed

on June 4th. These sources, although highly valuable to historians, can be biased and unreliable. Therefore, historians should exercise caution when evaluating these sources.

In order to counterbalance the aforementioned dilemma, I purposely limited the number of sources originated from the protestors. I also took advantage of my Chinese proficiency by looking through Chinese newspaper archives and talking with former protestors and former Party officials during the protest. These methods of acquiring evidence should have helped me gain a more balanced understanding of the democratic sentiments during the protest.

Apart from balancing different perspectives, historians who investigate this issue are under social and ethical pressures. If they suggest that there were democratic sentiments within the Party and the Army executing the martial law, many former protesters (especially families of victims who were killed during the June 4th incident) would accuse the historians of downplaying the Party's crime. In addition, the Western world almost unanimously agrees that the June 4th incident was a massacre and that the Party was the antagonist. Historians who propose otherwise are under significant ideological pressure. Therefore, historians should prevent these pressures from influencing the investigation. Any conclusions should be re-examined by other historians to ensure a higher degree of objectivity.

Index